THE ARCHITECTURE READER

THE ARCHITECTURE READER

ESSENTIAL WRITINGS FROM VITRUVIUS TO THE PRESENT

Edited By A. Krista Sykes

George Braziller Publishers

New York

Published in 2007 by George Braziller, Inc., New York

Copyright © 2007 by George Braziller, Inc.

Acknowledgments, Foreword, Introduction, and prefatory texts

Copyright © 2007 by A. Krista Sykes

See notes for information on copyright holders of all other texts

See captions for copyright holders of images

For information, please address the publisher:

George Braziller, Inc.

171 Madison Avenue

New York, New York 10016

www.georgebraziller.com

Library of Congress Cataloging-in-Publication Data

The Architecture reader : essential writings from Vitruvius to the present / edited by
A. Krista Sykes. p. cm.

Includes bibliographical references.

ISBN 978-0-8076-1579-9 (hardback) -- ISBN 978-0-8076-1580-5 (pbk.)

1. Architecture. 2. Architectural criticism. I. Sykes, A. Krista. II. Title.

NA2560.A71 2007

720--dc22   2006034835

Designed by Saira Kathpalia

Printed and bound in Singapore

First edition

TABLE OF CONTENTS

ACKNOWLEDGMENTS

Throughout the process of planning, compiling, and writing this text, I received assistance from many individuals who deserve recognition. I thank George Braziller for approaching me with the idea for this reader and for giving me the opportunity to undertake this project; Jessica Benko and Elizabeth Monroe for providing wonderful editorial commentary, much-needed advice, and overall guidance; Amy Finstein, Michael Hays, Robert Mark, John McMorrough, Brendan Moran, Mark Morris, Vincent Scully, and Julia Sluzenski for their insightful and valuable critiques of the manuscript; Lee Gray for his perceptive thoughts, indispensable counsel, and constant willingness to talk through the project; my parents and siblings for their never-failing support and assurance; and my cats for the entertainment and companionship. Finally, I am grateful to my husband, Joshua, for his patience, help, and encouragement throughout this and all other endeavors.

PREFACE

The writings that comprise this reader span more than two thousand years, include authors of many nationalities, and cover topics from primitive huts through, in the words of Shumon Basar, "poisonous mixtures." Additionally, the documents do not represent a single genre; they include journal articles, editorials, book chapters, lectures, interviews, and manifestos. Yet, among these excerpts, unifying characteristics exist. In these works, the authors—primarily architects—concern themselves with their own specific moment in time. They ponder, critique, and occasionally attack architectural norms and, in many cases, pose alternative methods of architectural thought and practice. As products of individuals active during different eras, these works demonstrate a broad array of attitudes toward architecture as both subject and discipline. Taken together, these texts provide a general overview of significant concepts encompassed by the field of architecture.

Regarding the selection of excerpts, it was crucial that the writings confront basic issues that endure throughout the history of architecture to our own era. For example, since the age of Vitruvius, architects have been concerned with the role that architecture plays in society. Thus, the social nature of the discipline, while subject to numerous interpretations, can be understood as a fundamental and recurring topic of architectural discourse. This leads to another aspect of the texts included in this reader. The discipline of architecture is inundated with specialized terminology that can render writings on architecture difficult to interpret. As an introductory collection of writings aimed toward non-architects, I attempted to include excerpts that would be accessible and of interest to those outside the field and that represent different approaches to architecture. It was not my intent, nor would it be possible, to present a comprehensive compilation of such approaches. Rather, I hoped to assemble noteworthy writings that, in most circumstances, have influenced the perception and creation of architecture through to our present day. Adolf Loos's essay "Ornament and

Crime" (1908) and Robert Venturi's text "Complexity and Contradiction in Architecture" (1966) are examples of such works. I also included a handful of excerpts that may not have had an immediately discernable effect within the discipline, but that nevertheless offer interesting and fruitful ideas for consideration. Daniel Libeskind's speech "Proof of Things Invisible" (1997) and Shumon Basar's article "The Poisonous Mixture" (2004) fall into this latter category.

The majority of the excerpts stem from the twentieth and twenty-first centuries. I made an effort to represent each decade within those eras, with the greatest concentration of texts falling in the last fifteen years. This emphasis reflects the proliferation of writing architects as well as my desire to convey the diversity that characterizes contemporary views of architecture. It also reveals my interest in the history and theory of twentieth-century architecture, particularly from the 1960s to the present.

However, I also strongly believe that our present is inevitably, if not consciously, informed by the past. Thus I included a number of significant texts predating the twentieth century, beginning with Vitruvius, the author of *The Ten Books on Architecture* (circa 25 B.C.E.), the only complete architectural treatise to survive intact from antiquity. As such, this work established the standard for all later architects who set out to write about architecture. The next excerpt, from Abbot Suger's account of the renovation of the Abbey Church of St.-Denis, dates from the Middle Ages. A selection from the Leon Battista Alberti architectural treatise of the mid-1400s, "On the Art of Building in Ten Books," follows Suger. The subsequent texts by Andrea Palladio (*The Four Books on Architecture*, 1570); Claude Perrault (*Ordonnance for the Five Kinds of Columns after the Method of the Ancients*, 1683); Etienne-Louis Boullée (*Architecture, Essay on Art*, 1770–1784); and Eugène-Emmanuel Viollet-le-Duc (*Dictionnaire raisonné*, 1854–1869) lead us toward the twentieth century. The exclusion of other architects is not meant to imply that they were insignificant or have left no lasting impression. For the purposes of this collection, however, I feel that the selections by Vitruvius, Suger, Alberti, Palladio,

Perrault, Boullée, and Viollet-le-Duc provide the most suitable foundation to prepare the reader for the contemporary excerpts, since each of these texts introduce or address issues that reappear throughout architectural discourse in general.

One other issue worthy of mention involves the decision to focus this collection on architecture without directly engaging issues of urbanism. In practice, architecture is inextricably intertwined with urbanism and attempting to divorce the two is somewhat artificial. For this book, however, I chose to deal almost exclusively with architecture in order to limit the size and scope of the collection. To include significant texts on urbanism would have proved impossible in the space allowed, while the incorporation of only a few writings would have done the topic an injustice, providing only a cursory glimpse into the complex and multifaceted subject. Hopefully the issues raised throughout this collection will prompt the reader to independently explore ideas of architecture and urbanism.

Indeed, we may conceive of the built environment in a multitude of ways if we take the time to think of it at all. The need for architectural and urban awareness is great, as is the need for wide-spread discussion. I hope that the issues broached in this book will inspire readers to thoughtfully consider what exists, what was before, and what may be in the coming years.

INTRODUCTION

The notion of architecture is quite complex. Two thousand years ago, the architect Vitruvius identified three branches of the discipline: "the art of building, the making of time-pieces, and the construction of machinery"[1]—everything from houses and roads to hydraulics and clocks. While the contemporary field of architecture is far more specialized, we still lack a consensus on what architecture encompasses; even the meaning of the term "architecture" can vary widely. Nevertheless, the basic concept of "architecture" generally relates to the design and fabrication of structures. Yet problems still arise when attempting to determine what structures today qualify as architecture. Is a bridge an architectural structure? An aqueduct? A fountain? Or does the term "architecture" apply only to buildings proper?

Another question appears with respect to buildings: what types of buildings qualify as architecture? Is there a difference between a work of architecture and a building? Some would say that the two are equivalent terms, interchangeable. Often, however, architects and scholars of architecture draw a distinction between architecture and building. The architectural historian Nikolas Pevsner opens his text *An Outline of European Architecture* with such a distinction, declaring: "A bicycle shed is a building; Lincoln Cathedral is a piece of architecture." Pevsner then qualifies this statement by explaining that, "Nearly everything that encloses space on a scale sufficient for a human being to move in is a building; the term architecture applies only to buildings designed with a view to aesthetic appeal."[2] So according to Pevsner, only certain buildings, those designed to be aesthetically appealing, can be considered architecture. Yet, this definition may raise a few objections. For example, Pevsner's idea of aesthetic appeal may differ quite dramatically from what I or you find aesthetically appealing. What about buildings Pevsner finds appealing and we do not? Are they still architecture? Or what about a bicycle shed that is "designed with a view to aesthetic appeal"? Does this bicycle shed ascend to the realm of architecture or does its utilitarian function preclude it from achieving the status of architecture?

A similar question arises regarding "anonymous" built environments. In 1964, the Austrian architect Bernard Rudofsky coordinated an exhibition at the Museum of Modern Art in New York entitled Architecture Without Architects. Featuring photographs of subterranean Chinese villages, African tree dwellings, and terraced Mediterranean housing, this show focused attention on a previously neglected aspect of the built environment: the "world of nonpedigreed architecture." While these creations were often appreciated for their ingenuity and functionality, historians had commonly excluded them from accounts of the architectural past, relegating such "primitive" structures "to the pages of geographic and anthropological magazines." Rudofsky's exhibition and accompanying publication, however, helped to extend the realm of architecture beyond the established "formal" canon to include indigenous and vernacular construction.[3] Indeed, architecture can exist without architects.

The "architecture without architects" concept raises a larger issue concerning the position of the architect, both past and present. What is an architect? What are the responsibilities of the architect? What should an architect's education entail? What skills must the architect possess? Elusive and ever changing, the answers to these questions mirror the shifting role of the architect and, in turn, influence our understanding of architecture as an object and as a discipline. Thus, a study of architecture necessitates a reflection upon the idea of the architect.

The Architect

Throughout time, people have defined the architect in different ways, alternately and sometimes simultaneously as designer, tradesman, artist, intellectual, and professional. Vitruvius, the author of *The Ten Books on Architecture* (written circa 25 B.C.E) presented the architect as an amalgam of all these traits. He believed that the architect's education should involve not only the study of drawing and geometry, but also history, medicine, astronomy, and law. In addition to this vast array of knowledge, Vitruvius's architect also needed the manual skill to construct his designs. Thus, according to Vitruvius, a successful architect was both a scholar and a craftsman.

During the Middle Ages, Vitruvius's notion of the architect was overshadowed by the concept of the master mason. As the name implies, the master mason was a trained craftsman, a member of a guild who rose to the top of his field through apprenticeship and experience, not scholarly study. Often a master mason served as a designer and on-site construction coordinator, procuring materials and directing workmen. Yet, it is somewhat problematic to speak of the medieval master mason as Vitruvius does of his architect, in part because few written records from this time period exist. Those documents that have survived tend to focus on financial and practical matters rather than theoretical and design issues. Furthermore, construction of large projects frequently spanned decades, if not centuries, making a succession of master masons necessary. Even when construction was completed rather quickly, the projects most often were associated with the architectural patron, not the designers or builders. Indeed, patrons frequently played a significant role in the final manifestation of a commissioned work, as did Abbot Suger in the renovation of the Church of St.-Denis (1140–1144). Such heavy patronal involvement further complicate considerations of the medieval architect.

A few centuries later, a different concept of the architect emerged in the writings of Leon Battista Alberti. Vitruvius's ghost clearly haunted Alberti, who in the mid-fifteenth century composed his own treatise, *On the Art of Building in Ten Books*. Alberti did not reproduce the work of Vitruvius, but rather used a humanist impulse to revise and update the material for his Renaissance audience. Like Vitruvius, Alberti also envisioned the architect as a man privileged with a classical education. However, Alberti felt that the arts, philosophy, and mathematics should be the primary emphases for schooling. He believed that more pragmatic concerns, such as legal and environmental issues, rest in the domain of the builder, who learns through experience, not formal study. This difference in prescribed education underlies an important distinction between Alberti's and Vitruvius's notions of the architect. Unlike Vitruvius's architect—not to mention the medieval master mason—Alberti's architect was not a craftsman. Rather, Alberti presented the Renaissance architect as a learned individual who designs but does not personally take part in construction. This separation of the architect and the building process—the notion of the gentleman architect posited by Alberti—has colored the perception of the architect to the present day. While this idea of the gentleman architect has had the effect of raising the status of the architect above that of the workman, it also has imposed limitations on the architect's accepted range of activity.

The breach between the architect and the process of production is somewhat analogous to the division of labor that arose during industrialization. The emergence of engineering as a distinct field sparked debates over the very nature of architecture and raised concerns regarding the future of the architect. Would the architect be surpassed or perhaps even replaced by the engineer? In the early 1920s, the Swiss architect Le Corbusier proposed an alternative: the architect must learn from the engineer who was in tune with the demands of contemporary existence. According to Le Corbusier, the architect, burdened by centuries of architectural convention, created traditional works neither relevant to nor appropriate for the conditions of twentieth-century life. Rather, Le Corbusier announced, the architect must rely not on historical decrees but, like the engineer, must state the problem to be solved and then devise a solution based on ideas of economy and propriety. In this way, the architect—in Le Corbusier's mind, the ultimate artist—could create beautiful architecture suitable for modern needs.

The great American architect Frank Lloyd Wright was also concerned with the creation of an appropriate architecture for his time. Wright believed the integrity of architecture, and of the architect, to be threatened by blind adherence to tradition and the growth of commercialization. As early as 1900, Wright expressed disgust with fellow architects who "[had] been caught in the commercial rush and whirl and hypnotized into trying to be commercial [themselves]."[4] Instead of designing works for early twentieth-century America, his colleagues, Wright felt, were, for the sake of profit and popularity, peddling architectural styles from foreign lands and past eras. As an alternative, Wright devised an original and unique architectural language that responded to the democratic intent and geographical particularities of the American Midwest. He viewed this "Prairie Style" architecture, perhaps best characterized by the Robie House (Chicago, 1909), as an artistic, practical, and dignified creation, not as a money-making tool. In this way, Wright felt he differed greatly from other architects of his day for whom success hinged on quantity instead of quality and on profit instead of propriety. For Wright, architecture was not a mere commodity, but a means of elevating humanity.

While Wright lamented the impact of commercialism on the architect, others such as Denise Scott Brown have found inspiration in commodification. Scott Brown feels that architects should learn from the commercial interests of the average person, that architects must examine what people buy in order to understand what they want. Such beliefs have led Scott Brown, along with her husband and business partner Robert Venturi, to study "everyday" environments—including New York subway stations, Las Vegas, and the suburb of Levittown, New Jersey—to further understand popular taste and the ways in which people inhabit and modify their surroundings. According to Scott Brown, such explorations are imperative for the socially conscious designer. It is the responsibility of the architect, she has asserted, to create an architecture that resonates with the common man, not one that caters to the elite members of society. Scott Brown's thoughts have signaled a shift from an attitude of superiority held by some modern architects toward the increasingly permissive pluralist and populist attitudes of the past few decades.

The architect Samuel Mockbee also was interested in the creation of architecture for the common man. With the founding of the Rural Studio in 1993, Mockbee initiated a program through Auburn University in which students designed and built housing for a poor community in Alabama. In an interview in 2001, Mockbee stated that the architect's greatest contemporary struggle involves remembering, in the midst of our corporate world, that it is people, not capital, who really matter. For Mockbee, the Rural Studio was not only a way to house economically deprived members of Hale County; it was also a way to cultivate a generation of socially sensitive architects who, as students, were provided with invaluable experience in both design and construction. The Rural Studio, based on Mockbee's philosophy, has thus helped to prompt a reconceptualization of the architect as a professional who, unlike Alberti's architect, can and perhaps even should take an active part in the construction process. In addition, Mockbee's sentiment regarding the social responsibilities of the profession echoes Frank Lloyd Wright's earlier call for a dignifying architecture of quality. The Rural Studio demonstrated that an architecture of quality need not be an architecture of expense. Working with a minimal budget, Mockbee and his students often employed non-traditional materials such as dirt-filled, stucco-covered tires, old street signs, and salvaged car windows to make what Mockbee called a "warm, dry, and noble" architecture.

While some architects aspire to a warm, dry, noble architecture, others aim to evoke the excitement born of the instability and apparent chaos of contemporary existence. For example, in the 1970s, Rem Koolhaas identified new opportunities for human activity that arose in New York City as a result of urban congestion. He continued this line of thought in his design for the Student Center at the Illinois Institute of

Technology in the late 1990s. In this project, Koolhaas and the Office for Metropolitan Architecture (OMA) interwove various and often conflicting zones of activity, allowing the "L" train to literally invade part of the building. Such designs simultaneously highlight and exacerbate the commotion of everyday life.

Disorder is not just accepted; it is embraced. This is Koolhaas's message to the contemporary architect, eloquently announced by the architect Shumon Basar in his article, "The Poisonous Mixture." The title of Basar's essay stems from a comment made by Koolhaas in a lecture at Columbia University in 1989. "Architecture," Koolhaas declared, "is a poisonous mixture of power and impotence."[5] Perhaps this concept provides a clue to the shifting definition of the architect throughout time. Could it be that the architect simply has been attempting to stave off feelings of helplessness in a world, and in a discipline, constantly in flux? This idea implies that different definitions of the architect—the architect as designer and tradesman; the architect as artist, intellectual, and professional—may not be so different after all.

Architecture and Nature

Nature plays a significant and multifaceted role in the architectural realm. At its most basic, nature, considered as the environment as a whole, provides a setting for architecture. Even in urban areas where the original landscape ceases to exist, architecture still interacts with the earth, the sky, the sun, and other natural elements. To assure the comfort of the occupants, responsible architects take into consideration such topographical and geographical information. The orientation of a building on its site, for example, can maximize the amount of natural light an interior receives, shelter the structure from prevalent winds, or provide visually appealing views of the surrounding environs. These concepts are nothing new; Vitruvius addressed issues concerning a building's placement within the environment, demonstrating that even two thousand years ago, architects were aware of the potential benefits to be derived from attention to the land.

In recent years, interest in a building's impact on the environment has grown considerably. Ideally, the creation and existence of any given structure would have no negative repercussions on the earth. Yet, through the processes of construction, daily operation, and demolition, buildings consume an astounding amount of the earth's energy and natural resources. As architects become increasingly aware of this problem, many have responded by adapting ideas of sustainability to inform their designs. For example, the Australian architect Glen Murcutt works with the specifics of the site and employs traditional Aboriginal techniques in his house designs. While Murcutt turns to local building customs to decrease the ecological impact of his work, the British architect Norman Foster utilizes advanced modern technology to create buildings that strive for self-sustainability. The architect William McDonough, in conjunction with the chemist Michael Braungart, has taken his concern for the environment beyond the realm of architecture proper, extending his efforts to all aspects of industrial production. These two men advocate a "cradle to cradle" paradigm that investigates and develops materials that can be used, recycled, and reused without producing tangible waste. Thus in the work of Murcutt, Foster, and McDonough and Braungart, we witness different methodologies derived from the same source: concern for the earth as a whole.

In a theoretical sense, nature and natural creations have long provided a model for architecture. In his treatise, Vitruvius cited the proportion and symmetry of the human body as an inspiration for architectural elements. His account of the Greek classical orders serves as one example of this tendency. He stated that the Doric, the most robust and massive of the orders, derived from the measurements of a man. The Ionic's more attenuated proportions and delicate features were modeled on a woman. The most slender of the orders, the Corinthian, echoed the lithe physique of a young maiden. Thus, the Greek classical orders as described by Vitruvius reflect both physical characteristics and symbolic meaning from nature via the study of the human body.

Centuries later, Alberti elaborated upon the relationship between architecture and nature in his discussion of *concinnitas*. This term concerns beauty as achieved through the harmonious correspondence among the parts of a composition and their relationship to the whole. *Concinnitas* is perhaps best described in the following passage from *On The Art of Building in Ten Books*: "Beauty is a form of sympathy and consonance of the parts within a body, according to definite number, outline, and position, as dictated by *concinnitas*, the absolute and fundamental rule in Nature. This is the main object of the art of building, and the source of her dignity, charm, authority, and worth."[6] According to Alberti, then, architecture—not to mention music and other arts—is governed by *concinnitas*, an underlying principle of nature. From similar natural inspiration, the American architect Frank Lloyd Wright later developed his idea of organic architecture, which strove, among other things, for the integration of the parts with the whole, as well as the building with the site.

For Viollet-le-Duc, natural organisms provided a structural model for architecture. From his studies of plants and animals, Viollet-le-Duc determined that the form and structure of each part of a creature was directly related to the function that part performed. For example, the shape of a bat's wing derives from its function. Nature has crafted the wing to facilitate the bat's flight, and each section of the wing contributes to the function of the whole; nothing is extraneous. Thus Viollet-le-Duc's understanding of appropriate architectural structure corresponds to nature's expression of structure. The ideas of structural clarity and rationality were continued in the work of the American architect Louis Sullivan, who also turned to nature as a model for design. These investigations led Sullivan to famously declared that "form ever follows function,"[7] a dictum that, somewhat modified, became a guiding principle of numerous modern architects.

The British social and architectural commentator John Ruskin adopted a different approach, finding in nature the perfect model for architectural ornament. Patterns extracted from actual flora and fauna could be rendered in stone by the skilled hands of craftsmen. Ruskin also appreciated the effects of nature's actions on a building. The weathering of the façade, the vegetation creeping through the cracks, the alterations made over the years—these aspects marked the passage of time. Regarding buildings from an older age, Ruskin declared, "*We have no right whatever to touch them.* They are not ours. They belong partly to those who built them, and partly to all the generations of mankind who are to follow us."[8] For Ruskin, architecture provided a record of the past to be interpreted in the present.

Architecture and the Past, Architecture and the Present

Architecture's relationship to the past and present raises a number of points for consideration. On the most basic level, we learn from studying history, from what has come before us. Alberti learned from Vitruvius, as did Palladio, Perrault, Boullée, and Viollet-le-Duc. We, in turn, learn from them all. We learn what works, what building types may be suitable for certain activities. We also learn what does not work, what materials fail under certain situations. History, however, can be a great constraint. Robert Venturi alludes to this dilemma in his book *Complexity and Contradiction in Architecture* when he discusses the growing complexities of twentieth-century life and the resulting demands on contemporary architecture.[9] It is not enough to abide by the rules of our fathers—in Venturi's case, the outmoded and simplistic notion that "form follows function." Venturi suggests that, at its best, architecture responds to present needs and conditions as well as information inherited from the past.

What information should we take from the past? How can this information shape an appropriate architecture in the present? What *is* an appropriate architecture for the present? Such inquiries rest at the center of architectural debates characterized by a wide range of responses. The Italian architect Antonio Sant'Elia, author of the "Manifesto of Futurist Architecture" (1914), sought to eradicate all traces of the past. Only an architecture based on the principles of speed, mechanization, and technological progress was fitting for the present. Such an environment would both cultivate and respond to a new futuristic society. However, John Ruskin was so discouraged by the negative effects of industrialization that he attempted to almost entirely discount the present. His nostalgic appreciation for the perceived social values of the medieval era prompted his call for an architecture modeled on that of fourteenth-century Venice.

Sant'Elia and Ruskin's positions represent extremes in the continuum of feelings about past and present aesthetics, skills, and ideologies. More commonly, architects rest somewhere in between, adopting both traditional and progressive aspects of architectural inspiration. For example, the German architect Bruno Taut, like Ruskin, yearned for a revived traditional notion of community, yet he relied on new materials such as glass and steel to create an architecture of social cohesiveness. Walter Gropius, a German architect recognized as the founder and original leader of the Bauhaus, turned to the medieval craft guild as a model for a cooperative artistic workshop. Gropius's new workshop, however, chose to interact with industry, to design and generate prototypes for factory production. Likewise, Le Corbusier drew upon both the past and the present. Interested in ideas of standardization, Le Corbusier identified a similar logic—the refinement of essential compositional elements—underlying both the classical Greek temple and the early twentieth-century automobile. This logic served in part as a foundation for Le Corbusier's reconceptualization of a house conducive to modern life. Thus, in the thought of Taut, Gropius, Le Corbusier, and many others, we find a marriage of the old and the new, the traditional and the progressive, the past and the present.

The past to which an architect looks may be quite distant. Indeed, in his search for a meaningful architecture, an architecture of harmony and strength in a world of chaos and instability, the twentieth-century architect Louis Kahn employed the visual mass and permanence manifested in the ruins of antiquity. Others architects such as Daniel Libeskind have discovered inspiration in the more recent past. Two of his most famous works, the Jewish Museum in Berlin and the Master Plan for the World Trade Center, draw upon the rich and tragic histories associated with the Holocaust and September 11th. In Libeskind's designs, the glaring absences left by these horrible events translate into physical reminders that simultaneously evoke the loss of the past and the hope of the present.

Another use of the past involves the adoption of historic stylistic elements in contemporary architecture. This technique of appropriating classical forms is often associated with postmodernism, an architectural movement spanning the 1960s through the 1980s.[10]   First theorized by Charles Jencks in the 1970s, the resurgence of classical elements was characterized in part as a backlash against modern architecture's perceived rejection of history and ornament. In defiance of the mandate "form follows function," architects such as Robert A. M. Stern, Michael Graves, and Philip Johnson turned to the past for inspiration, incorporating Doric columns, classical swags, and broken pediments into their present designs. Controversy abounded; admirers praised this work as ironic and witty while critics defamed it as superficial and simplistic. Regardless of various opinions, the postmodernist use of the past nevertheless focused attention on the difficult relationship between architecture and history, a theme that has persisted—and will no doubt continue to persist—throughout time.

Architecture as Science, Architecture as Art
Another frequent discussion surrounding architecture involves the categorization of the discipline and its product as *either* science *or* art. Even teaching institutions differ on their interpretations of architecture's "place"; in some schools, architectural instruction is allied with the studio arts, while in others it appears alongside engineering and technological studies. Yet in reality, it is extremely difficult—if not impossible—to separate the two, as architecture by its very nature incorporates elements of both science and art. This was clear to Vitruvius when he wrote that the architect must be versed

not only in drawing and handcraft, but also in what we would now consider more scientific realms such as astronomy, geology, and medicine. In the subsequent centuries, architects have stressed to varying degrees the "scientific" or the "artistic" within the discipline. In general, the distinction depends on the architect's personal views and predilections. Consequently, discussion about whether architecture is a science or an art is somewhat futile. It is more helpful to examine various ways in which architects have positioned their work with respect to the scientific and artistic realms.

Because the term "science" can refer to a broad domain, for the purposes of this discussion I will focus on a specific scientific area that has had a tremendous impact on architecture and design: technological and industrial development. During the late 1700s and early 1800s, industrialization and the availability of new materials, such as iron, glass, and steel, presented many opportunities for the creation of innovative architectural forms and new methods of production. The Crystal Palace, created by the greenhouse designer Joseph Paxton to accommodate England's Great Exhibition of 1851, incorporated a system of prefabrication and modular construction in order to erect the immense structure of cast iron and glass. Almost forty years later, new materials featured prominently in the Paris Exhibition of 1889 thanks to the iron Eiffel Tower, soaring 300 meters high, and the Galerie des Machines, a large, barrel-vaulted display hall composed of steel and glass. Another thirty years later, Le Corbusier relied on steel-reinforced concrete to create the Maison Domino (1915), a prototype for a factory-produced housing frame composed of thin vertical piers supporting concrete floor slabs. This experimentation with reinforced concrete became the foundation of Le Corbusier's "Five Points towards a New Architecture" (1926), developed in conjunction with his cousin Pierre Jeanneret, and ultimately contributed to Le Corbusier's concept of the house as "a machine for living in."

The machine has served both as a model for architecture and a tool for architectural production. Especially during the twentieth century, architecture has been based on or conceived as a machine, as a specialized and efficacious creation for a specific purpose. This was the case with R. Buckminster Fuller, whose quest to revolutionize the housing industry resulted in a one piece, lightweight, inexpensive aluminum home. Not only did he design his house to operate with mechanical efficiency, but he also intended for the house to be produced by factories that formerly made World War II supplies. Thus, Fuller's house was to be machinelike in its conception, function, and fabrication.

Such concepts of machinelike efficiency and production also pervaded the thoughts of the British architectural group Archigram, whose members in the 1960s devised a series of projects reliant on mechanical operation and technological innovation. For example, Peter Cook's Plug-in City of 1964 consisted of a basic urban infrastructure that would support "plug-in" or interchangeable parts. This scheme included prefabricated housing pods that could be moved via crane and inserted into various service outlets throughout the city. As elements of the pod became obsolete, they could be replaced with newer, more progressive parts that would better fit the owner's needs. Archigram's ideas could be described as hi-tech fantasies, many of which remain unbuildable to this day. Yet, the group's futuristic projects sparked the imagination of other architects. Archigram, as did Fuller, drew on the potential offered by mechanization and machine production to question traditional notions of architecture as stable, fixed, and permanent.

In more recent years, the machine in the form of the computer has emerged onto the architectural scene with dramatic results. In many cases, the computer has functioned as an addendum to conventional means of architectural creation; after designing on paper, architects could use various software programs to digitally model their work. Yet, architects such as Greg Lynn now use the computer as a design tool, not merely a presentation device. Lynn assimilates concepts from aeronautic and automobile design to create dynamic architectural forms that move beyond the rectilinear realm. He appears not to think in terms of line and plane, but of flow and force. The resulting structures—bulging, rippling, and asymmetrical—advertise this difference in Lynn's conception and formulation of architecture. Thus in both working method and final product, Lynn's architecture challenges conventional expectations. The Korean Presbyterian Church of New York, completed in 1999, serves as an example. Along with the firms of Garofalo Architects and Michael McInturf Architects, Lynn transformed a 1931 laundry factory into a visually and spatially unique church complex. Industrial materials such as aluminum panels wrap around and rise above the original masonry structure, creating a series of screens and reflective surfaces through which light filters into the building. The result is a progressive and almost otherworldly atmosphere that enlivens a formerly bleak site in Queens.

The American architect Frank Gehry also utilizes advanced software programs to design and construct his equally unique, and increasingly popular, structures. These twisting, turning, unfurling forms derive in part from the use of digital technology, but they are perhaps guided more by a creative act, by an artistic sense, by Gehry's "intuition." As an architect, Gehry acknowledges the importance and relevance of technology, as each of his complex buildings attests. Yet, Gehry feels that architecture is most certainly an art, and the architect is most certainly an artist. He clearly conveyed this message in his acceptance speech for the Pritzker Architecture Prize in 1989:

> Architecture must solve complex problems. We must understand and use technology, we must create buildings which are safe and dry, respectful of context and neighbors, and face all the myriad of issues of social responsibility, and even please the client.
>
> But then what? The moment of truth, the composition of elements, the selection of forms, scale, materials, color, finally, all the same issues facing the painter and the sculptor.[11]

The painter, the sculptor, the architect . . . for Gehry, these individuals are siblings, if not the same person. Indeed, throughout history, they have at times been the same individual. Michelangelo is perhaps the exemplar of the artist-architect. Another example of such a figure is Le Corbusier, an architect who reportedly split his day between painting and design. Michelangelo and Le Corbusier serve as prominent illustrations of the crossover between architecture and other artistic ventures, yet the phenomenon is hardly unique; contemporary examples of the artist-architect include Samuel Mockbee, a painter, Daniel Libeskind, a poet and musician, and Frank Gehry, often considered a sculptor.

Architects also derive inspiration from other artistic media. For example, Bernard Tschumi drew on cinematography, photography, and choreography to produce his "Manhattan Transcripts" (1976–1981), a series of images that probed the architectural relationships among space, movement, and events—considerations that would inform his design for the Parisian Parc de la Villette in the early 1980s. Similarly, Denise Scott Brown and Robert Venturi credit works of Pop Art, including Edward Ruscha's images of gas stations and Jasper Johns's superimposed American flags, with directing the pair's attention to the ordinary and the everyday, concerns that continue to condition their work forty years later. Gehry, too, cites artistic influences for his architectural creations ranging from Renaissance and Baroque painters to more contemporary artists. This includes his friends Claus Oldenberg and Coosje van Bruggen, with whom Gehry collaborated to create the Giant Binoculars that contain conference rooms and serve as an entrance to the Chiat/Day Building in Venice, CA (1985–1991). This inhabitable gateway serves as a clear reminder that, in many ways, art and architecture are inextricably intertwined.

Many architects believe that the relationship between architecture and art extends beyond compatibility or influence. Just as architecture inevitably incorporates elements of science—at the very least, gravity is an issue that affects built works—architecture, as an act of creativity and design, also encompasses aspects of art. This conceptual act stems from the will of the architect who is, in Gehry's opinion, fundamentally an artist. "Architecture," he declares, "is surely an art, and those who practice the art of architecture are surely architects."[12]

As I hope this introduction suggests, the relationship between architecture and art, and the relationships between architecture and nature, history, and science are neither clear nor direct. What makes these issues more complex is the human element that underlies all architectural production. Our interactions with our environment—man-made and natural—as well as our interactions with each other unavoidably factor into considerations of architecture, and into architecture's associations with society, politics, economics, psychology, and other aspects of life. With this in mind, my introductory discussion is necessarily brief and incomplete. My intention is not to provide an exhaustive account of architectural themes and influences. Rather I offer an overview of topics that weave throughout the following excerpts, our past and our present, and the entirety of architectural discourse.

---

[1] Vitruvius, "The Departments of Architecture," in *The Ten Books on Architecture*, vol.1, trans. Morris Hickey Morgan (New York: Dover Publications, Inc., 1960), 16.

[2] Nikolas Pevsner, *An Outline of European Architecture*, 7th ed. (London: Pelican Books, 1974), 15.

[3] Bernard Rudofsky, preface in *Architecture Without Architects: A Short Introduction to Non-Pedigreed Architecture* (Albuquerque: University of New Mexico Press, 2002).

[4] Frank Lloyd Wright, "The Architect," in *Collected Writings*, vol. 1, ed. Bruce Brooks Pfeiffer (New York: Rizzoli, 1992), 46.

[5] Rem Koolhaas, in Shumon Basar, "The Poisonous Mixture," in *Content,* ed. Rem Koolhaas and Brendan McGetrick (Cologne: Taschen GmbH, 2004), 67.

[6] Leon Battista Alberti, *On the Art of Building in Ten Books*, trans. Joseph Rykwert, Neil Leach, and Robert Tavernor (Cambridge: MIT Press, 1988), 303.

[7] Louis Sullivan, "The Tall Office Building Artistically Considered" in *America Builds: Source Documents in American Architecture and Planning*, ed. Leland M. Roth (New York: HarperCollins/Icon Editions, 1983), 345.

[8] John Ruskin, *The Seven Lamps of Architecture* (New York: Dover Publications, Inc., 1989), 197. Ruskin's emphasis.

[9] Robert Venturi, *Complexity and Contradiction in Architecture* (New York: Museum of Modern Art, 1966), 19.

[10] Postmodernism is understood as a cultural movement, not solely architectural. Jencks is credited with popularizing the preexisting term "postmodernism" with regard to architecture.

[11] Frank Gehry, "Frank Gehry's Acceptance Speech," The Pritzker Architecture Prize web site, http://www.pritzkerprize.com/gehry.htm

[12] Ibid.

Vitruvius, 1st Century b.c.e.

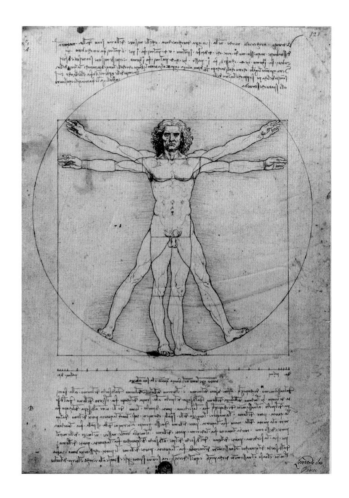

Leonardo da Vinci, *Vitruvian Man*, ca. 1492
Drawing of ideal proportions of the human figure
according to Vitruvius's treatise. Photo Credit: Alinari/Art Resource, NY

Little is known about the Roman architect and writer Vitruvius, including his full name (possibly Marcus Vitruvius Pollio) and his date of birth (approximately 80 B.C.E.). His treatise, *De aedeficatora* (translated as *On Architecture* and now known as *The Ten Books on Architecture*), is the only ancient text of its kind to survive intact. Written circa 25 B.C.E., this work disappeared for hundreds of years; its rediscovery in 1414 at the Swiss Monastery of St. Gall contributed to the renewed interest in classicism and humanism associated with the Renaissance as it took hold in Italy. Vitruvius's work drew primarily on the architecture of his Greek predecessors and addressed all aspects of the discipline from the training of architects through the construction of fortifications. According to Vitruvius, built architecture must encompass three requirements: *firmitas* (durability), *utilitas* (usefulness) and *venustas* (beauty). With this declaration, Vitruvius established the standards by which most subsequent architecture would be judged.

Another significant aspect of *The Ten Books on Architecture* involved the relationship between architecture and nature, and, by extension, architecture and man. Vitruvius positioned nature as the model for architecture; in particular, the proportion and symmetry of the human body inspired architectural designs. The perfection of the human body as discussed by Vitruvius was embodied in a late-fifteenth-century work by Leonardo da Vinci. The drawing—a man inscribed within a circle and square—referenced the harmonic proportions of the body while the title of the work—*Vitruvian Man*—memorialized Vitruvius and extended his influence beyond the realm of architecture.

The Ten Books on Architecture (ca. 25 B.C.E.)

Book I.

Chapter 1. The Education of the Architect

1. The architect should be equipped with knowledge of many branches of study and varied kinds of learning, for it is by his judgment that all work done by the other arts is put to test. This knowledge is the child of practice and theory. Practice is the continuous and regular exercise of employment where manual work is done with any necessary material according to the design of a drawing. Theory, on the other hand, is the ability to demonstrate and explain the productions of dexterity on the principles of proportion.

2. It follows, therefore, that architects who have aimed at acquiring manual skill without scholarship have never been able to reach a position of authority to correspond to their pains, while those who relied only upon theories and scholarship were obviously hunting the shadow, not the substance. But those who have a thorough knowledge of both, like men armed at all points, have the sooner attained their object and carried authority with them.

3. In all matters, but particularly in architecture, there are these two points—the thing signified, and that which gives it its significance. That which is signified is the subject of which we may be speaking; and that which gives significance is a demonstration on

---

Vitruvius, *The Ten Books on Architecture*, trans. Morris Hicky Morgan (New York: Dover Publications, Inc., 1960). Reprinted with permission of the publisher. For the Greek terms provided throughout Vitruvius's treatise, see Morris Hicky Morgan's translation from which this excerpt is derived.

scientific principles. It appears, then, that one who professes himself an architect should be well versed in both directions. He ought, therefore, to be both naturally gifted and amenable to instruction. Neither natural ability without instruction nor instruction without natural ability can make the perfect artist. Let him be educated, skilful [*sic*] with the pencil, instructed in geometry, know much history, have followed the philosophers with attention, understand music, have some knowledge of medicine, know the opinions of the jurists, and be acquainted with astronomy and the theory of the heavens.

4. The reasons for all this are as follows. An architect ought to be an educated man so as to leave a more lasting remembrance in his treatises. Secondly, he must have a knowledge of drawing so that he can readily make sketches to show the appearance of the work which he proposes. Geometry, also, is of much assistance in architecture, and in particular it teaches us the use of the rule and compasses, by which especially we acquire readiness in making plans for buildings in their grounds, and rightly apply the square, the level, and the plummet. By means of optics, again, the light in buildings can be drawn from fixed quarters of the sky. It is true that it is by arithmetic that the total cost of buildings is calculated and measurements are computed, but difficult questions involving symmetry are solved by means of geometrical theories and methods.

5. A wide knowledge of history is requisite because, among the ornamental parts of an architect's design for a work, there are many the underlying idea of whose employment he should be able to explain to inquirer. . . .

7. As for philosophy, it makes an architect high-minded and not self-assuming, but rather renders him courteous, just, and honest without avariciousness. This is very important, for no work can be rightly done without honesty and incorruptibility. . . .

8. Music, also, the architect ought to understand so that he may have knowledge of the canonical and mathematical theory. . . .

10. The architect should also have a knowledge of the study of medicine on account of the questions of climates, air, the healthiness and unhealthiness of sites, and the use of different waters. For without these considerations, the healthiness of a dwelling cannot be assured. And as for principles of law, he should know those which are necessary in the case of buildings having party walls, with regard to water dripping from the eaves, and also the laws about drains, windows, and water supply. And other things of this sort should be known to architects, so that, before they begin upon buildings, they may be careful not to leave disputed points for the householders to settle after the works are finished, and so that in drawing up contracts the interests of both employer and contractor may be wisely safe-guarded. For if a contract is skillfully drawn, each may obtain a release from the other without disadvantage. From astronomy we find the east, west, south, and north, as well as the theory of the heavens, the equinox, solstice, and courses of the stars. If one has no knowledge of these matters, he will not be able to have any comprehension of the theory of sundials.

11. Consequently, since this study is so vast in extent, embellished and enriched as it is with many different kinds of learning, I think that men have no right to profess themselves architects hastily, without having climbed from boyhood the steps of these studies and thus, nursed by the knowledge of many arts and sciences, having reached the heights of the holy ground of architecture. . . .

Chapter II. The Fundamental Principles of Architecture
1. ARCHITECTURE depends on Order, Arrangement, Eurythmy, Symmetry, Propriety, and Economy.

2. Order gives due measure to the members of a work considered separately, and sym-

metrical agreement to the proportions of the whole. It is an adjustment according to quantity. By this I mean the selection of modules from the members of the work itself and, starting from these individual parts of members, constructing the whole work to correspond. Arrangement includes the putting of things in their proper places and the elegance of effect which is due to adjustments appropriate to the character of the work. . . .

3. Eurythmy is beauty and fitness in the adjustments of the members. This is found when the members of a work are of a height suited to their breadth, of a breadth suited to their length, and, in a word, when they all correspond symmetrically.

4. Symmetry is a proper agreement between the members of the work itself, and relation between the different parts and the whole general scheme, in accordance with a certain part selected as standard. Thus in the human body there is a kind of symmetrical harmony between forearm, foot, palm, finger, and other small parts; and so it is with perfect buildings. . . .

5. Propriety is that perfection of style which comes when a work is authoritatively constructed on approved principles. It arises from prescription, from usage, or from nature. From prescription, in the case of hypaethral edifices, open to the sky, in honour of Jupiter Lightning, the Heaven, the Sun, or the Moon: for these are gods whose semblances and manifestations we behold before our very eyes in the sky when it is cloudless and bright. The temples of Minerva, Mars, and Hercules, will be Doric, since the virile strength of these gods makes daintiness entirely inappropriate to their houses. In temples to Venus, Flora, Proserpine, Spring-Water, and the Nymphs, the Corinthian order will be found to have peculiar significance, because these are delicate divinities and so its rather slender outlines, its flowers, leaves, and ornamental volutes will lend propriety where it is due. The construction of temples of the Ionic order to Juno, Diana, Father Bacchus, and the other gods of that kind, will be in keeping with

the middle position which they hold; for the building of such will be an appropriate combination of the severity of the Doric and the delicacy of the Corinthian.

6. Propriety arises from usage when buildings having magnificent interiors are provided with elegant entrance-courts to correspond; for there will be no propriety in the spectacle of an elegant interior approached by a low, mean entrance. Or, if dentils be carved in the cornice of the Doric entablature or triglyphs represented in the Ionic entablature over the cushion-shaped capitals of the columns, the effect will be spoilt by the transfer of the peculiarities of the one order of building to the other, the usage in each class having been fixed long ago.

7. Finally, propriety will be due to natural causes if, for example, in the case of all sacred precincts we select very healthy neighbourhoods with suitable springs of water in the places where the fanes are to be built, particularly in the case of those to Aesculapius and to Health, gods by whose healing powers great numbers of the sick are apparently cured. For when their diseased bodies are transferred from an unhealthy to a healthy spot, and treated with waters from health-giving springs, they will the more speedily grow well. The result will be that the divinity will stand in higher esteem and find his dignity increased, all owing to the nature of his site. There will also be natural propriety in using an eastern light for bedrooms and libraries, a western light in winter for baths and winter apartments, and a northern light for picture galleries and other places in which a steady light is needed; for that quarter of the sky grows neither light nor dark with the course of the sun, but remains steady and unshifting all day long.

8. Economy denotes the proper management of materials and of site, as well as a thrifty balancing of cost and common sense in the construction of works. This will be observed if, in the first place, the architect does not demand things which cannot be found or made ready without great expense. . . .

9. A second stage in Economy is reached when we have to plan the different kinds of dwellings suitable for ordinary householders, for great wealth, or for the high position of the statesman. A house in town obviously calls for one form of construction; that into which stream the products of country estates requires another; this will not be the same in the case of money-lenders and still different for the opulent and luxurious; for the powers under whose deliberations the commonwealth is guided dwellings are to be provided according to their special needs: and, in a word, the proper form of economy must be observed in building houses for each and every class.

Chapter III. The Departments of Architecture

. . . 2. All [structures] must be built with due reference to durability, convenience, and beauty. Durability will be assured when foundations are carried down to the solid ground and materials wisely and liberally selected; convenience, when the arrangement of the apartments is faultless and presents no hindrance to use, and when each class of building is assigned to its suitable and appropriate exposure; and beauty, when the appearance of the work is pleasing and in good taste, and when its members are in due proportion according to correct principles of symmetry. . . .

Book III.

Chapter I. On Symmetry: In Temples and in the Human Body

1. The design of a temple depends on symmetry, the principles of which must be most carefully observed by the architect. They are due to proportion. Proportion is a correspondence among the measures of the members of an entire work, and of the whole to a certain part selected as standard. From this result the principles of symmetry. Without symmetry and proportion there can be no principles in the design of any temple; that is, if there is no precise relation between its members, as in the case of those of a well shaped man.

2. For the human body is so designed by nature that the face, from the chin to the top

of the forehead and the lowest roots of the hair, is a tenth part of the whole height; the open hand from the wrist to the tip of the middle finger is just the same; the head from the chin to the crown is an eighth, and with the neck and shoulder from the top of the breast to the lowest roots of the hair is a sixth; from the middle of the breast to the summit of the crown is a fourth. If we take the height of the face itself, the distance from the bottom of the chin to the under side of the nostrils is one third of it; the nose from the under side of the nostrils to a line between the eyebrows is the same; from there to the lowest roots of the hair is also a third, comprising the forehead. The length of the foot is one sixth of the height of the body; of the forearm, one fourth; and the breadth of the breast is also one fourth. The other members, too, have their own symmetrical proportions, and it was by employing them that the famous painters and sculptors of antiquity attained to great and endless renown.

3. Similarly, in the members of a temple there ought to be the greatest harmony in the symmetrical relations of the different parts to the general magnitude of the whole. Then again, in the human body the central point is naturally the navel. For if a man be placed flat on his back, with his hands and feet extended, and a pair of compasses centered at his navel, the fingers and toes of his two hands and feet will touch the circumference of a circle described therefrom. And just as the human body yields a circular outline, so too a square figure may be found from it. For if we measure the distance from the soles of the feet to the top of the head, and then apply that measure to the outstretched arms, the breadth will be found to be the same as the height, as in the case of plane surfaces which are perfectly square.

4. Therefore, since nature has designed the human body so that its members are duly proportioned to the frame as a whole, it appears that the ancients had good reason for their rule, that in perfect buildings the different members must be in exact symmetrical relations to the whole general scheme. Hence, while transmitting to us the

proper arrangements for buildings of all kinds, they were particularly careful to do so in the case of temples of the gods, buildings in which merits and faults usually last forever.

2 ABBOT SUGER, 1081–1151

Ambulatory and chapels, Abbey Church, St.-Denis, France, 1140–44
Photo Credit: Foto Marburg/Art Resource, NY

In 1122, Suger was appointed the head of the Abbey Church of St.-Denis, an institution that for many centuries had been associated with the sovereigns of France. As the original ninth-century church was in need of enlargement and repair, Suger set out to create a magnificent and lavish religious building to surpass all others. Indeed, the new St.-Denis, as conceived by Suger but completed after his death, contained a number of structural, spatial, and aesthetic innovations. For example, exterior buttressing allowed the mass of the walls to dematerialize and be largely replaced by colorful stained glass. This was especially apparent in the newly devised double ambulatory (located at the far end of the church behind the altar and choir), an area replete with dazzling colored light that filtered in through stained glass windows. The increased transparency, brightly colored light, and novel planning configurations, as well as other specialized developments, caused many architectural historians to acknowledge the renovated St.-Denis, begun largely at Suger's behest, as the first truly Gothic structure. Suger's documentation of St.-Denis's reconstruction, excerpted below, provides a rare glimpse into a significant work of medieval architecture.

The Book of Sugar, Abbot of St.-Denis, On What Was Done Under His Adminis-
tration (1144–49)

XXV. Of the First Addition to the Church

. . . I found myself, under the inspiration of the Divine will and because of that inad-
equacy which we often saw and felt on feast days . . . (for the narrowness of the place
forced the women to run toward the altar upon the heads of the men as upon a pave-
ment with much anguish and noisy confusion), encouraged by the counsel of wise
men and by the prayers of many monks . . . to enlarge and amplify the noble church
consecrated by the Hand Divine; and I set out at once to begin this very thing. . . .
Thus we began work at the former entrance with the doors. We tore down a certain
addition asserted to have been made by Charlemagne on a very honorable occasion . . .
and we set our hand to this part. As is evident we exerted ourselves incessantly with
the enlargement of the body of the church as well as with the trebling of the entrance
and the doors, and with the erection of high and noble towers. . . .

The Other Little Book on the Consecration of the Church of St.-Denis (1144–46/47)

II. . . . Since in the front part, toward the north, at the main entrance with the main
doors, the narrow hall was squeezed in on either side by twin towers neither high nor
very sturdy but threatening ruin, we began, with the help of God, strenuously to work

---

Abbot Suger of St.-Denis, "On What Was Done Under His Administration" and "The Other Little Book on
the Consecration of the Church of St.-Denis, 1144–1149," in *The Book of Suger, Abbot of St.-Denis*, trans. and
ed. Erwin Panofsky (Princeton: Princeton University Press, 1946) 43–51, 89–91. 2nd ed. Gerda Panofsky-
Soergel (Princeton: Princeton University Press, 1979). Originally titled *Liber de rebus in administratione sua
gestis* (1144–1149) and *Libellus alter de consecratione ecclesiae Sancti Dionysii* (1144–1146/47), respectively.
Reprinted with permission of the publisher.

on this part, having laid very strong material foundations for a straight nave and twin towers, and most strong spiritual ones of which it is said: *For other foundation can no man lay than that is laid, which is Jesus Christ.* Leaning upon God's inestimable counsel and irrefragable aid, we proceeded with this so great and so sumptuous work to such an extent that, while at first, expending little, we lacked much, afterwards, expending much, we lacked nothing at all and even confessed in our abundance: *Our sufficiency is of God.* Through a gift of God a new quarry, yielding very strong stone, was discovered such as in quality and quantity had never been found in these regions. There arrived a skillful crowd of masons, stonecutters, sculptors and other workmen, so that—thus and otherwise—Divinity relieved us of our fears and favored us with Its goodwill by comforting us and by providing us with unexpected [resources]. . . .

In carrying out such plans my first thought was for the concordance and harmony of the ancient and the new work. . . .

[from *On What Was Done Under His Administration*]
XXVII. Of the Cast and Gilded Doors

Bronze casters having been summoned and sculptors chosen, we set up the Main doors on which are represented the Passion of the Savior and His Resurrection, or rather Ascension, with great cost and much expenditure for their gilding as was fitting for the noble porch. Also [we set up] others, new ones on the right side and the old ones on the left beneath the mosaic which, though contrary to modern custom, we ordered to be executed there and to be affixed to the tympanum of the portal. We also committed ourselves richly to elaborate the tower[s] and the upper crenelations of the front, both for the beauty of the church and, should circumstances require it, for practical purposes. Further we ordered the year of the consecration, lest it be forgotten, to be inscribed in copper-gilt letters in the following manner:

> For the splendor of the church that has fostered and exalted him.
> Suger has labored for the splendor of the church.

Giving thee a share of what is thine, O Martyr Denis,

He prays to thee to pray that he may obtain a share of Paradise.

The year was the One Thousand, One Hundred, and Fortieth

Year of the Word when [this structure] was consecrated.

The verses on the door, further, are these:

Whoever thou art, if thou seekest to extol the glory of these doors,

Marvel not at the gold and the expense but at the craftsmanship of the work.

Bright is the noble work; but, being nobly bright, the work

Should brighten the minds, so that they may travel, through the true lights,

To the True Light where Christ is the true door.

In what manner it be inherent in this world the golden door defines:

The dull mind rises in truth through that which is material

And, in seeing this light, is resurrected from its former submersion.

. . .

XXVIII. Of the Enlargement of the Upper Choir

In the same year, cheered by so holy and so auspicious a work, we hurried to begin the chamber of the divine atonement in the upper choir. . . . How much the Hand Divine Which operates in such matters has protected this glorious work is also surely proven by the fact that it allowed that whole magnificent building [to be completed] in three years and three months, from the crypt below to the summits of the vaults above, elaborated with the variety of so many arches and columns, including even the consummation of the roof. Therefore the inscription of the earlier consecration also defines, with only one word eliminated, the year of completion of this one, thus:

The year was One Thousand, One Hundred, Forty and Fourth of the Word when [this structure] was consecrated.

To these verses of the inscription we choose the following ones to be added:

> Once the new rear part is jointed to the part in front,
> The church shines with its middle part brightened.
> For bright is that which is brightly coupled with the bright,
> And bright is the noble edifice which is pervaded by the new light;
> Which stands enlarged in our time,
> I, who was Suger, being the leader while it was being accomplished.

Eager to press on my success, since I wished nothing more under heaven than to seek the honor of my mother church which with maternal affection had suckled me as a child . . . we devoted ourselves to the completion of the work and strove to raise and to enlarge the transept wings of the church [so as to correspond] to the form of the earlier and latter work that had to be joined by them.

3 Leon Battista Alberti, 1407–1476

While the Italian humanist Leon Battista Alberti excelled in multiple disciplines including art, music, mathematics, cryptography, and literature, his most renowned printed work, *De re aedificatoria*, belongs to the realm of architecture. Translated as *On the Art of Building in Ten Books*, this text (composed around 1450) is commonly recognized as the first modern treatise on architecture and the first encyclopedic architectural text since that of Vitruvius. Yet, as Joseph Rykwert points out, Vitruvius essentially compiled information about existing architecture; he wrote of "how the buildings . . . *were* built." In contrast, Alberti extrapolated from a number of sources, including the ruins of ancient Rome and Vitruvius's rediscovered text, to formulate principles for architectural production; he "[prescribed] how the buildings of the future [*were*] *to be* built." * Drawing upon ideas of harmony, variety and beauty as found in nature, Alberti redefined and introduced the classical orders for contemporary use. Upon its printing in 1486, *On the Art of Building in Ten Books* became a highly influential text for subsequent generations of architects.

As an architect, Alberti is credited with relatively few constructed works. Perhaps the most recognized are the façade of Santa Maria Novella in Florence (1456–70) and the Church of San Andrea in Mantua (1470–76). The former incorporates classical elements into medieval remnants of the preexisting façade, while the latter merges the flowing barrel-vaulted interior of the ancient Roman basilica, the tripartite motif of the triumphal arch, and the pediment of the temple to create a Renaissance interpretation of older building elements.

---

* Joseph Rykwert, "Introduction," in Leon Battista Alberti, *On the Art of Building in Ten Books,* trans. J. Rykwert, R. Tavernor, and N. Leach (Cambridge, MA: MIT Press, 1999), x. Rykwert's italics.

On the Art of Building in Ten Books (ca.1450, published 1486)

Prologue

Many and various arts, which help to make the course of our life more agreeable and cheerful, were handed down to us by our ancestors, who had acquired them by much effort and care. All of them seem to compete toward the one end, to be of the greatest possible use to humanity, yet we realize that each has some integral property, which shows it has a different advantage to offer from the others. For we are forced to practice some of these arts by necessity, while others commend themselves to us for their utility, and still others we appreciate because they deal with matters that are pleasant to know. I need not specify these arts: it is obvious which they are. Yet, if you reflect on it, you would not find one among all the most important arts that did not seek and consider its own particular ends, excluding anything else. If, however, you were eventually to find any that proved wholly indispensable and yet were capable of uniting use with pleasure as well as honor, I think you could not omit architecture from that category: architecture, if you think the matter over carefully, gives comfort and the greatest pleasure to mankind, to individual and community alike; nor does she rank last among the most honorable of the arts.

Before I go any farther, however, I should explain exactly whom I mean by an architect; for it is no carpenter that I would have you compare to the greatest exponents of other disciplines: the carpenter is but an instrument in the hands of the architect.

From Leon Battista Alberti, *On the Art of Building in Ten Books*, trans. Joseph Rykwert, Robert Tavernor, and Neil Leach (Cambridge, MA: MIT Press, 1999), 2–5, 23–24, 301–303, 315–317. © 1988 Joseph Rykwert, Robert Tavernor, and Neil Leach. Reprinted with permission of the publisher. Translators' commentary omitted from this reprinting.

Him I consider the architect, who by sure and wonderful reason and method, knows both how to devise through his own mind and energy, and to realize by construction, whatever can be most beautifully fitted out for the noble needs of man, by the movement of weights and the joining and massing of bodies. To do this he must have an understanding and knowledge of all the highest and most noble disciplines. This then is the architect. But to return to the discussion.

Some have said that it was fire and water which were initially responsible for bringing men together into communities, but we, considering how useful, even indispensable, a roof and walls are for men, are convinced that it was they that drew and kept men together. We are indebted to the architect not only for providing that safe and welcome refuge from the heat of the sun and the frosts of winter (that of itself is no small benefit), but also for his many other innovations, useful to both individuals and the public, which time and time again have so happily satisfied daily needs.

How many respected families both in our own city and in others throughout the world would have totally disappeared, brought down by some temporary adversity, had not their family hearth harbored them, welcoming them, as it were, into the very bosom of their ancestors? Daedalus received much praise from his contemporaries for having constructed a vault in Selinunte where a cloud of vapor emanated so warm and gentle that it induced a most agreeable sweat, and cured the body in an extremely pleasant manner. What of others? How could I list the devices—walks, swimming pools, baths, and so forth—that help to keep us healthy? Or even vehicles, mills, timepieces, and other smaller inventions, which nonetheless play so vital a role in our everyday lives? What of the methods of drawing up vast quantities of water from hidden depths for so many different and essential purposes? And of memorials, shrines, sanctuaries, temples, and the like, designed by the architect for divine worship and for the benefit of posterity? Finally, need I stress how, by cutting through rock, by tunneling through mountains or filling in valleys, by restraining the waters of the sea and lakes, and by draining marshes, through the building of ships, by altering the course and dredging the mouths of rivers, and through the construction of harbors and bridges, the architect has not only met the temporary needs of man, but also opened up new gateways to all the provinces of the world? As a result nations have been able to serve each other by exchanging fruit, spices, jewels, experience and knowledge, indeed anything that might improve our health and standard of living.

Nor should you forget ballistic engines and machines of war, fortresses and whatever else may have served to protect and strengthen the liberty of our country, and the good and honor of the state, to extend and confirm its dominion. It is my view moreover that, should you question all the various cities which within human memory have fallen into enemy hands by siege, and inquire who defeated and conquered them, they would not deny that it was the architect; and that they could easily have scorned an enemy armed with weapons alone but could no longer have resisted the power of invention, the bulk of war machines and the force of ballistic engines, with which the architect had harassed, oppressed, and overwhelmed them. On the other hand, those besieged would consider no protection better than the ingenuity and skill of the architect. Should you examine the various military campaigns undertaken, you would perhaps discover that the skill and ability of the architect have been responsible for more victories than have the command and foresight of any general; and that the enemy were more often overcome by the ingenuity of the first without the other's weapons, than by the latter's sword without the former's good counsel. And what is more important, the architect achieves his victory with but a handful of men and without loss of life. So much for the use of architecture.

But how congenial and instinctive the desire and thought for building may be to our minds is evident—if only because you will never find anyone who is not eager to build something, as soon as he has the means to do so; nor is there anyone who, on making some discovery in the art of building, would not gladly and willingly offer and broadcast his advice for general use, as if compelled to do so by nature. It often happens that we ourselves, although busy with completely different things, cannot prevent our minds and imagination from projecting some building or other. Or again, when we see some other person's building, we immediately look over and compare the individual dimensions, and to the best of our ability consider what might be taken away, added, or altered, to make it more elegant, and willingly we lend our advice. But if it has been well designed and properly executed, who would not look at it with great pleasure and joy? Need I mention here not only the satisfaction, the delight, but even the honor that architecture has brought to citizens at home or abroad? Who would not boast of having built something? We even pride ourselves if the houses we live in have been constructed with a little more care and attention than usual. When you erect a wall or portico of great elegance and adorn it with a door, columns, or roof, good citizens approve and express joy for their own sake, as well as for yours, because they realize that you have used your wealth to increase greatly not only your own honor and glory, but also that of your family, your descendants, and the whole city. . . .

To conclude, then, let it be said that the security, dignity, and honor of the republic depend greatly on the architect: it is he who is responsible for our delight, entertainment, and health while at leisure, and our profit and advantage while at work, and in short, that we live in a dignified manner, free from any danger. In view then of the delight and wonderful grace of his works, and of how indispensable they have proved, and in view of the benefit and convenience of his inventions, and their service to posterity, he should no doubt be accorded praise and respect, and be counted among those most deserving of mankind's honor and recognition. . . .

Book I. Chapter IX

All the power of invention, all the skill and experience in the art of building, are called upon in compartition; compartition alone divides up the whole building into the parts by which it is articulated, and integrates its every part by composing all the lines and angles into a single, harmonious work that respects utility, dignity, and delight. If (as the philosophers maintain) the city is like some large house, and the house is in turn like some small city, cannot the various parts of the house—atria, *xysti*, dining rooms, porticoes, and so on—be considered miniature buildings? Could anything be omitted from any of these, through inattention and neglect, without detracting from the dignity and worth of the work? The greatest care and attention, then, should be paid to studying these elements, which contribute to the whole work, so as to ensure that even the most insignificant parts appear to have been formed according to the rules of art. . . .

The parts ought to be so composed that their overall harmony contributes to the honor and grace of the whole work, and that effort is not expended in adorning one part at the expense of all the rest, but that the harmony is such that the building appears a single, integral, and well-composed body, rather than a collection of extraneous and unrelated parts.

Moreover, in fashioning the members, the moderation shown by nature ought to be followed; and here, as elsewhere, we should not so much praise sobriety as condemn unruly passion for building: each part should be appropriate, and suit its purpose. For every aspect of building, if you think of it rightly, is born of necessity, nourished by convenience, dignified by use; and only in the end is pleasure provided for, while pleasure itself never fails to shun every excess. Let the building then be such that its members want no more than they already have, and what they have can in no way be faulted.

Then again, I would not wish all the members to have the same shape and size, so that there is no difference between them: it will be agreeable to make some parts large, and good to have some small, while some are valuable for their very mediocrity. It will be equally pleasing to have some members defined by straight lines, others by curved ones, and still others by a combination of the two, provided, of course, that the advice on which I insist is obeyed and the mistake is avoided of making the building appear like some monster with uneven shoulders and sides. Variety is always a most pleasing spice, where distant objects agree and conform with one another; but when it causes discord and difference between them, it is extremely disagreeable. Just as in music, where deep voices answer high ones, and intermediate ones are pitched between them, so they ring out in harmony, a wonderfully sonorous balance of proportioned results, which increases the pleasure of the audience and captivates them; so it happens in everything else that serves to enchant and move the mind.

This whole process should respect the demands of use and convenience, and follow the methods sanctioned by those who are experienced: to contravene established customs often detracts from the general elegance, while conforming to them is considered advantageous and leads to the best results. Although other famous architects seem to recommend by their work either the Doric, or the Ionic, or the Corinthian, or the Tuscan division as being the most convenient, there is no reason why we should follow their design in our work, as though legally obliged; but rather, inspired by their example, we should strive to produce our own inventions, to rival, or, if possible, to surpass the glory of theirs. . . .

Book IX. Chapter V
. . . The great experts of antiquity . . . have instructed us that a building is very like an animal, and that Nature must be imitated when we delineate it. Let us investigate, then, why some bodies that Nature produces may be called beautiful, others less beautiful, and even ugly. . . .

When you make judgments on beauty, you do not follow mere fancy, but the workings of a reasoning faculty that is inborn in the mind. It is clearly so, since no one can look at anything shameful, deformed, or disgusting without immediate displeasure and aversion. What arouses and provokes such a sensation in the mind we shall not inquire in detail, but shall limit our consideration to whatever evidence presents itself that is relevant to our argument. For within the form and figure of a building there resides some natural excellence and perfection that excites the mind and its immediately recognized by it. I myself believe that form, dignity, grace, and other such qualities depend on it, and as soon as anything is removed or altered, these qualities are themselves weakened and perish. Once we are convinced of this, it will not take long to discuss what may be removed, enlarged, or altered, in the form and figure. For every body consists entirely of parts that are fixed and individual; if these are removed, enlarged, reduced, or transferred somewhere inappropriate, the very composition will be spoiled that gives the body its seemly appearance.

From this we may conclude, without my pursuing such questions any longer, that the three principle components of that whole theory into which we inquire are number, what we might call outline, and position. But arising from the composition and connection of these three is a further quality in which beauty shines full face: our term for this is *concinnitas;* which we say is nourished with every grace and splendor. It is the task and aim of *concinnitas* to compose parts that are quite separate from each other by their nature, according to some precise rule, so that they correspond to one another in appearance.

That is why when the mind is reached by way of sight or sound, or any other means, *concinnitas* is instantly recognized. It is our nature to desire the best, and to cling to it with pleasure. Neither in the whole body nor in its parts does *concinnitas* flourish as much as it does in Nature herself; thus I might call it the spouse of the soul and of reason. It has a vast range in which to exercise itself and bloom—it runs through man's entire life and government, it molds the whole of Nature. Everything that Nature produces is regulated by the law of *concinnitas*, and her chief concern is that whatever she produces should be absolutely perfect. Without *concinnitas* this could hardly be achieved, for the critical sympathy of the parts would be lost. So much for this.

If this is accepted, let us conclude as follows. Beauty is a form of sympathy and consonance of the parts within a body, according to definite number, outline, and position, as dictated by *concinnitas*, the absolute and fundamental rule in Nature. This is the main object of the art of building, and the source of her dignity, charm, authority, and worth.

All that has been said our ancestors learned through observation of Nature herself; so they had no doubt that if they neglected these things, they would be unable to attain all that contributes to the praise and honor of the work; not without reason they declared that Nature, as the perfect generator of forms, should be their model. And so, with the utmost industry, they searched out the rules that she employed in producing things, and translated them into methods of building. By studying in Nature the patterns both for whole bodies and for their individual parts, they understood that at their very origins bodies do not consist of equal portions, with the result that some are slender, some fat, and others in between; and observing the great difference in purpose and intention between one building and another, . . . they concluded that, by the same token, each should be treated differently.

Following Nature's own example, they also invented three different ways of ornamenting a house, their names taken from the nations who favored one above the others, or even invented each, as it is said. One kind was fuller, more practical and enduring: this they called Doric. Another was slender and full of charm: this they named Corinthian. The one that lay in between, as though composed of both, they called the Ionic; they devised these for the body as a whole. When they observed the particular contribution of each of the three factors mentioned above, number, outline, and position, in the production of beauty, they established how to employ them, having studied nature's works. . . .

Book IX. Chapter X
. . . A great matter is architecture, nor can everyone undertake it. He must be of the

greatest ability, the keenest enthusiasm, the highest learning, the widest experience, and, above all, serious, of sound judgment and counsel, who would presume to call himself an architect. The greatest glory in the art of building is to have a good sense of what is appropriate. For to build is a matter of necessity; to build conveniently is the product of both necessity and utility; but to build something praised by the magnificent, yet not rejected by the frugal, is the province only of an artist of experience, wisdom, and thorough deliberation.

Moreover, to make something that appears to be convenient for use, and that can without doubt be afforded and built as projected, is the job not of the architect so much as the workman. But to preconceive and to determine in the mind and with judgment something that will be perfect and complete in its every part is the achievement of such a mind as we seek. Through his intellect he must invent, through experience recognize, through judgment select, through deliberation compose, and through skill effect whatever he undertakes. I maintain that each is based on prudence and mature reflection. But as for other virtues, in him I expect no more humanity, good nature, modesty, honesty, than in any other person given to any form of vocation; for anyone who lacks these qualities, in my opinion, does not deserve to be called a man. But above all he must avoid any frivolity, obstinacy, ostentation, or presumption, and anything that might lose him good will or provoke enmity among his fellow citizens.

Finally, I would have him take the same approach as one might toward the study of letters, where no one would be satisfied until he had read and examined every author, good and bad, who had written anything on the subject in which he was interested. Likewise, wherever there is a work that has received general approval, he should inspect it with great care, record it in drawing, note its numbers, and construct models and examples of it; he should examine and study the order, position, type, and number of the individual parts, especially those employed by the architects of the biggest and most important buildings, who, it might be conjectured, were exceptional men, in that they were given control of so great an expenditure. . . .

The architect should strive constantly to exercise and improve his ability through keen and animated interest in the noble arts; in this way he should gather and store in his mind anything of note, either dispersed and scattered abroad, or hidden in the remotest recesses of Nature, that might lend his works remarkable praise and glory. . . .

[The architect] should therefore develop his ability through practice and experience in any matter that might make some commendable contribution to his knowledge; and he should not think it his only duty to possess that skill without which he could not be what he professes to be, but he should apply himself to gain understanding and appreciation of all the noble arts so far as they are relevant, which understanding should be so ready and so serviceable that he will have no need of any further learning in this field; and he must not abandon his study, nor cool his application, until he feels that he is very close to those who are awarded the highest praise. He should not consider himself satisfied until he has employed every faculty with which art and talent have endowed him, and assimilated everything to the best of his ability so that he attains the highest degree of praise for it.

Of the arts the ones that are useful, even vital, to the architect are painting and mathematics. I am not concerned whether he is versed in any others. I will not hear those who say that an architect ought to be an expert in law, because he must deal with the rules for containing water, establishing boundaries, and proclaiming the intention to build, and with the many other legal constraints encountered during the course of building. Nor do I demand that he should have an exact understanding of the stars, simply because it is best to make libraries face Boreas, and baths the setting sun. Nor do I say that he ought to be a musician, because he must place sounding vases in a theater; nor an orator, to instruct his client on what he proposes to do. Let him have insight, experience, wisdom, and diligence in the matters to be discussed, and he will give an articulate, accurate, and informed account of them, which is the most important thing in oratory.

Yet he should not be inarticulate, nor insensitive to the sound of harmony; and it is enough that he does not build on public land, or on another person's property; that he does not obstruct the light; that he does not transgress the servitudes on rain dripping from the eaves, on watercourses, and on rights of way, except where there is provision; and that he has a sound knowledge of the winds, their direction, and their names; still, I would not criticize him for being better educated. But he should forsake painting and mathematics no more than the poet should ignore tone and meter. Nor do I imagine that a limited knowledge of them is enough.

But I can say this of myself: I have often conceived of projects in the mind that seemed quite commendable at the time; but when I translated them into drawings, I found several errors in the very parts that delighted me most, and quite serious ones; again, when I return to drawings, and measure the dimensions, I recognize and lament my carelessness; finally, when I pass from the drawings to the model, I sometimes notice further mistakes in the individual parts, even over the numbers. For all this I would not expect him to be a Zeuxis in his painting, or a Nichomachus in arithmetic, or an Archimedes in geometry. Let it be enough that he has a grasp of those elements of painting of which we have written; that he has sufficient knowledge of mathematics for the practical and considered application of angles, numbers, and lines, such as that discussed under the topic of weights and the measurements of surfaces and bodies, which some called *podismata* and *embata*. If he combines enthusiasm and diligence with a knowledge of these arts, the architect will achieve favor, wealth, fame for posterity, and glory.

4 ANDREA PALLADIO, 1508–1580

Andrea Palladio, Villa Rotonda, Vicenza, Italy, 1550s
Photo Credit: Cameraphoto Arte, Venice/Art Resource, NY

Andrea Palladio, originally named Andrea di Pietro della Gondola, first established himself as a stonemason in Vicenza. In the mid-1530s, he came under the patronage of the amateur architect Giangiorgio Trissino, a wealthy Renaissance scholar who bestowed the name Palladio upon Andrea and encouraged him undertake a classical education in the arts and mathematics. With Trissino as a mentor, Palladio immersed himself in the writings of Vitruvius and traveled to Rome to study the great architectural works of Roman antiquity. Through his illustrations of ancient structures and his own architectural designs—first country villas, the most famous of which may be the Villa Capra (1566–71), also known as the Villa Rotunda) and later larger religious buildings such as the Church of San Giorgio Maggiore (1564–80)—Palladio became well known throughout the Venetian region. Yet, perhaps his greatest architectural contribution is *I Quattro Libri dell'Architettura*, a text Palladio began in the 1550s and finally published in 1570. In this treatise, known in English as *The Four Books on Architecture*, Palladio discussed his architectural philosophy and offered practical guidance for builders, thoroughly illustrated with woodcuts of his works. Unlike Alberti's architectural writings, Palladio's text was intended for a nonacademic audience, for anyone involved in construction. This lack of pretension no doubt contributed to the work's popularity; within the next century, portions of *I Quattri Libri* had been translated into multiple languages. In eighteenth-century England, Palladio's work was extremely admired, generating numerous classical designs in a style often referred to as "Palladian," thus memorializing one of the most influential architects of the Italian Renaissance.

The Four Books on Architecture (ca. mid-1550s, published 1570)

The First Book on Architecture: Foreword to the Readers

Guided by a natural inclination, I dedicated myself to the study of architecture in my youth, and since I always held the opinion that the ancient Romans, as in many other things, had also greatly surpassed all those who came after them in building well, I elected as my master and guide Vitruvius, who is the only ancient writer on this art. I set myself the task of investigating the remains of the ancient buildings that have survived despite the ravages of time and the cruelty of the barbarians, and finding them much worthier of study than I had first thought, I began to measure all their parts minutely and with the greatest care. I became so assiduous an investigator of such things that, being unable to find anything that was not made with fine judgment and beautiful proportions, I repeatedly visited various parts of Italy and abroad in order to understand the totality of buildings from their parts and commit them to drawings. Accordingly, seeing how different the usual manner of building is from the things that I had observed in those structures and had read about in Vitruvius and Leon Battista Alberti and the other excellent writers who came after Vitruvius, and also from those which I myself built recently, which have been greatly appreciated and praised by those who employed me, I considered it worthy of man, who is not born for himself alone but also to be of use to others, to make public the designs of those buildings that I have collected over such a long period and at such personal risk, and to expound briefly what it is about them that seemed to me to be most worthy of consideration, and also the rules that I have followed and still follow when building; so that those who read my books may benefit from what is useful in them and supply themselves

Andrea Palladio, *The Four Books on Architecture*, trans. Robert Tavernor and Richard Schofield (Cambridge, MA: MIT Press, 1997), 5–7. © 1997 Massachusetts Institute of Technology. Reprinted with permission of the publisher. Translators' commentary omitted from this reprinting.

those things (of which perhaps there will be many) which I will have overlooked; so that, little by little, one may learn to set aside those strange abuses, barbarous inventions, and pointless expenses and (most importantly) avoid the common failures of various kinds that have been seen in many buildings. . . . I hope therefore that this manner of building will, to the benefit of all, soon achieve that level so desirable in all the arts. . . . [Since] I must publish the results of those labors which, since my youth, I have devoted to studying and measuring the ancient buildings that I knew about with as much care as I was capable of, and take this occasion to discuss architecture as briefly, methodically, and clearly as I could, I thought it would be most appropriate to begin with private houses; for it is plausible that they supplied the models [ragione] for public buildings, since it is very likely that man previously lived by himself, and then, seeing that he needed the help of other men in providing those things which would make him happy (if happiness is to be found down here), he quite naturally longed for and loved the company of other men: so they formed settlements from a number of houses and from settlements cities in which there were public places and buildings; and also because, of all the branches of architecture, none is more essential to man nor more often built than this. I shall discuss, therefore, private houses, and will then proceed to public buildings. I shall deal briefly with roads, bridges, squares, prisons, basilicas (that is, places of judgment), xysti, palaestrae, which were places where men took exercise, temples, theaters and amphitheaters, arches, baths, aqueducts, and finally I shall deal with the fortification of cities, and with harbors. In all these books I shall avoid being long-winded and will simply provide the advice [avertenza] that seems essential to me, and will make use of those terms widely used nowadays by craftsmen. For my part, I can promise no more than long labor, great diligence, and the devotion which I put into understanding and practicing what I offer; if it pleases God that I have not worked in vain I shall give thanks for his goodness, with all my heart, while still remaining greatly indebted to those who, through their own ingenious inventions and the experience they gained, have bequeathed us the rules of this art, for they opened up an easier and more direct route to the study of new things, and (thanks to them) we know of many things that would perhaps have remained hidden. This first part will be divided into two books; the first will be concerned with the preparation of materials and, once prepared, how and in what form they are to be used from the foundations up to the roof; and where those universal rules, which should be followed in all public as well as private structures, should be applied. The second will be concerned with the types [qualità] of buildings suitable to various classes of men; first I will discuss buildings in the city and then well-chosen and convenient sites required for buildings in the country [villa] and how they are to be laid out [compartire]. And, as we have very few ancient examples to refer to in this part, I will include plans and elevations [impiede] of many buildings which I designed [ordinare] for various gentlemen, and the designs of houses of the ancients with the most noteworthy parts of them following Vitruvius' teachings about how they were to be made.

Chapter I. On What Must Be Considered and Prepared Before Building Can Start
One must consider carefully every aspect of the plan [pianta] and elevations [impiede] of a building before starting to build. There are three things in every building (as Vitruvius says) that have to be considered, without which none deserve credit; these are usefulness or convenience [commodità], durability, and beauty. For one could not describe as perfect a building which was useful, but only briefly, or one which was inconvenient for a long time, or, being both durable and useful, was not beautiful. Convenience will be provided for when each member [membro] is given its appropriate position, well situated, no less than dignity requires nor more than utility demands; each member will be correctly positioned when the loggias [loggia], halls, rooms, cellars, and granaries are located in their appropriate places. Durability will be guaranteed when all the walls are plumb vertical, thicker below than above, and have sound and strong foundations; and further, when the columns above stand vertically over those below and all the solid openings, such as doors and windows, are one above the other: so that solid is above solid and void above void. Beauty will derive from a graceful shape and the relationship of the whole to the parts, and of the parts among themselves and to the whole, because buildings must appear to be like complete and well-defined

bodies, of which one member [membro] matches another and all the members are necessary for what is required. Having weighed up these things by mean of drawings and the model, one must carefully calculate the entire cost involved, making provision for the money in good time and preparing the materials that are likely needed, so that, when building, nothing is missing or hinders the completion of the work; for the patron [edificatore] will get great credit and the whole building will be at a great advantage if it is built at the appropriate pace, and all its walls, having been built up at the same height together, settle to the same extent, for then they will not develop those cracks seen so often in buildings which were constructed at different times and brought to their conclusion haphazardly. Then, once the most skillful craftsmen available have been chosen, so that the work may be carried out in the best possible manner according to their advice, provision should be made for timber, stone, sand, lime, and metals; on the subject of these materials one should heed the following rule [avertenza] that, for instance, to make the woodwork of the ceilings [travamenta, solaro] of halls and rooms, a sufficient quantity of beams should be provided so that, when putting them all in place, there is a space as wide as a beam and a half between them. Similarly, with stone, bear in mind that the jambs [erta] of the doors and windows do not require pieces of stone thicker than one fifth of the width of the opening nor less than one sixth. And if the ornament of a building is to be supplied by columns or pilasters [pilastri], their bases, capitals, and architraves should be stone, and the other parts of brick [pietro cotta]. As to walls, take care to make them thinner as they rise; such a rule should ensure the cost is reasonable and cut expenses considerably. Since I will talk in detail about all these subjects in their proper place, it is enough for now to have mentioned these general considerations here and to have made, as it were, a sketch of the whole building. But because, as well as the quantity one must also consider the type [qualità] and quality when choosing the best material, much will be gained from having experienced the buildings of others, because, having learned from them, we can already decide what is appropriate and suited to our own needs.

5 CLAUDE PERRAULT, 1613–1688

Claude Perrault, east front of the Louvre, Paris, 1666–70
View along the Quai du Louvre
Photo Credit: Réunion des Musées Nationaux/Art Resource, NY

Claude Perrault began his career as a physician interested in the study of anatomy, natural history, and physics. He received no formal architectural training, but nevertheless was involved in a number of architectural endeavors. His design for the East Façade of the Louvre (1665–80), at that time the Parisian royal residence, is his most well known. In combination, the East Façade's distinctive paired colonnade, raised basement level, and central crowning pediment inspired a number of works built throughout Europe and the United States, including Charles Garnier's Paris Opera (1857–74) and Charles Bulfinch's State House in Boston (1795–98). Perrault's notoriety also stemmed from his 1673 French translation of Vitruvius's *Ten Books on Architecture* as well as Perrault's 1683 publication, *Ordonnance des cinq espèces de colonnes selon la méthode des Anciens*, or *Ordonnance for the Five Kinds of Columns after the Method of the Ancients*. In the latter treatise, excerpted below, Perrault argued against the existence of universally fixed proportions arising from nature that, when changed, destroy architectural beauty. Disagreeing with this notion of absolute beauty based upon proportion, Perrault identified two types of beauty: positive and arbitrary. Positive beauty, according to Perrault, results from an inherent quality that is pleasing to everyone, such as rich materials or the precise execution of a work. Arbitrary beauty, however, stems not from innate qualities but from culturally conditioned preferences. With this distinction between positive and arbitrary beauty, Perrault provided an alternate framework through which architecture, and popular taste, could be viewed.

Ordonnance for the Five Kinds of Columns after the Method of the Ancients (1683)

Preface

The ancients rightly believed that the proportional rules that give buildings their beauty were based on the proportions of the human body and that just as nature has suited a massive build to bodies made for physical labor while giving a slighter one to those requiring adroitness and agility, so in the art of building, different rules are determined by the different intentions to make a building more massive or more delicate. Now these different proportions together with their appropriate ornaments are what give rise to the different architectural orders, whose characters, defined by variations in ornament, are what distinguish them most visibly but whose most essential differences consist in the relative size of their constituent parts.

These differences between the orders that are based, with little exactitude or precision, on their proportions and characters are the only well-established matters in architecture. Everything else pertaining to the precise measurement of their members or the exact outline of their profiles still has no rule on which all architects agree; each architect has attempted to bring these elements to their perfection chiefly through the things that proportion determines. As a result, in the opinion of those who are knowledgeable, a number of architects have approached an equal degree of perfection in different ways. This shows that the beauty of a building, like that of the human body, lies less in the exactitude of unvarying proportion and the relative size of constituent

Claude Perrault, *Ordonnance for the Five Kinds of Columns after the Method of the Ancients*, trans. Indra Kagis McEwen (Los Angeles: The Getty Center for the History of Art and the Humanities, 1993) 47–48, 50–51, 53–54. © 1993 The Getty Center for the History of Art and the Humanities, the J. Paul Getty Trust, Los Angeles. Reprinted with permission of the publisher.

parts than in the grace of its form, wherein nothing other than a pleasing variation can sometimes give rise to a perfect and matchless beauty without strict adherence to any proportional rule. A face can be both ugly and beautiful without any change in proportions, so that an alteration of the features—for example, the contraction of the eyes and the enlargement of the mouth—can be the same when one laughs or weeps, with a result that can be pleasing in one case and repugnant in the other; whereas, the dissimilar proportions of two different faces can be equally beautiful. Likewise, in architecture, we see works whose differing proportions nevertheless have the grace to elicit equal approval from those who are knowledgeable and possessed of good taste in architectural matters.

One must agree, however, that although no single proportion is indispensable to the beauty of a face, there still remains a standard from which its proportion cannot stray too far without destroying its perfection. Similarly, in architecture, there are not only general rules of proportion, such as those that, as we have said, distinguish one order from anther, but also detailed rules from which one cannot deviate without robbing an edifice of much of its grace and elegance. Yet these proportions have enough latitude to leave architects free to increase or decrease the dimensions of different elements according to the requirements occasioned by varying circumstances. . . . It is . . . also for this very reason that all those who have written about architecture contradict one another, with the result that in the ruins of ancient buildings and among the great number of architects who have dealt with the proportions of the orders, one can find agreement neither between any two buildings nor between any two authors, since none has followed the same rules.

This shows just how ill-founded is the opinion of people who believe that the proportions supposed to be preserved in architecture are as certain and invariable as the proportions that give musical harmony its beauty and appeal, proportions that do not depend on us but that nature has established with absolutely immutable precision and that cannot be changed without immediately offending even the least sensitive ear. For if this were so, those works of architecture that do not have the true and natural proportions that people claim they can have would necessarily be condemned by common consensus, at least by those whom extensive knowledge has made most capable of discernment. . . .

Now, even though we often like proportions that follow the rules of architecture without knowing why, it is nevertheless true that there must be some reason for this liking. The only difficulty is to know if this reason is always something positive, as in the case of musical harmonies, of it, more usually, it is simply founded on custom and whether that which makes the proportions of a building pleasing is not the same as that which makes the proportions of a fashionable costume pleasing. For the latter have nothing positively beautiful or inherently likable, since when there is a change in custom or in any other of the nonpositive reasons that make us like them, we like them no longer, even though the proportions themselves remain the same.

In order to judge rightly in this case, one must suppose two kinds of beauty in architecture and know which beauties are based on convincing reasons and which depend only on prejudice. I call beauties based on convincing reasons those whose presence in works is bound to please everyone, so easily apprehended are their value and quality. They include the richness of materials, the size and magnificence of the building, the precision and cleanness of the execution, and symmetry, which in French signifies the kind of proportion that produces an unmistakable and striking beauty. For there are two kinds of proportions. One, difficult to discern, consists in the proportional relationship between the parts, such as that between the size of various elements, either with respect to one another or to the whole, of which an element may be, for instance, a seventh, fifteenth, or twentieth part. The other kind of proportion, called symmetry, is very apparent and consists in the relationship the parts have collectively as a result of the balanced correspondence of their size, number, disposition, and order. . . .

Against the beauties I call positive and convincing, I set those I call arbitrary, because they are determined by our wish to give a definite proportion, shape, or form to things that might well have a different form without being misshapen and that appear agreeable not by reasons within everyone's grasp but merely by custom and the association the mind makes between two things of a different nature. By this association the esteem that inclines the mind to things whose worth it knows also inclines it to those things whose worth it does not know and little by little induces it to value both equally. This principle is the natural basis for belief, which is nothing but the result of a predisposition not to doubt the truth of something we do not know if it is accompanied by our knowledge and good opinion of the person who assures us of it. It is also prejudice that makes us like the fashions and the patterns of speech that custom has established at court, for the regard we have or the worthiness and patronage of people in the court makes us like their clothing and their way of speaking, although these things in themselves have nothing positively likable, since after a time they offend us without their having undergone any inherent change.

It is the same in architecture, where there are things such as the usual proportions between capitals and their columns that custom alone makes so agreeable that we could not bear their being otherwise, even though in themselves they have no beauty that must infallibly please us or necessarily elicit our approval. . . .

. . . [Neither] imitation of nature, nor reason, nor good sense in any way constitutes the basis for the beauty people claim to see in proportion and in the orderly disposition of the parts [of a work of architecture]; indeed, it is impossible to find any source other than custom for the pleasure they impart. Since those who first invented these proportions had no rule other than their fancy (*fantaisie*) to guide them, as their fancy changed they introduced new proportions, which in turn were found pleasing. . . .

The first works of architecture manifested richness of materials; grandeur, opulence, and precision of workmanship; symmetry (which is a balanced and fitting correspondence of parts that maintain the same arrangement and position); good sense in matters where it is called for; and other obvious reasons for beauty. As a result, these works seemed so beautiful and were so admired and revered that people decided they should serve as the criteria for all others. And inasmuch as they believed it impossible to add to or to change anything in all these positive beauties without diminishing the beauty of the whole, they found it unimaginable that the proportions of these works could be altered without ill effect; whereas, they could, in fact, have been otherwise without injury to the other beauties. In the same way, when a person passionately loves a face whose only perfect beauty lies in its complexion, he also believes its proportions could not be improved upon, for just as the great beauty of one part makes him love the whole, so the love of the whole entails the love of its parts.

It is therefore true that in architecture there is positive beauty and beauty that is only arbitrary, even though it appears to be positive due to prejudice, against which one guards oneself with great difficulty. It is also true that even though good taste is founded on a knowledge of both kinds of beauty, a knowledge of arbitrary beauty is usually more apt to form what we call taste and is that which distinguishes true architects from the rest.

ETIENNE-LOUIS BOULLÉE, 1728–1799

Born and raised in Paris, Etienne-Louis Boullée initially pursued painting before turning to architecture. He trained and practiced in a neoclassical idiom, but relatively little of his work was actually constructed. Rather, Boullée's reputation rests largely on his work as a teacher, theorist, and designer of visionary projects. In his treatise *Architecture, Essai sur l'art* (*Architecture, Essay on Art*), written in the 1790s but unpublished until the mid-1950s, Boullée espoused his view of architecture as a highly poetic and psychological art grounded in nature. He believed the sphere, a naturally occurring form and Boullee's "image of perfection," supported this assertion. According to Boullée, the sphere's appealing qualities—symmetry, regularity, and variety—have an "immeasurable hold over our senses"; these immutable qualities, in Boullée's estimation, derive from nature.

Boullée's visionary projects employed a stripped neoclassical vocabulary that has come to be associated with French revolutionary architecture. His designs relied heavily on geometric forms and the ways in which they would be modeled by light and shadow; they also drew on the permanence and emotive power of ancient Egyptian monuments. For example, Boullée's project for Newton's Cenotaph (1784), a funerary monument to the British scientist and mathematician, involves a gigantic sphere 500 feet in diameter embedded within a cylindrical base. At its center, this sphere would contain the tomb of Newton, as well as a suspended globe representing both the sun and moon. Boullée intended the Cenotaph to symbolize the universe and communicate with those experiencing the structure. This idea of *architecture parlante*, or "speaking architecture," discussed by Boullée's contemporary, Claude Nicolas Ledoux, gained renewed interest in the latter half of the twentieth century after the 1953 publication of Boullée's *Architecture, Essay on Art*.

Architecture, Essay on Art (1770–84)

Introduction

What is architecture? Shall I join Vitruvius in defining it as the art of building? Indeed, no, for there is a flagrant error in this definition. Vitruvius mistakes the effect for the cause.

In order to execute, it is first necessary to conceive. Our earliest ancestors built their huts only when they had a picture of them in their minds. It is this product of the mind, this process of creation, that constitutes architecture and what can consequently be defined as the art of designing and bringing to perfection any building whatsoever. Thus, the art of construction is merely an auxiliary art which, in our opinion, could appropriately be called the scientific side of architecture.

Art, in the true sense of the word, and science, these we believe have their place in architecture.

The majority of authors writing on this subject confine themselves to discussing the technical side. That is natural if we think about it a little. It was necessary to study safe building methods before attempting to build attractively. And since the technical side is of paramount importance and consequently the most essential, it was natural that this aspect should be dealt with first.

Etienne-Louis Boullée, *Architecture, Essay on Art*, in Helen Rosenau, *Boullée & Visionary Architecture* (London: Academy Editions; New York: Harmony Books, 1976), 83, 85–87.

Moreover, it must be admitted that the beauty of art cannot be demonstrated like a mathematical truth; although this beauty is derived from nature, to sense it and apply it fruitfully certain qualities are necessary and nature is not very generous with them.

What do we find in books on architecture? Ruins of ancient temples that we know were excavated in Greece. However perfect these examples may be, they are not sufficient to provide a complete treatise on art. . . .

And now Reader, let me ask you, "Am I not to some extent justified in maintaining that architecture is still in its infancy, for we have no clear notion of its basic principles?"

In common with all education me, I admit that tact and sensibility can result in excellent work. I admit that even artists who have not acquired sufficient knowledge to search out the basic principles at the root of their art will nevertheless be competent, provided they are guided by that gift of Nature that permits men to choose wisely.

But it is nonetheless true that there are few authors who have considered architecture from the artistic point of view; what I mean is that few authors have attempted to study in depth that side of architecture that I term art, in the strict sense of the word. We have some precepts based on good examples but these are few and far between. . . .

The Present Problem
Is architecture merely fantastic art belonging to the realm of pure invention or are its basic principles derived from Nature?

Allow me first of all to challenge the existence of any art form that is pure invention.

If by the strength of his mind and the techniques it devises, a man could arouse in us with his art those sensations we experience when we look at nature, such art would be far superior to anything we possess, for we are limited to more or less imperfect [imitations]. But there is no art that we can create alone, for if such an art existed it would mean that the Divine Being, the creator of Nature, had endowed us with a quality that is part of His own essential being.

What, therefore, could Perrault have meant by a purely inventive art? Don't we derive all our ideas from nature? And does not genius for us lie in the forceful manner in which our senses are reminded of nature?. . .

Let us listen to a modern Philosopher [John Locke] who tells us, "All our ideas, all our perceptions come to us via external objects. External objects make different impressions on us according to whether they are more or less analogous with the human organism." I should add that we consider "*beautiful*" those objects that most resemble the human organism and that we reject those which, lacking this resemblance, do not correspond to the human condition.

On the Essential Quality of Volumes. On Their Properties. On Their Analogy with the Human Organism
. . . [A] sphere is, in all respects, the image of perfection. It combines strict symmetry with the most perfect regularity and the greatest possible variety; its form is developed to the fullest extent and is the simplest that exists; its shape is outlined by the most agreeable contour and, finally, the light effects that it produces are so beautifully graduated that they could not possibly be softer, more agreeable or more varied. These

unique advantages, which the sphere derives from nature, have an immeasurable hold over our senses.

A great man (Montesquieu) once said, "Symmetry is pleasing because it is the image of clarity and because the mind, which is always seeking understanding, easily accepts and grasps all that is symmetrical."[1] I would add that symmetry is pleasing because it is the image of order and perfection.

Variety is pleasing because it satisfied a spiritual need which, by its very nature, likes to be stimulated and sustained by what is new. And it is variety that makes things appear new to us. It therefore follows that variety puts new life into our faculties by offering us new pleasures and it is as pleasing to us in the objects that are part of any given volume, as it is in the light effects so produced.

Grandeur, too, always pleases us whatever form it takes for we are ever eager to increase our pleasure and would like to embrace the Universe.

Finally, the image of Grace is one which, deep in our hearts, is the most pleasing of all. . . .

Consideration of How We Can with Certitude Define the Basic Principles of an Art and of Architecture in Particular

What constitute to perfection the principles of any given art are those principles from which no deviation is possible. . . .

---

[1] Here Boullée refers to the article "Goût" on page 764 of Montesquieu's *Encyclopédie* (1757).

What . . . is the primary law on which architectural principles are based?

Let us consider an example of architecture that has been imperfectly observed and lacks proportion. This will certainly be a defect but the defect will not necessarily be such an eyesore that we cannot bear to look at the building. . . .

In architecture a lack of proportion is not generally very obvious except to the eye of the connoisseur. It is thus evident that although proportion is one of the most important elements constituting beauty in architecture, it is not the primary law from which its basic principles derive. Let us try, therefore, to discover what it is impossible not to admit in architecture, and that from which there can be no deviation without creating a real eyesore.

Let us imagine a man with a nose that is not in the middle of his face, with eyes that are not equidistant, one being higher than the other, and whose limbs are also ill-matched. It is certain that we would consider such a man hideous. Here we have an example that can readily be applied to the subject under discussion. If we imagine a Palace with an off-centre front projection, with no symmetry and with windows set at varying intervals and different heights, the overall impression would be one of confusion and it is certain that to our eyes such a building would be both hideous and intolerable.

It is easy for the reader to surmise that the basic rule and the one that governs the principles of architecture, originates in regularity. . . .

. . . Symmetrical compositions are true and pure. The slightest disorder, the slightest confusion becomes intolerable. Order must be in evidence and paramount in any composition based on symmetry. In short, the wheel of reason should never desert an architect's genius for he should always make a rule of the excellent maxim, "Nothing is beautiful if all is not judicious."

7 EUGÈNE-EMMANUEL VIOLLET-LE-DUC, 1814–1879

West façade of Notre-Dame, Paris, France, ca. 1200–50
Photo Credit: Scala/Art Resource, NY

The French architect Eugène-Emmanuel Viollet-le-Duc is well known for his restoration work on Gothic monuments such as Sainte-Chappelle and Notre Dame in Paris. Yet, his legacy rests on his theoretical writings. Deeply influenced by buildings of the Middle Ages, Viollet-le-Duc championed Gothic architecture as a model for the designers of his day. However, he did not call for a Gothic revival, but rather emphasized the governing logic behind medieval architecture. In particular, Viollet-le-Duc identified the direct correlation between the form and structure of the Gothic cathedral. Ultimately, Gothic builders aspired to construct the lightest, tallest, most graceful works possible. This meant a dematerialization of the building itself, a reduction of the building's mass in favor of vast amounts of glass. Every feature of the Gothic cathedral, from the elongated compound piers to its ribbed groin vaults, needed to function structurally. All forms, even seemingly ornamental elements, were direct manifestations of the building's structure. According to Viollet-le-Duc, the underlying principles of this structure stem from the logic and rationality of nature, the harmony of parts, proportion, and use, evident in natural creations. Viollet-le-Duc discussed this universal principle of structural rationalism as well as other architectural theories in his ten-volume *Dictionnaire raisonné de l'architecture française du XI au XVI siècle* (literally, the *Reasoned Dictionary of French Architecture of the 11th to the 16th Centuries*, but often called the *Dictionnaire raisonné*) of 1854–69 and his two volume *Entretiens sur l'architecture* (*Discourses on Architecture*) of 1858–72. Viollet-le-Duc's notion of structural rationalism was particularly influential for modern architects of the late-nineteenth and early-twentieth centuries.

Dictionnaire raisonné (1854–68)

STYLE, s.m. There is *style*; then there are the *styles*. Styles enable us to distinguish different schools and epochs from one another. The styles of Greek, Roman, Byzantine, Romanesque, and Gothic architecture differ from each other in ways that make it easy to classify the monuments produced by these various types of art. . . .

We will speak here of *style* only as it belongs to art understood as a conception of the human mind. Just as there is only *Art* in this sense, so there is only one *Style*. What, then, is style in this sense? It is, in a work of art, the manifestation of an ideal based on a principle.

Style can also be understood as mode; that is, to make the form of an art appropriate to its objective. In art, then, there is *absolute style*; there is also *relative style*. The first dominates the entire artistic conception of an object; the second can be modified depending upon the purpose of the object. The style appropriate for a church would not be appropriate for a private dwelling; this is relative style. Yet a house can reveal the imprint of an artistic expression (just as can a temple or a barracks) that is independent of the object itself, an imprint belonging to the artist or, more precisely, to the principle that he took as a starting point: this is *style*. . . .

Style is for a work of art what blood is for the human body: it develops the work, nourishes it, gives it strength, health, and duration; it gives it, as the saying goes, the real blood that is common to all humans. Although each individual has very different

---

Eugène-Emmanuel Viollet-le-Duc, "Style," in *Dictionnaire raisonné*, trans. Kenneth D. Whitehead (New York: George Braziller, Inc., 1990). Reprinted with permission from the publisher.

physical and moral qualities, we must nevertheless speak of style when it is a question of the artist's power to give body and life to works of art, even when each work of art still has its own proper character. . . .

. . . Architecture as an art is a human creation. Such is our inferiority that, in order to achieve this type of creation, we are obliged to proceed as nature proceeds in the things she creates. We are obliged to employ the same elements and the same logical method as nature; we are obliged to observe the same submission to certain natural laws and to observe the same transitions. When the first man traced in the sand with a stick a circle pivoting upon its axis, he in no way *invented* the circle; he merely discovered a figure already existing. All discoveries in geometry have resulted from observations, not creations. The angles opposite the vertex of a triangle did not have to wait to be discovered by somebody in order to be equal to each other.

Architecture, this most human of creations, is but an application of principles that are born outside us—principles that we appropriate by observation. Gravitational force existed before we did; we merely deduced the statics of it. Geometry, too, was already existent in the universal order; we merely took note of its laws, and applied them. The same thing is true of all aspects of the architectural art; proportions—indeed, even decoration—must arise out of the great natural order whose principles we must appropriate in the measure that human intelligence permits us to do so. It was not without reason that Vitruvius said that the architect had to be in possession of most of the knowledge of his time, and for his part he put philosophy at the head of all knowledge. Among the ancients, of course, philosophy included all of the sciences of "observation," whether in the moral order or in the physical order.

If, therefore, we succeed in acquiring some little knowledge of the great principles of the universal natural order, we will quickly realize that all creation is developed in a very logical way and, very probably, is subject to laws anterior to any creative idea.

So much is this the case that we might well claim: "In the beginning, numbers and geometry existed!" Certainly the Egyptians and, after them, the Greeks understood things that way; for them, numbers and geometric figures were sacred. We believe that the style the Egyptians and Greeks achieved—for style is never lacking in their artistic productions—was due to the religious respect they had for the principles to which universal creation itself was the first to be subject, that universal creation which itself is style *par excellence*.

In questions of this order, however, we need to bring forward some simple and obvious demonstration. We are not here concerned with philosophy; we are concerned with bringing some great and fundamental principles within our grasp—simple principles, in fact. Style is able to enter into architectural work only when it operates in accordance with these fundamental principles.

There are those who appear to be persuaded that artists are simply born with the faculty to produce works with style and that all they have to do is to open themselves to a sort of inspiration of which they are not the masters. This idea would appear to be too broadly general in its sweep; it is, nevertheless, favored by the fuzzy-minded. It is not an idea, however, that ever seems to have been favored or, indeed, even admitted in those epochs that knew best how to produce the works of art that have been most noted for their style. On the contrary, in those times it was believed that the most perfect kind of artistic creation was the consequence of a profound observation of the principles on which art can and must be based. (It was, of course, also granted that artists did possess artistic faculties.)

We will leave it open to poets and painters to decide whether what we call inspiration can or cannot get along without a long and profound observation of nature. As far as architecture is concerned, however, this particular pursuit is compelled on its scientific side to observe the imperatives that rule it; it is obliged from the very first to seek the elements and the principles on which it will be based, and then to deduce from them with an utterly rigorous logic all the consequences that follow. It happens to be the truth that we cannot pretend to proceed with a power greater than that possessed by universal creation itself, for we act at all only by the virtue of our observation of the laws of that creation. Once we have recognized that nature (however we suppose nature herself to have been inspired) has never so much as joined two single atoms together without being subject to a completely logical rule; once we have recognized that nature always proceeds with mathematical exactitude from the simple to the complex, without ever abandoning its first principles—once we have recognized these things, we will surely have to be allowed to smile broadly if we then find an architect waiting for an *inspiration* without first having some recourse to his reason. . . .

. . . If we were to follow through and examine all the phases of creation in our world, both organic and inorganic, we would quickly find it to be the case that, in all of nature's various works, however different they may be in appearance, the same logical order proceeding from a fundamental principle is followed; this is an *a priori* law, and nature never deviates from it. And it is to this natural method that is owing the "style" with which all of nature's works are imbued. From the largest mountain down to the finest crystal, from the lichen to the oaks of our forests, from the polyp to human beings, everything in terrestrial creation does indeed possess style—that is to say, a perfect harmony between the results obtained and the means employed to achieve them.

This is the example that nature has provided for us, the example we must follow when, with the help of our intelligence, we presume to create anything ourselves.

What we call imagination is in reality only one aspect of our human mind. It is the part of the mind that is alive even while the body is asleep; it is through that same part of the mind that, in dreams, we see spread out before us bizarre scenes consisting of impossible facts and events that have no connection one with the other. This part of ourselves that is imagination still does not sleep when we are awake; but we generally regulate it by means of our reason. We are not the masters of our imagination; it distracts us unceasingly and turns us away from whatever is occupying us, although it seems to escape entirely and float freely only during sleep. However, we are the masters of our reason. Our reason truly belongs to us; we nourish it and develop it. With constant exercise, we are able to make out of it an attentive "operator" for ourselves, able to regulate our actions and ensure that our accomplishments are both lively and lasting.

Thus, even while we recognize that a work of art may exist in an embryonic state in the imagination, we must also recognize that it will not develop into a true and viable work of art without the intervention of reason. It is reason that will provide the embryonic work with the necessary organs to survive, with the proper relationships between its various parts, and also with what in architecture we call its proper proportions. Style is the visible sign of the unity and harmony of all the parts that make up the whole work of art. Style originates, therefore, in an intervention of reason.

The architecture of the Egyptians, like that of the Greeks, possessed style because both architectures were derived by means of an inflexible logical progression from the principle of stability on which both were based. One cannot say the same of all the constructions of the Romans during the Roman Empire. As for the architecture of the Middle Ages, it, too, possessed style once it had abandoned the debased traditions of antiquity—that is, in the period from the twelfth to the fifteenth centuries. It possessed style because it proceeded according to the same kind of logical order that we have observed at work in nature. Thus, just as in viewing a single leaf it is possible to reconstruct the entire plant, and in viewing an animal bone, the animal itself, it is also possible to deduce the members of an architecture from the view of an architectural profile . . . Similarly, the nature of the finished construction can be derived from an architectural member. . . .

. . . [Style] as well as the beautiful, we must insist, resides not merely in forms, but in the harmony of a form with reference to an end in view, to a result to be achieved. If a form clearly delineates an object and makes understandable the purpose for which that object was produced, then it is a beautiful form. It is for this reason that the creations of nature are always beautiful in the eyes of the observer. The correct application of a form to its object and to its use or function, and the harmony that necessarily always accompanies such a correct application, can only evoke our admiration, whether we observe it in a stately oak tree or in the smallest of insects. We will discover style in the mechanisms of the wings of a bird of prey, just as we will discover style in the curves of a body of a fish; in these cases style clearly results from mechanisms or curves so aptly designed that flight results in one case and swimming in the other. It hardly concerns us if someone points out that a bird has wings in order to be able to fly or that this bird is able to fly only because of its wings; the fact is that the wings are a perfect machine, which produces flight. This machine represents a precise expression of the function that it fulfills. We other artists need go no further than this. . . .

. . . Now, style is inherent in an architectural art when that art is practiced in accordance with a logical and harmonious order, whether in its details or as a whole, whether in its principles or in its form; nothing in such an architectural art is ever left to chance or fantasy. It is, however, nothing but fantasy that guides an artist if, for example, he provides a wall that has no need of it with an architectural order; or if he provides with a buttress a column already erected with a view toward carrying a load. It is fantasy that includes in the same building concave bays along with square bays terminating with horizontal beam members; or that inserts projecting cornices or ledges between the floors of a building where there are no roof drains; or that raises up pediments over bays opening on a wall; or that cuts into an upper story in order to make a door opening for the people or vehicles that must pass through the door; and so on. If it is not fantasy that leads to the construction of such things, so contrary to reason, then it must be what is commonly called *taste*. But is it a proof of good taste in architecture not to proceed in accordance with reason? Architecture, after all, is an art that is destined to satisfy, before everything else, material needs that are perfectly well defined; and architecture is obliged to make use of materials whose qualities result from laws to which we must necessarily submit.

It is an illusion to imagine that there can be style in architectural works whose features are unexplained and unexplainable; or that there can be style where the form is nothing but the product of memory crammed with a number of different motifs taken from here or from there. It would be equally valid to say that there could be style in a literary work of which the chapters or, indeed, even the sentences were nothing but a loose collection of words borrowed from ten different authors, all writing on different subjects. . . .

Style is the consequence of a principle pursued methodically; it is a kind of emanation from the form of the work that is not consciously sought after. Style that is sought after is really nothing else but *manner*. Manner becomes dated; style never does.

When an entire population of artists and artisans is strongly imbued with logical principles in accordance with which form is the consequence of the object as well as its purpose, then style will be present in the works that issue from their hands, from the most ordinary vase to the most monumental building, from the simplest household utensil to the costliest piece of furniture. We admire this unity in the best of Greek antiquity, and we find the same kind of thing again in the best of what the Middle Ages produced, though the two types of art are different because the two civilizations that produced them were different. We cannot appropriate to ourselves the style of the Greeks, because we are not Athenians. Nor can we re-create the style of our predecessors in the Middle Ages, for the simple reason that time has moved on. We can only affect the manner of the Greeks or of the artists of the Middle Ages; that is to say, we can only produce pastiches. If we cannot accomplish what they did, we can at least proceed as they did by allowing ourselves to become penetrated with principles that are true and natural principles—just as they were imbued with true and natural principles. If we succeed in doing this, our works will possess style without our having to seek after it.

8 LOUIS SULLIVAN, 1856–1924

During the late-nineteenth century, Louis Sullivan played a central role in the development of an American architecture that rejected the use of historicist styles. As discussed in the excerpt below, Sullivan felt that architecture should draw on a principle he discerned in nature, namely, that "form ever follows function." At its most basic, this dictum implies that a building's form, like an eagle's wing, must reflect its function or use. For example, Sullivan's Wainwright Building in St. Louis, Missouri (1890) has three distinct zones that correspond to the presumed interior activities. The ground floor, dedicated to commercial purposes, features large windows for product display. The smaller, regular windows of the middle floors relate to the individual offices housed within, while the uppermost floor, occupied by mechanical equipment for the building, has no need for daylight and thus is marked by small round voids surrounded by vegetal-like ornament. Indeed, Sullivan's designs often included ornamental motifs derived from nature, as function for Sullivan involved not only the practical use of the building by its occupants, but also their psychological and aesthetic experience of the building. Furthermore, function encompassed the efficiency and durability of the building itself. It is not surprising, then, that Sullivan embraced modern technology, in particular steel frame construction, which allowed for increased floor space, flexible arrangement of the interiors, and a maximum amount of light due to amplified fenestration. Thus, Sullivan combined ideas of nature and technology in his search for a unique American architecture, a philosophy that set him apart from his contemporary architects and would inspire the work of Frank Lloyd Wright.

"The Tall Office Building Artistically Considered" (1896)

. . . All things in nature have a shape, that is to say, a form, an outward semblance, that tells us what they are, that distinguishes them from ourselves and from each other.

Unfailingly in nature these shapes express the inner life, the native quality of the animal, tree, bird, fish, that they present to us; they are so characteristic, so recognizable, that we say, simply, it is "natural" it should be so. Yet the moment we peer beneath this surface of things, the moment we look through the tranquil reflection of ourselves and the clouds above us, down into the clear, fluent, unfathomable depth of nature, how startling is the silence of it, how amazing the flow of life, how absorbing the mystery. Unceasingly the essence of things is taking shape in the matter of things, and this unspeakable process we call birth and growth. Awhile the spirit and the matter fade away together, and it is this that we call decadence, death. These two happenings seem jointed and interdependent, blended into one like a bubble and its iridescence, and they seem borne along upon a slowly moving air. This air is wonderful past all understanding.

Yet to the steadfast eye of one standing upon the shore of things, looking chiefly and most lovingly upon that side on which the sun shines and that we feel joyously to be life, the heart is ever gladdened by the beauty, the exquisite spontaneity, with which life seeks and takes on its forms in an accord perfectly responsive to its needs. It seems ever as though the life and the form were absolutely one and inseparable so adequate is the sense of fulfillment.

Louis Sullivan, "The Tall Office Building Artistically Considered," in *America Builds*, ed. Leland Roth (New York: Icon/Harper and Row, 1983), 344–46. © Leland M. Roth. Reprinted with permission from the publisher.

Whether it be the sweeping eagle in his flight or the open apple-blossom, the toiling work-horse, the blithe swan, the branching oak, the winding stream at its base, the drifting clouds, over all the coursing sun, form ever follows function, and this is the law. Where function does not change form does not change. The granite rocks, the ever-brooding hills, remain for ages; the lightning lives, comes into shape, and dies in a twinkling.

It is the pervading law of all things organic, and inorganic, of all things physical and metaphysical, of all things human and all things superhuman, of all true manifestations of the head, of the heart, of the soul, that the life is recognizable in its expression, that form ever follows function. This is the law.

Shall we, then, daily violate this law in our art? Are we so decadent, so imbecile, so utterly weak of eyesight, that we cannot perceive this truth so simple, so very simple? It is indeed a truth so transparent that we see through it but do not see it? Is it really then, a very marvelous thing, or is it rather so commonplace, so everyday, so near a thing to us, that we cannot perceive that the shape, form, outward expression, design or whatever we may choose, of the tall office building should in the very nature of things follow the functions of the building, and that where the function does not change, the form is not to change?

Does this not readily, clearly, and conclusively show that the lower one or two stories will take on a special character suited to the special needs, that the tiers of typical offices, having the same unchanging function, shall continue in the same unchanging form, and that as to the attic, specific and conclusive as it is in its very nature, its function shall equally be so in force, in significance, in continuity, in conclusiveness of outward expression? From this results, naturally, spontaneously, unwittingly, a three-part division, not from any theory, symbol, or fancied logic.

And thus the design of the tall office building takes its place with all other architectural types made when architecture, as has happened once in many years, was a living art. Witness the Greek temple, the Gothic cathedral, the medieval fortress.

And thus, when native instinct and sensibility shall govern the exercise of our beloved art; when the known law, the respected law, shall be that form ever follows function; when our architects shall cease struggling and prattling handcuffed and vainglorious in the asylum of a foreign school; when it is truly felt, cheerfully accepted, that this law opens up the airy sunshine of green fields, and gives to us a freedom that the very beauty and sumptuousness of the outworking of the law itself as exhibited in nature will deter any sane, any sensitive man from changing into license, when it becomes evidence that we are merely speaking a foreign language with a noticeable American accent, whereas each and every architect in the land might, under the benign influence of this law, express in the simplest, most modest, most natural way that which it is in him to say; that he might really and would surely develop his own characteristic individuality, and that the architectural art with him would certainly become a living form of speech, a natural form of utterance, giving surcease to him and adding treasures small and great to the growing art of his land; when we know and feel that Nature is our friend, not our implacable enemy—that an afternoon in the country, an hour by the sea, a full open view of one single day, through dawn, high noon, and twilight, will suggest to us so much that is rhythmical, deep, and eternal in the vast art of architecture, something so deep, so true, that all the narrow formalities, hard-and-fast rules, and strangling bonds of the schools cannot stifle it in us—then it may be proclaimed that we are on the high-road to a natural and satisfying art, and architecture that will soon become a fine art in the true, the best sense of the word, an art that will live because it will be of the people, for the people, and by the people.

9 FRANK LLOYD WRIGHT, 1867–1959

Frank Lloyd Wright, Robie House, Chicago, IL, 1908–10
Photo from *The Early Work of Frank Lloyd Wright: The "Ausgeführte Bauten" of 1911*
(NY: Dover Publications, 1982), 122

The American architect Frank Lloyd Wright began his career as a draughtsman in the office of Louis Sullivan and his partner, Dankmar Adler (1844–1900). During this time, Wright absorbed many lessons from Sullivan, including the older architect's appreciation for nature and his rejection of historicist styles. Wright developed very specific ideas about architecture, and he communicated them through numerous designs, lectures, and publications. Wright's architectural activity spanned more than six decades, during which time he developed a highly unique architecture inspired by varied sources such as the nineteenth-century American Shingle Style and the art and architecture of Japan. Wright produced masterpieces such as the Dana-Thomas House in Springfield, Illinois (1902–04); the Kauffman House, otherwise known as Fallingwater, in Bear Run, Pennsylvania (1936–37); and the Guggenheim Museum in New York City (1946–59). Each of these works represents a different phase of Wright's practice, but all demonstrate his desire for an organic architecture in which all parts contribute to a unified whole.

Wright began to express this natural philosophy quite early in his career with the development of his Prairie Style homes. Exemplified by the Robie House in Chicago, Illinois (1908–10), Wright's Prairie Style works are generally characterized by long, low, horizontal roofs that echo the flat landscape of American Midwest. A vertical chimney often anchors the building to its site, establishing the hearth as the symbolic, if not the literal, center of the family dwelling. As Wright discussed in the article excerpted below, other features such as a raised foundation, screen windows, built-in furniture, and interior flowing spaces contribute to the Prairie Style. Furthermore, Wright embraced new materials and technology, viewing the machine not as a threat to the architect's creativity but rather as a tool to assist him in his task of creating harmonious, integrated, and original works. Throughout his life, Wright maintained this philosophy as he consistently sought to develop an architecture reflective of American democracy and individuality, inspired by the integrity of the artist and of the land.

"In the Cause of Architecture" (1908)

. . . Primarily, Nature furnished the materials for architectural motifs out of which the architectural forms as we know them to-day have been developed, and, although our practice for centuries has been for the most part to turn from her, seeking inspiration in books and adhering slavishly to dead formulae, her wealth of suggestion is inexhaustible; her riches greater than any man's desire. I know with what suspicion the man is regarded who refers matters of fine art back to Nature. I know that it is usually an ill-advised return that is attempted, for Nature in external, obvious aspect is the usually accepted sense of the term and the nature that is reached. But given inherent vision there is no source so fertile, so suggestive, so helpful aesthetically for the architect as a comprehension of natural law. As Nature is never right for a picture so is she never right for the architect—that is, not ready-made. Nevertheless, she has a practical school beneath her more obvious forms in which a sense of proportion may be cultivated, when Vignola and Vitruvius fail as they must always fail. It is there that he may develop that sense of reality that translated to his own field in terms of his own work will lift him far above the realistic in his art; there he will be inspired by sentiment that will never degenerate to sentimentality and he will learn to draw with a surer hand the every-perplexing line between the curious and the beautiful.

A sense of the organic is indispensable to an architect; where can he develop it so surely as in this school? A knowledge of the relations of form and function lies at the root of his practice; where else can he find the pertinent object lessons Nature so readily fur-

Frank Lloyd Wright, "In the Cause of Architecture," in *Architectural Record* 23, no. 3 (1908). Reprinted in *The Origins of Modern Architecture: Selected Essays from Architectural Record*, ed. Eric Uhlfelder (New York: Dover Publications, Inc., 1998), 50–53, 57–58, 60. Reprinted with permission from the publisher.

nishes? Where can he study the differentiations of form that go to determine character as he can study them in the trees? Where can that sense of inevitableness characteristic of a work of art be quickened as it may be by intercourse with nature in this sense?

Japanese art knows this school more intimately than that of any people. In common use in their language there are many words like the word "edaburi," which, translated as near as may be, means the formative arrangement of the branches of a tree. We have no such word in English, we are not yet sufficiently civilized to think in such terms, but the architect must not only learn to think in such terms but he must learn in this school to fashion his vocabulary for himself and furnish it in a comprehensive way with useful words as significant as this one. . . .

In 1894, with this text from Carlyle at the top of the page—"The Ideal is within thy-self, thy condition is but the stuff thou art to shape that same Ideal out of"—I formulated the following "propositions." I set them down here much as they were written then, although in the light of experience they might be stated more completely and succinctly.

I. Simplicity and Repose are qualities that measure the true value of any work of art. But simplicity is not in itself an end nor is it a matter of the side of a barn but rather an entity with a graceful beauty in its integrity from which discord, and all that is meaningless, has been eliminated. A wild flower is truly simple. Therefore:

> 1. A building should contain as few rooms as will meet the conditions which give it rise and under which we live, and which the architect should strive continually to simplify; then the ensemble of the rooms should be carefully considered that comfort and utility may go hand in hand with beauty. Beside the entry and necessary work rooms there need be but three rooms on the ground floor of any house, living room, dining room and kitchen, with the

possible addition of a "social office"; really there need be but one room, the living room with requirements otherwise sequestered from it or screened within it by means or architectural contrivances.

2. Openings should occur as integral features of the structure and form, if possible, its natural ornamentation.

3. An excessive love of detail has ruined more fine things from the standpoint of fine art or fine living than any one human shortcoming—it is hopelessly vulgar. Too many houses, when they are not little stage settings or scene paintings, are mere notion stores, bazaars or junk-shops. Decoration is dangerous unless you understand it thoroughly and are satisfied that it means something good in the scheme as a whole, for the present you are usually better off without it. Merely that it "looks rich" is no justification for the use of ornament.

4. Appliances or fixtures as such are undesirable. Assimilate them together with all appurtenances into the design of the structure.

5. Pictures deface walls oftener than they decorate them. Pictures should be decorative and incorporated in the general scheme as decoration.

6. The most truly satisfactory apartments are those in which most or all of the furniture is built in as a part of the original scheme considering the whole as an integral unit.

II. There should be as many kinds (styles) of houses as there are kinds (styles) of people and as many differentiations as there are different individuals. A man who has individuality (and what man lacks it?) has a right to its expression in his own environment.

III. A building should appear to grow easily from its site and be shaped to harmonize with its surroundings if Nature is manifest there, and if not try to make it as quiet, substantial and organic as She would have been were the opportunity Hers.[1]

We of the Middle West are living on the prairie. The prairie has a beauty of its own and we should recognize and accentuate this natural beauty, its quiet level. Hence, gently sloping roofs, low proportions, quiet sky lines, suppressed heavy-set chimneys and sheltering overhangs, low terraces and out-reaching walls sequestering private gardens.

IV. Colors require the same conventionalizing process to make them fit to live with that natural forms do; so go to the woods and fields for color schemes. Use the soft, warm, optimistic tones of earths and autumn leaves in preference to the pessimistic blues, purples or cold greens and grays of the ribbon counter; they are more wholesome and better adapted in most cases to good decoration.

V. Bring out the nature of the materials, let their nature intimately into your scheme. Strip the wood of varnish and let it alone—stain it. Develop the natural texture of the plastering and stain it. Reveal the nature of the wood, plaster, brick or stone in your designs; they are all by nature friendly and beautiful. No treatment can be really a matter of fine art when these natural characteristics are, or their nature is, outraged or neglected.

VI. A house that has character stands a good chance of growing more valuable as it grows older while a house in the prevailing mode, whatever that mode may be, is soon out of fashion, stale and unprofitable.

---

[1] In this I had in mind the barren town lots devoid of tree or natural incident, town houses and board walks only in evidence.

Buildings like people must first be sincere, must be true and then withal as gracious and lovable as may be.

Above all, integrity. The machine is the normal tool of our civilization, give it work that it can do well—nothing is of greater importance. To do this will be to formulate new industrial ideals, sadly needed. . . .

In the hope that some day America may live her own life in her own buildings, in her own way, that is, that we may make the best of what we have for what it honestly is or may become, I have endeavored in this work to establish a harmonious relationship between ground plan and elevation of these buildings, considering the one as a solution and the other an expression of the conditions of a problem of which the whole is a project. I have tried to establish an organic integrity to begin with, forming the basis for the subsequent working out of a significant grammatical expression and making the whole, as nearly as I could, consistent.

What quality of style the buildings may possess is due to the artistry with which the conventionalization as a solution and an artistic expression of a specific problem within these limitations has been handled. The types are largely a matter of personal taste and may have much or little to do with the American architecture for which we hope.

From the beginning of my practice the question uppermost in my mind has been not "what style" but "what is style?" and it is my belief that the chief value of the work illustrated here will be found in the fact that if in the face of our present day conditions any given type may be treated independently and imbued with the quality of style, then a truly noble architecture is a definite possibility, so soon as Americans really demand it of the architects of the rising generation.

I do not believe we will ever again have the uniformity of type which has characterized the so-called great "styles." Conditions have changed; our ideal is Democracy, the highest possible expression of the individual as a unit not inconsistent with a harmonious whole. The average of human intelligence rises steadily, and as the individual unit grows more and more to be trusted we will have an architecture with richer variety in unity than has ever arisen before; but the forms must be born out of our changed conditions, they must be *true* forms, otherwise the best that tradition has to offer is only an inglorious masquerade, devoid of vital significance or true spiritual value. . . .

The present industrial condition is constantly studied in the practical application of these architectural ideals and the treatment simplified and arranged to fit modern processes and to utilize to the best advantage the work of the machine. The furniture takes the clean cut, straight-line forms that the machine can render far better than would be possible by hand. Certain facilities, too, of the machine, which it would be interesting to enlarge upon, are taken advantage of and the nature of the materials is usually revealed in the process.

Nor is the atmosphere of the result in it completeness new and hard. In most of the interiors there will be found a quiet, a simple dignity that we imagine is only to be found in the "old" and it is due to the underlying organic harmony, to the each in all and the all in each throughout. This is the modern opportunity—to make a building, together with its equipment, appurtenances and environment, an entity which shall constitute a complete work of art, and a work of art more valuable to society as a whole than has before existed because discordant conditions endured for centuries are smoothed away; everyday life here finds a expression germane to its daily existence; an idealization of the common need sure to be uplifting and helpful in the same sense that pure air to breathe is better than air poisoned with noxious gases.

An artist's limitations are his best friends. The machine is here to stay. It is the forerunner of the democracy that is our dearest hope. There is no more important work before the architect now [than] to use this normal tool of civilization to the best advantage instead of prostituting it as he has hitherto done in reproducing with murderous ubiquity forms born of other times and other conditions and which it can only serve to destroy. . . .

As for the future—the work shall grow more truly simple; more expressive with fewer lines, fewer forms; more articulate with less labor; more plastic; more fluent, although more coherent; more organic. It shall grow not only to fit more perfectly the methods and processes that are called upon to produce it, but shall further find whatever is lovely or of good repute in method or process, and idealize it with the cleanest, most virile stroke I can imagine. As understanding and appreciation of life matures and deepens, this work shall prophesy and idealize the character of the individual it is fashioned to serve more intimately, no matter how inexpensive the result must finally be. It shall become in its atmosphere as pure and elevating in its humble way as the trees and flowers are in their perfectly appointed way, for only so can architecture be worthy [of] its high rank as a fine art, or the architect discharge the obligation he assumes to the public—imposed upon him by the nature of his own profession.

Adolf Loos, 1870–1933 10

Although the architect Adolf Loos was born in Brno, Moravia, he spent the majority of his career in Vienna. He built relatively little but gained notoriety through his impassioned and often sarcastic writings on architecture and society. For example, in his essay "Ornament and Crime" (1908), excerpted below, Loos criticized the use of ornament on moral grounds. He believed "the evolution of culture [to be] synonymous with the removal of ornamentation from objects of everyday use." According to this theory of societal development, the application of decoration to utilitarian objects such as jackets, bicycles, or buildings was an affront to human progress. Yet, this "degenerate" behavior registered as criminal when modern people wasted time, money, and effort to create unnecessary and inappropriate ornament. Related to this concept was Loos's assertion that architecture was fundamentally shelter—a useful object—and thus was not art. While architects such as Walter Gropius sought to merge art and life, to infuse everyday objects with an aesthetic beauty, Loos argued for the strict separation of art and life. For Loos, architecture belonged to life.

"Ornament and Crime" (1908)

In the womb the human embryo goes through all phases of development the animal kingdom has passed through. And when a human being is born, his sense impressions are like a new-born dog's. In childhood he goes through all changes corresponding to the stages in the development of humanity. At two he sees with the eyes of a Papuan, at four with those of a Germanic tribesman, at six of Socrates, at eight of Voltaire. At eight he becomes aware of violet, the color discovered by the eighteenth century; before that, violets were blue and the purple snail was red, Even today physicists can point to colors in the solar spectrum which have been given a name, but which it will be left to future generations to discern.

A child is amoral. A Papuan too, for us. The Papuan slaughters his enemies and devours them. He is not a criminal. But if a modern person slaughters someone and devours him, he is a criminal or a degenerate. The Papuan covers his skin with tattoos, his boat, his oars, in short everything he can lay his hands on. He is no criminal. The modern person who tattoos himself is either a criminal or a degenerate. There are prisons in which eighty percent of the inmates have tattoos. People with tattoos not in prison are either latent criminals or degenerate aristocrats.

The urge to decorate one's face and anything else within reach is the origin of the fine arts. It is the childish babble of painting. But all art is erotic.

A person of our times who gives way to the urge to daub the walls with erotic symbols is a

Adolf Loos, *Ornament and Crime, Selected Essays*, trans. Michael Mitchell (Riverside, CA: Ariadne Press, 1998), 167–75. Reprinted with permission from the publisher.

criminal or a degenerate. What is natural in the Papuan or the child is a sign of degeneracy in a modern adult. I made the following discovery, which I passed on to the world: *the evolution of culture is synonymous with the removal of ornamentation from objects of everyday use. . . .*

. . . I do not accept the objection that ornament is a source of increased pleasure in life for cultured people, the objection expressed in the exclamation, "But if the ornament is beautiful!" For me, and with me for all people of culture, ornament is not a source of increased pleasure in life. When I want to eat a piece of gingerbread, I choose a piece that is plain, not a piece shaped like a heart, or a baby, or a cavalryman, covered over and over with decoration, A fifteenth-century man would not have understood me, but all modern people will. The supporters of ornament think my hunger for simplicity is some kind of mortification of the flesh. No, my dear Professor of Applied Arts, I am not mortifying the flesh at all. I find the gingerbread tastes better like that.

It is easy to reconcile ourselves to the great damage and depredations the revival of ornament had done to our aesthetic development, since no one and nothing, not even the power of the state, can hold up the evolution of mankind. It can only be slowed down. We can afford to wait. But in economic respects it is a crime, in that it leads to the waste of human labor, money, and materials. That is damage time cannot repair. . . .

Ornament means wasted labor and therefore wasted health. That was always the case. Today, however, it also means wasted material, and both mean wasted capital.

As there is no longer any organic connection between ornament and our culture, ornament is no longer an expression of our culture. The ornament being created now bears no relationship to us, nor to any human being, or to the system governing the world today. It has no potential for development. . . . In the past the artist was a healthy, vigorous figure, always at the head of humanity. The modern ornamental artist, however, lags behind or is a pathological case. After three years even he himself disowns his own products. Cultured people find them intolerable straight away, others become aware of it only after a number of years. . . . Modern ornament has no parents and no offspring, no past and no future. Uncultivated people, for whom the greatness of our age is a closed book, greet it rapturously and then disown it after a short time.

Humanity as a whole is healthy, only a few are sick. But these few tyrannize the worker, who is so healthy he is incapable of inventing ornaments. They compel him to execute the ornaments they have invented, in a wide variety of different materials.

The changing fashion in ornament results in a premature devaluation of the product of the worker's labor; his time and the materials used are wasted capital. I have formulated the following principle: *The form of an object should last, that is, we should find it tolerable as long as the object itself lasts.* I will explain: A suit will change its style more often than a valuable fur. A woman's ball outfit, intended for one night alone, will change its style more quickly than a desk. Woe betide us, however, if we have to change a desk as quickly as a ball outfit because we can no longer stand the old style. Then we will have wasted the money we paid for the desk.

Ornamental artists and craftsmen are well aware of this, and in Austria they try to show this deficiency in a positive light. They say, "A consumer who has furnishings he cannot stand after ten years, and thus is forced to refurnish his apartment every ten years, is better than one who buys something only when the old one becomes worn out with use. Industry needs that. The rapid changes in fashion provide employment for millions."

This seems to be the secret of the Austrian economy. When a fire breaks out, how often does one hear someone say, "Thank God! Now there is work for people again." Just set a house on fire, set the Empire on fire, and everyone will be rolling in money! Just keep on making furniture we chop up for firewood after three years, mountings we have to melt down after four, because even at auction they will not fetch a tenth of the cost of labor and materials, and we will get richer and richer!

Not only the consumer bears the loss, it is above all the producer. Nowadays, putting decoration on objects which, thanks to progress, no longer need to be decorated, means a waste of labor and an abuse of material. If all objects would last as long in aesthetic terms as they last physically, the consumer would be able to pay a price for them that would allow the worker to earn more money and work shorter hours. For an object from which I am convinced I will get full use until it is worn out I am quite happy to pay four times the price of another I could buy. I am happy to pay forty crowns for my shoes, even though there are shoes for ten in another shop. But in those trades that languish under the yoke of the ornamental artist, no value is put on good or bad work-manship. Work suffers because no one is willing to pay for it at its true value.

And that is a good thing too, since these ornamented objects are bearable only when they are shoddily produced. I find it easier to accept a fire when I hear it is only worth-less rubbish that is being destroyed. I can enjoy the trumpery in the *Künstlerhaus* [The Association of Viennese Artists] because I know it takes a few days to put it up and one day to tear it down. But throwing coins instead of stones, lighting a cigar with a bank note, crushing up and drinking a pearl, I find unaesthetic. . . .

A modern person, who regards ornament as a symptom of the artistic superfluity of previous ages and for that reason holds it sacred, will immediately recognize the un-healthy, the forced—painfully forced—nature of modern ornament. Ornament can no longer be produced by someone living on the cultural level of today. It is different for individuals and people who have not yet reached that level.

The ideal I preach is the aristocrat. What I mean by that is the person at the peak of humanity, who yet has a profound understanding of the problems and aspirations of those at the bottom. One who well understands the way the African works patterns into his cloth according to a certain rhythm, so the design appears only when the fabric is taken off the loom; likewise the Persian weaving his rug, the Slovak peasant woman making her lace, the old woman making marvelous needlework from silk and glass beads. The aristocrat lets them carry on in their own accustomed way, he knows the time they spend on their work is sacred to them. The revolutionary would go and tell them it was all pointless, just as he would drag an old woman away from the wayside shrine, telling her there is no God. But the atheist among the aristocrats still raises his hat when he passes a church.

My shoes are covered with decoration formed by sawtooth patterns and holes. Work done by the shoemaker, work he has not been paid for. Imagine I go to the shoemaker and say, "You charge thirty crowns for a pair of shoes. I will pay you forty-eight." It will raise the man to such a transport of delight he will thank me through his work-manship and the material used, making them of a quality that will far outweigh my extra payment. He is happy, and happiness is a rare commodity in his house. He has found someone who understands him, who respects his work, and does not doubt his honesty. He can already see the finished shoes in his mind's eye. He knows where the best leather is to be found at the moment, he knows which of his workers he will entrust with the task, and the shoes will have all the sawtooth patterns and holes an elegant pair of shoes can take. And then I say, "But there is one condition. The shoes must be completely plain." I will drag him down from the heights of bliss to the depths of hell. He will have less work, and I have taken away all his pleasure in it.

The ideal I preach is the aristocrat. I can accept decoration on my own person if it brings pleasure to my fellow men. It brings pleasure to me, too. I can accept the African's ornament, the Persian's, the Slovak peasant woman's, my shoemaker's, for it provides the high point of their existence, which they have no other means of achiev-ing. *We* have the art that has superseded ornament. After all the toil and tribulations of the day, we can go to hear Beethoven or *Tristan*. My shoemaker cannot. I must not take his religion away from him, for I have nothing to put in its place. But anyone who goes to the *Ninth* and then sits down to design a wallpaper pattern is either a fraud or a degenerate.

The disappearance of ornament has brought about an undreamed-of blossoming in the other arts. Beethoven's symphonies would never have been written by a man who had to dress in silk, velvet, and lace. Those who go around in velvet jackets today are not artists, but clowns or house painters. We have become more refined, more subtle. When men followed the herd they had to differentiate themselves through color, modern man uses his dress as a disguise. His sense of his own individuality is so immensely strong it can no longer be expressed in dress. Lack of ornamentation is a sign of intellectual strength. Modern man uses the ornaments of earlier or foreign cultures as he likes and as he sees fit. He concentrates his own inventive power on other things.

Antonio Sant'Elia, 1888–1916

The Italian architect Antonio Sant'Elia is best known for the "Manifesto of Futurist Architecture" (1914) and the associated sketches of the *Città Nuova*, his visionary metropolis of the future. As a member of the Italian Futurist movement founded by Filippo Tommaso Marinetti, Sant'Elia called for the renunciation of tradition and convention, a divorce from all things of the past. He and his fellow Futurists advocated an entirely new way of life based on technology, progress, and speed. Sant'Elia's drawings of the *Città Nuova* depict a multilevel city of colossal, terraced towers in which transmission antennas, electric wires, external elevators, skywalks, and a sense of modernity abound. Sant'Elia's crusade for the future far exceeded his contemporaries' conceptions of modernity, making the proclamations of Le Corbusier and Gropius appear conservative in comparison. A glorification of battle and violence, viewed as the necessary means of eradicating the past, accompanied the Futurist cries for progress. Unfortunately, Sant'Elia became a victim of this philosophy, perishing on the fields of World War I. Nevertheless, despite the brevity of his life and his few built works, Sant'Elia's visions of the future as discussed in his manifesto and embodied in the *Città Nuova* influenced subsequent generations of architects.

"Manifesto of Futurist Architecture" (1914)

No architecture has existed since 1700. A moronic mixture of the most various stylistic elements used to mask the skeletons of modern houses is called modern architecture. The new beauty of cement and iron are profaned by the superimposition of motley decorative incrustations that cannot be justified either by constructive necessity or by our (modern) taste, and whose origins are in Egyptian, Indian or Byzantine antiquity and in that idiotic flowering of stupidity and impotence that took the name of NEOCLASSICISM.

These architectonic prostitutions are welcomed in Italy, and rapacious alien ineptitude is passed off as talented invention and as extremely up-to-date architecture. Young Italian architects (those who borrow originality from clandestine and compulsive devouring of art journals) flaunt their talents in the new quarters of our towns, where a hilarious salad of little ogival columns, seventeenth-century foliation, Gothic pointed arches, Egyptian pilasters, rococo scrolls, fifteen-century cherubs, swollen caryatids, take the place of style in all seriousness, and presumptuously put on monumental airs. The kaleidoscopic appearance and reappearance of forms, the multiplying of machinery, the daily increasing needs imposed by the speed of communications, by the concentration of population, by hygiene, and by a hundred other phenomena of modern life, never cause these self-styled renovators of architecture a moment's perplexity or hesitation. They persevere obstinately with the rules of Vitruvius, Vignola

---

Antonio Sant'Elia, "Manifesto of Futurist Architecture," trans. Caroline Tisdall, in Umberto Apollonio, ed., *Futurist Manifestos*, trans. R. Brain, R. W. Flint, J. C. Higgitt, C. Tisdall (London: Thames & Hudson, Ltd., 1973), 160, 169–172. Original © 1970 by Verlag M. Dumont Schauberg and Gabriele Mazzotta editore. Reprinted with permission of Viking Penguin, a division of the Penguin Group, Inc.

and Sansovino plus gleanings from any published scrap of information on German architecture that happens to be at hand. Using these, they continue to stamp the image of imbecility on our cities, our cities which should be the immediate and faithful projection of ourselves.

And so this expressive and synthetic art has become in their hands a vacuous stylistic exercise, a jumble of ill-mixed formulae to disguise a run-of-the-mill traditionalist box of bricks and stone as a modern building. As if we who are accumulators and generators of movement, with all our added mechanical limbs, with all the noise and speed of our life, could live in streets built for the needs of men four, five or six centuries ago.

This is the supreme imbecility of modern architecture, perpetuated by the venal complicity of the academies, the internment camps of the intelligentsia, where the young are forced into the onanistic recopying of classical models instead of throwing their minds open in the search for new frontiers and in the solution of the new and pressing problem: THE FUTURIST HOUSE AND CITY. The house and the city that are ours both spiritually and materially, in which our tumult can rage without seeming a grotesque anachronism.

The problem posed in *Futurist* architecture is not one of linear rearrangement. It is not a question of finding new mouldings and frames for windows and doors, of replacing columns, pilasters and corbels with caryatids, flies and frogs. Neither has it anything to do with leaving a façade in bare brick, or plastering it, or facing it with stone or in determining formal differences between the new building and the old one. It is a question of tending the healthy growth of the Futurist house, of constructing it with all the resources of technology and science, satisfying magisterially all the demands of our habits and our spirit, trampling down all that is grotesque and antithetical (tradition, style, aesthetics, proportion), determining new forms, new lines, a new harmony of profiles and volumes, an architecture whose reason for existence can be found solely in the unique conditions of modern life, and in its correspondence with the aesthetic values of our sensibilities. This architecture cannot be subjected to any law of historical continuity. It must be new, just as our state of mind is new.

The art of construction has been able to evolve with time, and to pass from one style to another, while maintaining unaltered the general characteristics of architecture, because in the course of history changes of fashion are frequent and are determined by the alternations of religious conviction and political disposition. But profound changes in the state of the environment are extremely rare, changes that unhinge and renew, such as the discovery of natural laws, the perfecting of mechanical means, the rational and scientific use of material. In modern life the process of stylistic development in architecture has been brought to a halt. ARCHITECTURE NOW MAKES A BREAK WITH TRADITION. IT MUST PERFORCE MAKE A FRESH START.

Calculations based on the resistance of materials, on the use of reinforced concrete and steel, exclude 'architecture' in the classical and traditional sense. Modern constructional materials and scientific concepts are absolutely incompatible with the disciplines of historical styles, and are the principal cause of the grotesque appearance of 'fashionable' buildings in which attempts are made to employ the lightness, the superb grace of the steel beam, the delicacy of reinforced concrete, in order to obtain the heavy curve of the arch and the bulkiness of marble.

The utter antithesis between the modern world and the old is determined by all those things that formerly did not exist. Our lives have been enriched by elements the possibility of whose existence the ancients did not even suspect. Men have identified material contingencies, and revealed spiritual attitudes, whose repercussions are felt in a thousand ways. Principal among these is the formation of a new ideal of beauty that is still obscure and embryonic, but whose fascination is already felt even by the masses. We have lost our predilection for the monumental, the heavy, the static, and we have enriched our sensibility with a *taste for the light, the practical, the ephemeral and the swift*. We no longer feel ourselves to be the men of the cathedrals, the palaces and the podiums. We are the men of the great hotels, the railway stations, the immense streets, colossal ports, covered markets, luminous arcades, straight roads and beneficial demolitions.

We must invent and rebuild the Futurist city like an immense and tumultuous shipyard, agile, mobile and dynamic in every detail; and the Futurist house must be like a gigantic machine. The lifts must no longer be hidden away like tapeworms in the niches of stairwells; the stairwells themselves, rendered useless, must be abolished, and the lifts must scale the lengths of the façades like serpents of steel and glass. The house of concrete, glass and steel, stripped of paintings and sculpture, rich only in the innate beauty of its lines and relief, extraordinarily 'ugly' in its mechanical simplicity, higher and wider according to need rather than the specifications of municipal laws. It must soar up on the brink of a tumultuous abyss: the street will no longer lie like a doormat at ground level, but will plunge many storeys down into the earth, embracing the metropolitan traffic, and will be linked up for necessary interconnections by metal gangways and swift-moving pavements.

THE DECORATIVE MUST BE ABOLISHED. The problem of Futurist architecture must be resolved, not by continuing to pilfer from Chinese, Persian or Japanese photographs or fooling around with the rules of Vitruvius, but through flashes of genius and through scientific and technical expertise. Everything must be revolutionized. Roofs and underground spaces must be used; the importance of the façade must be diminished; issues of taste must be transplanted from the field of fussy moulding, finicky capitals and flimsy doorways to the broader concerns of BOLD GROUPINGS AND MASSES, AND LARGE SCALE DISPOSITION OF PLANES. Let us make an end of monumental, funereal and commemorative architecture. Let us overturn monuments, pavements, arcades and flights of steps; let us sink the streets and squares; let us raise the level of the city.

I COMBAT AND DESPISE:

1. All the pseudo-architecture of the avant-garde, Austrian, Hungarian, German and American;

2. All classical architecture, solemn, hieratic, scenographic, decorative, monumental, pretty and pleasing;

3. The embalming, reconstruction and reproduction of ancient monuments and palaces;

4. Perpendicular and horizontal lines, cubical and pyramidical forms that are static, solemn, aggressive and absolutely excluded from our utterly new sensibility;

5. The use of massive, voluminous, durable, antiquated and costly materials.

AND PROCLAIM:

1. That Futurist architecture is the architecture of calculation, of audacious temerity and of simplicity; the architecture of reinforced concrete, of steel, glass, cardboard, textile fibre, and of all those substitutes for wood, stone and brick that enable us to obtain maximum elasticity and lightness;

2. That Futurist architecture is not because of this an arid combination of practicality and usefulness, but remains art, i.e., synthesis and expression;

3. That oblique and elliptic lines are dynamic, and by their very nature possess an emotive power a thousand times stronger than perpendiculars and horizontal; and that no integral, dynamic architecture can exist that does not include these;

4. That decoration as an element superimposed on architecture is absurd, and that THE DECORATIVE VALUE OF FUTURIST ARCHITECTURE DEPENDS SOLELY ON THE USE AND ORIGINAL ARRANGEMENT OF RAW OR BARE OR VIOLENTLY COLOURED MATERIALS;

5. That, just as the ancients drew inspiration for their art from the elements of nature, we—who are materially and spiritually artificial—must find that inspiration in the elements of the utterly new mechanical world we have created, and of which architecture must be the most beautiful expression, the most complete synthesis, the most efficacious integration;

6. That architecture as the art of arranging forms according to pre-established criteria is finished;

7. That by the term architecture is meant the endeavour to harmonize the environment with Man with freedom and great audacity, that is to transform the world of things into a direct projection of the world of the spirit;

8. From an architecture conceived in this way no formal or linear habit can grow, since the fundamental characteristics of Futurist architecture will be its impermanence and transience. THINGS WILL ENDURE LESS THAN US. EVERY GENERATION MUST BUILD ITS OWN CITY. This constant renewal of the architectonic environment will contribute to the victory of Futurism which has already been affirmed by WORDS-IN-FREEDOM, PLASTIC DYNAMISM, MUSIC WITHOUT QUADRATURE AND THE ART OF NOISES, and for which we fight without respite against traditionalist cowardice.

Geoffrey Scott, 1884–1929 12

In 1907, the English scholar and writer Geoffrey Scott moved to Florence, Italy, where he became part of the literary circle surrounding the American Mary Berenson and her husband Bernard, an art historian and critic. Alongside the British landscape architect Cecil Pinsent, Scott took part in the garden design for the Berenson's villa, I Tatti. Scott would be involved in a few other minor design projects throughout his life, but his fame stems from his writing, particularly his 1914 text, *The Architecture of Humanism: A Study in the History of Taste*. In this work, Scott addressed the declining appreciation for humanist principles established by Renaissance architecture. He traced the perceived shift from humanist values to five underlying "fallacies"—the natural, picturesque, mechanical, ethical, and biological—prevalent in nineteenth- and early twentieth-century thought, principles that supplanted humanism as the basis for architecture. Scott felt that the concepts governing architecture should derive from the human body and human experience, not scientific, functional, or moral concerns. Drawing on the aesthetic theory of empathy, Scott declared *"We have transcribed ourselves into terms of architecture . . . {and} architecture into terms of ourselves."* This "dual transcription," he concluded, "is the humanism of architecture." Scott's understanding of humanism and its role in architecture is particularly striking when considered alongside the more functionalist approaches to architecture that gained currency in the years surrounding World War I.

The Architecture of Humanism (1914)

Chapter VIII. Humanist Values

I. Architecture, simply and immediately perceived, is a combination, revealed through light and shade, of spaces, of masses, and of lines. These few elements make the core of architectural experience. . . .

The spaces, masses and lines of architecture, as perceived, are appearances. We may infer from them further facts about a building which are not perceived; facts about construction, facts about history or society. But the art of architecture is concerned with their immediate aspect; it is concerned with them as appearances.

And these appearances are related to human functions. Through these spaces we can conceive ourselves to move; these masses are capable, like ourselves, of pressure and resistance; these lines, should we follow or describe them, might be our path and our gesture.

Conceive for a moment a 'top-heavy' building or an 'ill-proportioned' space. No doubt the degree to which these qualities will be found offensive will vary with the spectator's sensibility to architecture; but sooner or later, if the top-heaviness or the disproportion is sufficiently pronounced, every spectator will judge that the building or the space is ugly, and experience a certain discomfort from their presence. So much will be conceded.

Geoffrey Scott, *The Architecture of Humanism: A Study in the History of Taste* (London: Constable and Co., Ltd., 1924) 157–63. Reprinted with permission of W.W. Norton & Company, Inc. Scott's footnotes have been omitted from this excerpt; the italics are his.

Now what is the cause of this discomfort? It is often suggested that the top-heavy building and the cramped space are ugly because they suggest the idea of instability, the idea of collapse, the idea of restriction, and so forth. But these ideas are not in themselves disagreeable. . . .

. . . [Our] discomfort in the presence of such architecture cannot spring merely from the idea of restriction or instability.

But neither does it derive from an actual weakness or restriction in our immediate experience. It is disagreeable to have our movements thwarted, to lose strength or to collapse; but a room fifty feet square and seven feet high does not restrict our actual movements, and the sight of a granite building raised (apparently) on a glass shop-front does not cause us to collapse.

There is instability—or the appearance of it; but it is in the building. There is discomfort, but it is in ourselves. What then has occurred? The conclusion seems evident. The concrete spectacle has done what the mere idea could not: it has stirred our physical memory. It has awakened in us, not indeed an actual state of instability or of being overloaded, but that condition of spirit which in the past has belonged to our actual experiences of weakness, of thwarted effort or incipient collapse. We have looked at the building and identified ourselves with its apparent state. *We have transcribed ourselves into terms of architecture*.

But the 'states' in architecture with which we thus identify ourselves need not be actual. The actual pressures of a spire are downward, yet no one speaks of a 'sinking' spire. A spire, when well designed, appears—as common language testifies—to soar. We identify ourselves, not with its actual downward pressure, but its apparent upward impulse. So, too, by the same excellent—because unconscious—testimony of speech, arches 'spring,' vistas 'stretch,' domes 'swell,' Greek temples are 'calm,' and baroque façades 'restless.' The whole of architecture is, in fact, unconsciously invested by us with human movement and human moods. Here, then, is a principle complementary to the one just stated. We *transcribe architecture into terms of ourselves.*

This is the humanism of architecture. The tendency to project the image of our functions into concrete forms is the basis, for architecture, of creative design. The tendency to recognize, in concrete forms, the image of those functions is the true basis, in its turn, of critical appreciation.

II. . . . This 'rising' of towers and 'springing' of arches, it will be said—these different movements which animate architecture—are mere metaphors of speech. . . .

. . . But a metaphor, when it is so obvious as to be universally employed and immediately understood, presupposes a true and reliable experience to which it can refer. . .

. . . [When] we speak of a tower as 'standing' or 'leaning' or 'rising,' or say of a curve that it is 'cramped' or 'flowing,' the words are the simplest and most direct description we can give of our impression. . . . [Art] addresses us through immediate impressions rather than through the process of reflection, and this universal metaphor of the body, a language profoundly felt and universally understood, is its largest opportunity. A metaphor is, by definition, the transcription of one thing into terms of another, and this in fact is what the theory under discussion claims. It claims that architectural art is the transcription of the body's states into forms of building.

. . . The processes of which we are least conscious are precisely the most deep-seated and universal and continuous, as, for example, the process of breathing. And this habit of projecting the image of our own functions upon the outside world, of reading the outside world in our own terms, is certainly ancient, common, and profound. It is, in fact, the *natural* way of perceiving and interpreting what we see. It is the way of the child in whom perpetual pretence and 'endless imitation' are a spontaneous method of envisaging the world. It is the way of the savage, who believes in 'animism,' and conceives every object to be invested with powers like his own. It is the way of the primitive peoples, who in the elaborate business of the dance give a bodily rendering to their beliefs and desires long before thought has accurately expressed them. It is the way of a superbly gifted race like the Greeks, whose mythology is one vast monument to just this instinct. It is the way of the poetic mind at all times and places, which [humanizes] the external world, not in a series of artificial conceits, but simply so perceiving it. To perceive and interpret the world scientifically, as it actually is, is a later, a less 'natural,' a more sophisticated process, and one from which we still relapse even when we say the sun is rising. The scientific perception of the world is forced upon us; the humanist perception of it is ours by right. The scientific method is intellectually and practically useful, but the naïve, the anthropomorphic way which [humanizes] the world and interprets it by analogy with our own bodies and our own wills, is still the aesthetic way; it is the basis of poetry, and it is the foundation of architecture.

13 LE CORBUSIER, 1887–1966

Le Corbusier, Villa Savoye, Poissy, France, 1928–29
© 2007 Artist Rights Society (ARS), New York/ADAGP, Paris/FLC
Photo Credit: Anthony Scibilia/Art Resource, NY

Le Corbusier, born Charles-Edouard Jeanneret in the Swiss town of Le Chaux-de-Fonds, forced a reconsideration of functional and aesthetic expectations in architecture; he is thus recognized as one of the most brilliant and influential architects of the twentieth century. Particularly intrigued by the possibilities of standardization and industrial production, in 1915 Le Corbusier devised the Maison Domino, an inexpensive, mass-producible housing frame composed of reinforced-concrete slab floors and vertical point supports. Two years later, he moved to Paris where he adopted the name Le Corbusier and began writing articles he would later publish together as *Vers une Architecture* (1923, translated as *Towards a New Architecture*). In this text, Le Corbusier urged architects to reconsider the accepted notion of the house and with it, the possibilities of twentieth-century life. Much as engineers devised the airplane to allow man to fly, Le Corbusier felt that architects must recreate the house for man to live in modern terms, with updated social ideals of space, hygiene, and technology; like the machine, the house should efficiently function in the service of its occupants. To support his argument Le Corbusier highlighted mechanized objects such as the airplane as models for contemporary architectural thought.

During the early 1920s, Le Corbusier collaborated with his cousin, **Pierre Jeanneret** (1896–1967). Together they expanded Le Corbusier's ideas concerning mass production and mechanization to formulate "Five Points towards a New Architecture" (1926). In place of conventional construction methods that relied on a buried foundation, load-bearing walls, and a pitched roof, Le Corbusier and Jeanneret proposed a new building system that incorporated structural *pilotis* (stilts of reinforced concrete), an open interior plan, an enclosing but non-load-bearing façade, strip or ribbon windows, and a flat rooftop garden. This set of revolutionary principles challenged traditional notions of structure and aesthetics, and established a new approach to architectural design.

Towards a New Architecture (1923)

Eyes Which Do Not See
II. Airplanes

> *There is a new spirit: it is a spirit of construction and of synthesis guided by a clear conception.*
> *Whatever may be thought of it, it animates to-day the greater part of human activity.*
> *A GREAT EPOCH HAS BEGUN*
>
> Programme of *l'Espirit Nouveau*
> No. 1, October, 1920.

There is one profession and one only, namely architecture, in which progress is not considered necessary, where laziness is enthroned, and in which the reference is always to yesterday.

Everywhere else, taking thought for the morrow is almost a fever and brings its inevitable solution: if a man does not move forward he becomes bankrupt.

But in architecture no one ever becomes bankrupt. A privileged profession, alas!

* * *

The airplane is indubitably one of the products of the most intense selection in the range of modern industry.

Le Corbusier, *Towards a New Architecture*, trans. Frederick Etchells (New York: Dover Publications, Inc., 1986), 109–27. Reprinted with permission from the publisher.

The War was an insatiable "client," never satisfied, always demanding better. The orders were to succeed at all costs and death followed a mistake remorselessly. We may then affirm that the airplane mobilized invention, intelligence and daring: *imagination* and *cold reason*. It is the same spirit that built the Parthenon.

Let us look at things from the point of view of architecture, but in the state of mind of the inventor of airplanes.

The lesson of the airplane is not primarily in the forms it has created, and above all we must learn to see in an airplane not a bird or a dragon-fly, but a machine for flying; the lesson of the airplane lies in the logic which governed the enunciation of the problem and which led to its successful realization. When a problem is properly stated, in our epoch, it inevitably finds its solution.

The problem of the house has not yet been stated.

One commonplace among Architects (the younger ones): *the construction must be shown.*

Another commonplace amongst them: *when a thing responds to a need, it is beautiful.*

But . . . To show the construction is all very well for an Arts and Crafts student who is anxious to prove his ability. The Almighty has clearly shown our wrists and our ankles, but there remains all the rest!

When a thing responds to a need, it is not beautiful; it satisfies all one part of our mind, the primary part, without which there is no possibility of richer satisfactions; let us recover the right order of events.

Architecture has another meaning and other ends to pursue than showing construction and responding to needs (and by "needs" I mean utility, comfort and practical arrangement).

ARCHITECTURE is the art above all others which achieves a state of platonic grandeur, mathematical order, speculation, the perception of the harmony which lies in emotional relationships. This is the AIM of architecture.

But let us return to our chronology.

If we feel the need of a new architecture, a clear and settled organism, it is because, as things are, the sensation of mathematical order cannot touch us since *things no longer respond to a need*, and because there is no longer real construction in architecture. An extreme confusion reigns. Architecture as practiced provides no solution to the present-day problem of the dwelling-house and has no comprehension of the structure of things. It does not fulfill the very first conditions and so it is not possible that the higher factors of harmony and beauty should enter in.

The architecture of to-day does not fulfill the necessary and sufficient conditions of the problem.

The reason is that the problem has not been stated as regards architecture. There has been no salutary war as in the case of the airplane.

But you will say, the Peace has set the problem in the reconstruction of the North of France. But then, we are totally disarmed, we do not know how to build in a modern way—materials, systems of construction, THE CONCEPTION OF THE DWELLING, all are lacking. Engineers have been busy with barrages, with bridges, with Atlantic liners, with mines, with railways. Architects have been asleep.

The airplane shows us that a problem well stated finds its solution. To wish to fly like a bird is to state the problem badly, and Ader's "Bat" never left the ground. To invent a flying machine having in mind nothing alien to pure mechanics, that is to say, to search for a means of suspension in the air and a means of propulsion, was to put the problem properly: in less than ten years the whole world could fly.

LET US STATE THE PROBLEM

Let us shut our eyes to what exists.

A house: a shelter against heat, cold, rain, thieves and the inquisitive. A receptacle for light and sun. A certain number of cells appropriated to cooking, work and personal life.

A room: a surface over which one can walk at ease, a bed on which to stretch yourself, a chair in which to rest or work, a work-table, receptacles in which each thing can be put at once in its right place.

The number of rooms: one for cooking and one for eating. One for work, one to wash yourself in and one for sleep.

Such are the standards of the dwelling.

Then why do we have the enormous and useless roofs on pretty suburban villas? Why the scanty windows with their little panes; why large houses with so many rooms locked up? Why the mirrored wardrobes, the washstands, the commodes? And then, why the elaborate bookcases? The consoles, the china cabinets, the dressers, the sideboards? Why the enormous glass chandeliers? The mantelpieces? Why the draped curtains? Why the damasked wall-papers thick with colour, with their motley design?

Daylight hardly enters your homes. Your windows are difficult to open. There are no ventilators for changing the air such as we get in any dining-car. Your chandeliers hurt the eyes. Your imitation stone stucco and your wall-papers are an impertinence, and no good modern picture could ever be hung on your walls, for it would be lost in the welter of your furnishings.

Why do you not demand from your landlord:

1. Fittings to take underclothing, suits and dresses in our bedroom, all of one depth, of a comfortable height and as practical as an "Innovation" trunk;

2. In your dining-room fittings to take china, silver and glass, shutting tightly and with a sufficiency of drawers in orders that "clearing away" can be done in an instant, and all these fittings "built in" so that round your chairs and table you have room enough to move and that feeling of space which will give you the calm necessary to good digestion;

3. In your living-room *fittings to hold your books and protect them from dust and to hold your collection of paintings and works of art.* And in such a way that the walls of your room are unencumbered. You could then bring out your pictures one at a time when you want them.

As for your dressers, and your mirrored wardrobes, you can sell all these to one of those young nations which have lately appeared on the map. There *Progress* rages, and they are dropping the traditional home (with its fittings, etc.) to live in an up-to-date house *à l'européenne* with its imitation stone stucco and its mantelpieces.

Let us repeat some fundamental axioms:

(a) *Chairs are made to sit in.* There are rush-seated church chairs at 5s., luxuriously upholstered arm-chairs at £20 and adjustable chairs with a movable reading-desk, a shelf for your coffee cup, an extending foot rest, a back that raises and lowers with a handle, and gives you the very best position either for work or a nap, in a healthy, comfortable and right way. Your *bergères*, your Louis XVI *canseuses*, bulging through their tapestry covers, are these machines for sitting in? Between ourselves, you are more comfortable at your club, your bank or in your office.

(b) *Electricity gives light*. We can have concealed lighting, or we can have diffused and projected lighting. One can see as clearly as in broad daylight without ever hurting one's eyes.

A hundred-candle-power lamp weighs less than two ounces, but there are chandeliers weighing nearly two hundredweight with elaborations in bronze or wood, and so huge that they fill up all the middle of the room; the upkeep of these horrors is a terrible task because of the flies. These chandeliers are also very bad for the eyes at night.

(c) *Windows serve to admit light, "a little, much or not at all," and to see outside.* There are windows in sleeping-cars which close hermetically or can be opened at will; there are the great windows of modern cafés which close hermetically or can be entirely opened by means of a handle which causes them to disappear below ground; there are the windows in dining cars which have little louvres opening to admit air "a little, much, or not at all," there is modern plate glass which has replaced bottle-glass and small panes; there are roll shutters which can be lowered gradually and will keep out the light at will according to the spacing of their slats. But architects still use only windows like those at Versailes or Compiègne, Louis X, Y or Z which shut badly, have tiny panes, are difficult to open and have their shutters outside; if it rains in the evening one gets wet through in trying to close them.

(d) *Pictures are made to be looked at and meditated on.* In order to see a picture to advantage, it must be hung suitably and in the proper atmosphere. The true collector of pictures arranges them in a cabinet and hangs on the wall the particular painting he wants to look at; but your walls are a riot of all manner of things.

(e) *A house is made for living in.*—"No!"—"But of course!"—"Then you are a Utopian!"

Truth to tell, the modern man is bored to tears in his home; so he goes to his club. The modern woman is bored outside her boudoir; she goes to tea-parties. The modern man and woman are bored at home; they go to night-clubs. But lesser folk who have no clubs gather together in the evening under the chandelier and hardly dare to walk through the labyrinth of their furniture which takes up the whole room and is all their fortune and their pride.

The existing plan of the dwelling-house takes no account of man and is conceived as a furniture store. This scheme of things, favourable enough so the trade of Tottenham Court Road, is of ill omen for society. It kills the spirit of the family, of the home; there are no homes, no families and no children, for living is much too difficult a business.

The temperance societies and the anti-Malthusians should address an urgent appeal to architects; they should have the MANUAL OF THE DWELLING printed and distributed to mothers of families and should demand the resignation of all the professors in the architectural schools.

THE MANUAL OF THE DWELLING

Demand a bathroom looking south, one of the largest rooms in the house or flat, the old drawing-room for instance. One wall to be entirely glazed, opening if possible on to a balcony for sun baths; the most up-to-date fittings with a shower-bath and gymnastic appliances.

An adjoining room to be a dressing-room in which you can dress and undress. Never undress in your bedroom. It is not a clean thing to do and makes the room horribly untidy. In this room demand fitments for your linen and clothing, not more than 5 feet in height, with drawers, hangers, etc.

Demand one really large living room instead of a number of small ones.

Demand bare walls in your bedroom, your living room and your dining-room. Built-in fittings to take the place of much of the furniture, which is expensive to buy, takes up too much room and needs looking after.

If you can, put the kitchen at the top of the house to avoid smells.

Demand concealed or diffused lighting.

Demand a vacuum cleaner.

Buy only practical furniture and never buy decorative "pieces." If you want to see bad taste, go into the houses of the rich. Put only a few pictures on your walls and none but good ones.

Keep your odds and ends in drawers or cabinets.

The gramophone or the pianola or wireless will give you exact interpretations of first-rate music, and you will avoid catching cold in the concert hall, and the frenzy of the virtuoso.

Demand ventilating panes to the windows in every room.

Teach your children that a house is only habitable when it is full of light and air, and when the floors and walls are clear. To keep your floors in order eliminate heavy furniture and thick carpets.

Demand a separate garage to your dwelling.

Demand the maid's room should not be an attic. Do not park your servants under the roof.

Take a flat which is one size smaller than what your parents accustomed you to. Bear in mind economy in your actions, your household management and in your thoughts.

Conclusion. Every modern man has the mechanical sense. The feeling for mechanics exists and is justified by our daily activities. This feeling in regard to machinery is one of respect, gratitude and esteem.

Machinery includes economy as an essential factor leading to minute selection. There is a moral sentiment in the feeling for mechanics.

The man who is intelligent, cold and calm has grown wings to himself.

Men—intelligent, cold and calm—are needed to build the house and to lay out the town.

"Five Points Towards a New Architecture" (1926)

The theoretical considerations set out below are based on many years of practical experience on building sites.

Theory demands concise formulation.

The following points in no way relate to aesthetic fantasies or a striving for fashionable effects, but concern architectural facts that imply an entirely new kind of building, from dwelling house to palatial edifices.

1. The supports. To solve a problem scientifically means in the first place to distinguish between its elements. Hence in the case of a building a distinction can immediately be made between the supporting and the non-supporting elements. The earlier foundations, on which the building rested without a mathematical check, are replaced by individual foundations and the walls by individual supports. Both supports and support foundations are precisely calculated according to the burdens they are called upon to carry. These supports are spaced out at specific, equal intervals, with no thought for the interior arrangement of the building. They rise directly from the floor to 3, 4, 6, etc. metres and elevate the ground floor. The rooms are thereby removed from the dampness of the soil; they have light and air; the building plot is left to the garden, which consequently passes under the house. The same area is also gained on the flat roof.

Le Corbusier and Pierre Jeanneret, "Five Points Towards a New Architecture," from Ulrich Conrads, ed., *Programs and Maifestoes on 20th Century Architecture*, trans. M. Bullock (Cambridge, MA: MIT Press, 1970) 99–101. Text in Conrads quoted from *Towards a New Architecture* (London, 1927). English translation © 1970 Lund Humphries, London, and the Massachusetts Institute of Technology, Cambridge, Massachusetts. Reprinted with permission from the MIT Press.

2. **The roof gardens**. The flat roof demands in the first place systematic utilization for domestic purposes: roof terrace, roof garden. On the other hand, the reinforced concrete demands protection against changing temperatures. Over-activity on the part of the reinforced concrete is prevented by the maintenance of a constant humidity on the roof concrete. The roof terrace satisfies both demands (a rain-dampened layer of sand covered with concrete slabs with lawns in the interstices; the earth of the flowerbeds in direct contact with the layer of sand). In this way the rain water will flow off extremely slowly. Waste pipes in the interior of the building. Thus a latent humidity will remain continually on the roof skin. The roof gardens will display highly luxuriant vegetation. Shrubs and even small trees up to 3 or 4 metres tall can be planted. In this way the roof garden will becomes the most favored place in the building. In general, roof gardens mean to a city the recovery of all the built-up area.

3. **The free designing of the ground-plan.** The support system carries the intermediate ceilings and rises up to the roof. The interior walls may be placed wherever required, each floor being entirely independent of the rest. There are no longer any supporting walls but only membranes of any thickness required. The result of this is absolute freedom in designing the ground-plan; that is to say, free utilization of the available means, which makes it easy to offset the rather high cost of reinforced concrete construction.

4. **The horizontal window.** Together with the intermediate ceilings the supports form rectangular openings in the façade through which light and air enter copiously. The window extends from support to support and thus becomes a horizontal window. Stilted vertical windows consequently disappear, as do unpleasant mullions. In this way, rooms are equably lit from wall to wall. Experiments have shown that a room thus lit has an eight times stronger illumination than the same room lit by vertical windows with the same window area.

The whole history of architecture revolves exclusively around the wall apertures.

Through use of the horizontal window reinforced concrete suddenly provides the possibility of maximum illumination.

5. **Free design of the façade**. By projecting the floor beyond the supporting pillars, like a balcony all round the building, the whole façade is extended beyond the supporting construction. It thereby loses its supportive quality and the windows may be extended to any length at will, without any direct relationship to the interior division. . . . The façade may thus be designed freely.

The five essential points set out above represent a fundamentally new aesthetic. Nothing is left to us of the architecture of past epochs, just as we can no longer derive benefit from the literary and historical teaching given in schools.

Constructional Considerations
Building construction is the purposeful and consistent combination of building elements.

Industries and technological undertakings are being established to deal with the production of these elements.

Serial manufacture enables these elements to be made precise, cheap and good. They can be produced in advance in any number required.

Industries will see to the completion and uninterrupted perfecting of the elements.

Thus the architect has at his disposal a box of building units. His architectural talent can operate freely. It alone, through the building programme, determines his architecture.

The age of the architects is coming.

WALTER GROPIUS, 1883–1969

Walter Gropius, Bauhaus, Dessau, Germany, 1926–27
© 2007 Artist Rights Society (ARS), New York/VG Bild-Kunst, Bonn
Photo Credit: Vanni/Art Resource, NY

Throughout his life, the German architect Walter Gropius promoted collaboration between artists and industry. As a member of the Deutsche Werkbund, an organization dedicated to the qualitative improvement of German manufactured goods, Gropius recognized that standardization and factory production could lead to the availability of inexpensive, everyday items for public consumption. The promise for architecture was equally great; modular construction, made possible by creative design and the industrial production of building materials, could grant the common man access to affordable quality housing. These thoughts contributed to Gropius's 1919 founding of the Bauhaus, a school that sought to unify the arts under the rubric of design. Student training was based on an apprentice-like system that emphasized an understanding of craft and materials, as well as functionalism, composition, and aesthetics. Another focus concerned the reality of mechanical reproduction. Indeed, the Bauhaus eventually served as a workshop geared toward the creation of prototypes for industrial production, a concept Gropius discussed in "Principles of Bauhaus Production," reproduced below. Under Gropius's leadership, the Bauhaus fostered an alliance between the artist and industry, a relationship that helped raise the standards for machine-made goods and thus provide society with inexpensive, high-quality products. Gropius later carried these social and cooperative interests to the United States where he established the design firm aptly named The Architects' Collaborative.

"Principles of Bauhaus Production" (1926)

The Bauhaus wants to serve in the development of present-day housing, from the simplest household appliances to the finished dwelling.

In the conviction that household appliances and furnishings must be rationally related to each other, the Bauhaus is seeking—by systematic practical and theoretical research into formal, technical, and economic fields—to derive the design of an object from its natural functions and relationships.

Modern man, who no longer dresses in historical garments but wears modern clothes, also needs a modern home appropriate to him and his time, equipped with all the modern devices of daily use.

An object is defined by its nature. In order, then, to design it to function correctly—a container, a chair, or a house—one must first of all study its nature; for it must serve its purpose perfectly, that is, it must fulfill its function usefully, be durable, economical, and 'beautiful.' This research into the nature of objects leads to the conclusion that by resolute consideration of modern production methods, constructions, and materials, forms will evolve that are often unusual and surprising, since they deviate from the conventional (consider, for example, the changes in the design of heating and lighting fixtures).

Walter Gropius, "Principles of Bahaus Production," from H. Wingler, *The Bauhaus: Weimar, Dessau, Berlin, Chicago*, trans. Wolfgang and Basil Gilbert (Cambridge, MA: MIT Press, 1969), 109–10. © 1969 by the Massachusetts Institute of Technology. Reprinted with permission from the publisher.

It is only through constant contact with newly evolving techniques, with the discovery of new materials, and with new ways of putting things together, that the creative individual can learn to bring the design of objects into a living relationship with tradition and from that point to develop a new attitude toward design, which is:

> a resolute affirmation of the living environment of machines and vehicles;
>
> the organic design of things based on their own present-day laws, without romantic gloss and wasteful frivolity;
>
> the limitation to characteristic, primary forms and colors, readily accessible to everyone;
>
> simplicity in multiplicity, economical utilization of space, material, time, and money.

The creation of standard types for all practical commodities of everyday use is a social necessity.

On the whole, the necessities of life are the same for the majority of people. The home and its furnishings are mass consumer goods and their design is more a matter of reason than a matter of passion. The machine—capable of producing standardized products—is an effective device which, by means of mechanical aids—steam and electricity—can free the individual from working manually for the satisfaction of his daily needs and can provide him with mass-produced products that are cheaper and better than those manufactured by hand. There is no danger that standardization will force a choice upon the individual, since due to natural competition the number of available types of each object will always be ample to provide the individual with a choice of design that suits him best.

The Bauhaus workshops are essentially laboratories in which prototypes of products suitable for mass production and typical of our time are carefully developed and constantly improved.

In these laboratories, the Bauhaus wants to train a new kind of collaborator for industry and the crafts, who has an equal command of both technology and form.

To reach the object of creating a set of standard prototypes which meet all the demands of economy, technology, and form requires the selection of the best, most versatile, and most thoroughly educated men who are well grounded in the workshop experience and who are imbued with an exact knowledge of the design elements of form and mechanics and their underlying laws.

The Bauhaus represents the opinion that the contrast between industry and the crafts is much less marked by the difference in the tools they use than by the division of labor in industry and unity of the work in the crafts. But the two are constantly getting closer to each other. The crafts of the past have changed, and the future crafts will be merged in a new productive unity in which they will carry out the experimental work for industrial production. Speculative experiments in laboratory workshops will yield models and prototypes for productive implementation in factories.

The prototypes that have been completed in the Bauhaus workshops are being reproduced by outside firms with whom the workshops are closely related.

The production of the Bauhaus thus does not represent any kind of competition for either industry or crafts but rather provides them with impetus for their development. The Bauhaus does this by bringing creatively talented people with ample practical experience into the actual course of production, to take over the preparatory work for production, from industry and the crafts. The products reproduced from prototypes that have been developed by the Bauhaus can be offered at a reasonable price only by utilization of all the modern, economical methods of standardization (mass production by industry) and by large-scale sales. The dangers of a decline in the quality of the product by comparison to the prototype, in regard to quality of material and workmanship, as a result of mechanical reproduction will be countered by all available means. The Bauhaus fights against the cheap substitute, inferior workmanship, and the dilettantism of the handicrafts, for a new standard of quality work.

15 HENRY-RUSSELL HITCHCOCK, 1903–1987, AND PHILIP JOHNSON, 1906–2005

Ludwig Mies van der Rohe, Barcelona Pavilion, International Exposition, Barcelona, 1929
© 2007 Artist Rights Society (ARS), New York/VG Bild-Kunst, Bonn
Photo Credit: Digital Image © The Museum of Modern Art/Licensed by SCALA/Art Resource, NY

In 1932, the Museum of Modern Art (MOMA) in New York staged Modern Architecture—International Exhibition. Using models, photographs, and the occasional plan, this show presented a new architectural aesthetic that, during the past few decades, had been developed largely by European practitioners such as Le Corbusier, Mies van der Rohe, Walter Gropius, and J. J. P. Oud. With Philip Johnson, who had recently earned his undergraduate degree in philosophy from Harvard University, the architectural historian Henry-Russell Hitchcock organized the exhibition. Together Hitchcock and Johnson prepared an accompanying catalog—*The International Style: Architecture since 1922*—that further defined the work on display. In their text, excerpted below, Hitchcock and Johnson listed three characteristics of this new "International Style" architecture: an emphasis on volume instead of mass, an organization based on regularity instead of classical axial symmetry, and a prohibition of applied ornament. Significantly, this summary focused on formal characteristics and made no mention of the desired social improvements that led to the development of this new architectural language.

The majority of the work included in the MOMA exhibition was dominated by European architects, but the designs of a few Americans, including Frank Lloyd Wright, did appear. However, the show and catalog emphasized the sleek and novel appearance of the International Style, featuring buildings executed in steel, glass, and concrete. Presented as a coherent and fashionable body of work, the International Style, along with the accompanying formal principles enunciated by Hitchcock and Johnson, had a tremendous impact on American architecture through the mid-twentieth century, strongly influencing commercial, civic, and residential design.

The International Style: Architecture since 1922 (1932)

Introduction

The Idea of Style

The light and airy systems of construction of the Gothic cathedrals, the freedom and slenderness of their supporting skeleton, afford, as it were, a presage of a style that began to develop in the nineteenth century, that of metallic architecture. With the use of metal, and of concrete reinforced by metal bars, modern builders could equal the most daring feats of Gothic architects without endangering the solidity of the structure. In the conflict that obtains between the two elements of construction, solidity and open space, everything seems to show that the principle of free spaces will prevail, that the palaces and houses of the future will be flooded with air and light. Thus the formula popularized by Gothic architecture has a great future before it. Following on the revival of Græco-Roman architecture which prevailed from the sixteenth century to our own day, we shall see, with the full application of different materials, a yet more enduring rebirth of the Gothic style.

Salomon Reinach, APOLLO, 1904

Since the middle of the eighteenth century there have been recurrent attempts to achieve and to impose a controlling style in architecture such as existed in the earlier epochs of the past. The two chief of these attempts were the Classical Revival and the Mediæval Revival. Out of the compromises between these two opposing schools and difficulties of reconciling either sort of revivalism with the new needs and the new methods of construction of the day grew the stylistic confusion of the last hundred years.

Henry-Russell Hitchcock and Philip Johnson, *The International Style: Architecture Since 1922* (New York: W. W. Norton & Company, Inc., 1995), 33–37 and 44–49. © 1932 by W. W. Norton & Company, Inc.; renewed © 1960 by Henry-Russell Hitchcock and Philip Johnson. Reprinted with permission of the publisher.

The nineteenth century failed to create a style of architecture because it was unable to achieve a general discipline of structure and of design in the terms of the day. The revived "styles" were but a decorative garment to architecture, not the interior principles according to which it lived and grew. On the whole the development of engineering in building went on regardless of the Classical or Mediæval architectural forms which were borrowed from the past. Thus the chaos of eclecticism served to give the very idea of style a bad name in the estimation of the first modern architects of the end of the nineteenth and the beginning of the twentieth century.

In the nineteenth century there was always not one style, but "styles," and the idea of "styles" implied a choice. The individualistic revolt of the first modern architects destroyed the prestige of the "styles," but it did not remove the implication that there was a possibility of choice between one aesthetic conception of design and another. In their reaction against revivalism these men sought rather to explore a great variety of free possibilities.

The result, on the whole, added to the confusion of continuing eclecticism, although the new work possessed a general vitality which the later revivalists had quite lost. The revolt from stylistic discipline to extreme individualism at the beginning of the twentieth century was justified as the surest issue from an impasse of imitation and sterility. The individualists decried submission to fixed aesthetic principles as the imposition of a dead hand upon the living material of architecture, holding up the failure of the revivals as a proof that the very idea of style was an unhealthy delusion.

Today the strict issue of reviving the styles of the distant past is no longer one of serious consequence. But the peculiar traditions of imitation and modification of the styles of the past, which eclecticism inherited from the earlier Classical and Mediæval Revivals, have not been easily forgotten. The influence of the past still most to be feared is that of the nineteenth century with its cheapening of the very idea of style. Modern architecture has nothing but the healthiest lessons to learn from the art of the further past, if that art be studied scientifically and not in a spirit of imitation. Now that it is possible to emulate the great styles of the past in their essence without imitating their surface, the problem of establishing one dominant style, which the nineteenth century set itself in terms of alternative revivals, is coming to a solution.

The idea of style, which began to degenerate when the revivals destroyed the disciplines of the Baroque, has become real and fertile again. Today a single new style has come into existence. The aesthetic conceptions on which its disciplines are based derive from the experimentation of the individualists. They and not the revivalists were the immediate masters of those who have created the new style. This contemporary style, which exists throughout the world, is unified and inclusive, not fragmentary and contradictory like so much of the production of the first generation of modern architects. In the last decade it has produced sufficient monuments of distinction to display its validity and its vitality. It may fairly be compared in significance with the styles of the past. In the handling of the problems of structure it is related to the Gothic, in the handling of the problems of design it is more akin to the Classical. In the preeminence given to the handling of function it is distinguished from both.

The unconscious and halting architectural developments of the nineteenth century, the confused and contradictory experimentation of the beginning of the twentieth, have been succeeded by a directed evolution. There is now a single body of discipline, fixed enough to permit individual interpretation and to encourage general growth.

The idea of style as the frame of potential growth, rather than as a fixed and crushing mould, has developed with the recognition of underlying principles such as archaeologists discern in the great styles of the past. The principles are few and broad. They are not mere formulas of proportion such as distinguish the Doric from the Ionic order, they are fundamental, like the organic verticality of the Gothic or the rhythmical symmetry of the Baroque. There is, first, a new conception of architecture as volume rather than as mass. Secondly, regularity rather than axial symmetry serves as the chief means of ordering design. These two principles, with a third proscribing arbitrary applied decoration, mark the productions of the international style. This new style is not international in the sense that the production of one country is just like that of another. Nor is it so rigid that the work of various leaders is not clearly distinguishable. The international style has become evident and definable only gradually as different innovators throughout the world have successfully carried out parallel experiments.

In stating the general principles of the contemporary style, in analyzing their derivation from structure and their modification by function, the appearance of a certain dogmatism can hardly be avoided. In opposition to those who claim that a new style of architecture is impossible or undesirable, it is necessary to stress the coherence of the results obtained within the range of possibilities thus far explored. For the international style already exists in the present; it is not merely something the future may hold in store. Architecture is always a set of actual monuments, not a vague corpus of theory. . . .

It is particularly in the early work of three men, Walter Gropius in Germany, Oud in Holland, and Le Corbusier in France, that the various steps in the inception of the new style must be sought. These three with Mies van der Rohe in Germany remain the great leaders of modern architecture.

Gropius' factory at Alfeld, built just before the War, came nearer to an integration of the new style than any other edifice built before 1922. In industrial architecture the tradition of the styles of the past was not repressive, as many factories of the nineteenth century well illustrate. The need for using modern construction throughout and for serving function directly was peculiarly evident. Hence it was easier for Gropius to advance in this field beyond his master, Behrens, than it would have been in any other. The walls of the Alfeld factory are screens of glass with spandrels of metal at the floor levels. The crowning band of brickwork does not project beyond these screens. The purely mechanical elements are frankly handled and give interest to a design fundamentally so regular as to approach monotony. There is no applied ornamental decoration except the lettering. The organization of the parts of the complex structure is ordered by logic and consistency rather than by axial symmetry.

Yet there are traces still of the conceptions of traditional architecture. The glass screens are treated like projecting bays between the visible supports. These supports are sheathed with brick so that they appear like the last fragments of the solid masonry wall of the past. The entrance is symmetrical and heavy. For all its simplicity it is treated with a decorative emphasis. Gropius was not destined to achieve again so fine and so coherent a production in the contemporary style before the Bauhaus in 1926. There he profited from the intervening aesthetic experimentation of the Dutch Neoplasticists. The Bauhaus is something more than a mere development from the technical triumph of the Alfeld factory.

During the years of the War, Oud in Holland came into contact with the group of Dutch cubist painters led by Mondriaan and Van Doesburg, who called themselves Neoplasticists. Their positive influence on his work at first was negligible. Oud remained for a time still a disciple of Berlage, whose half-modern manner he had previously followed rather closely. He profited also by his study of the innovation of Wright, whose work was already better known in Europe than in America. Then he sought consciously to achieve a Neoplasticist architecture and, from 1917 on, the influence of Berlage and Wright began to diminish. At the same time he found in concrete an adequate material for the expression of new conceptions of form. Oud's projects were increasingly simple, vigorous and geometrical. On the analogy of abstract painting he came to realize the aesthetic potentialities of planes in three dimensions with which Wright had already experimented. He reacted sharply against the picturesqueness of the other followers of Berlage and sought with almost Greek fervor to arrive at a scheme of proportions ever purer and more regular.

In his first housing projects carried out for the city of Rotterdam in 1918 and 1919 he did not advance as far as in his unexecuted projects. But at Oud-Mathenesse in 1921–

22, although he was required to build the whole village in traditional materials and to continue the use of conventional roofs, the new style promised in his projects came into being. The avoidance of picturesqueness, the severe horizontality of the composition, the perfect simplicity and consistency which he achieved in executing a very complex project, all announced the conscious creation of a body of aesthetic disciplines.

Oud-Mathenesse exceeded Gropius' Alfeld factory in significance if not in impressiveness. Gropius made his innovations primarily in technics, Oud in design. He undoubtedly owed the initial impetus to the Neoplasticists, but his personal manner had freed itself from dependence on painting. The models Van Doesburg made of houses in the early twenties, in collaboration with other Neoplasticists, with their abstract play of volumes and bright colors, had their own direct influence in Germany.

But the man who first made the world aware that a new style was being born was Le Corbusier. As late as 1916, well after his technical and sociological theorizing had begun, his conceptions of design were still strongly marked by the Classical symmetry of his master Perret. His plans, however, were even more open than those of Wright. In his housing projects of the next few years he passed rapidly beyond his master Perret and beyond Behrens and Loos, with whom he had also come in contact. His *Citrohan* house model of 1921 was the thorough expression of a conception of architecture as radical technically as Gropius' factory and as novel aesthetically as Oud's village. The enormous window area and the terraces made possible by the use of ferroconcrete, together with the asymmetry of the composition, undoubtedly produced a design more thoroughly infused with a new spirit, more completely freed from the conventions of the past than any thus far projected.

The influence of Le Corbusier was the greater, the appearance of a new style the more remarked, because of the vehement propaganda which he contributed to the magazine *L'Esprit Nouveau*, 1920–1925. Since then, moreover, he has written a series of books effectively propagandizing his technical and aesthetic theories. In this way his name

149

has become almost synonymous with the new architecture and it has been praised or condemned very largely in his person. But he was not, as we have seen, the only innovator nor was the style as it came generally into being after 1922 peculiarly his. He crystallized; he dramatized; but he was not alone in creating.

When in 1922 he built at Vaucresson his first house in the new style, he failed to equal the purity of design and the boldness of construction of the *Citrohan* project. But the houses that immediately followed this, one for the painter Ozenfant, and another for his parents outside Vevey, passed further beyond the transitional stage than anything that Oud or Gropius were to build for several more years. Ozenfant's sort of cubism, called Purism, had perhaps inspired Le Corbusier in his search for sources of formal inspiration for a new architecture. But on the whole Le Corbusier in these early years turned for precedent rather to steamships than to painting. Some of his early houses, such as that for the sculptor Miestchaninoff at Boulogne-sur-Seine, were definitely naval in feeling. But this marine phase was soon over like Oud's strictly Neoplasticist phase, or the Expressionist period in the work of the young architects of Germany. Various external influences helped to free architecture from the last remnants of a lingering traditionalism. The new style displayed its force in the rapidity with which it transmuted them beyond recognition.

Mies van der Rohe advanced toward the new style less rapidly at first than Gropius. Before the War he had simplified, clarified, and lightened the domestic style of Behrens to a point that suggests conscious inspiration from Schinkel and Persius. After the War in two projects for skyscrapers entirely of metal and glass he carried technical innovation even further than Gropius, further indeed than anyone has yet gone in practice. These buildings would have been pure volume, glazed cages supported from within, on a scale such as not even Paxton in the nineteenth century would have dreamed possible. However, in their form, with plans based on clustered circles or sharp angles, they were extravagantly Romantic and strongly marked by the contemporary wave of Expressionism in Germany.

It was in Mies' projects of 1922 that his true significance as an aesthetic innovator first appeared. In a design for a country house he broke with the conception of the wall as a continuous plane surrounding the plan and built up his composition of sections of intersecting planes. Thus he achieved, still with the use of supporting walls, a greater openness even than Le Corbusier with his ferroconcrete skeleton construction. Mies' sense of proportions remained as serene as before the War and even more pure. This project and the constructions of Oud and Le Corbusier in this year emphasize that it is just a decade ago that the new style came into existence.

The four leaders of modern architecture are Le Corbusier, Oud, Gropius and Mies van der Rohe. But others as well as they, Rietveld in Holland, Lureat in France, even Mendelsohn in Germany, for all his lingering dalliance with Expressionism, took parallel steps of nearly equal importance in the years just after the War. The style did not spring from a single source but came into being generally. The writing of Oud and Gropius, and to a greater degree that of Le Corbusier, with the frequent publication of their projects of these years, carried the principles of the new style abroad. These projects have indeed become more famous than many executed buildings.

From the first there were also critics, who were not architects, to serve as publicists. Everyone who was interested in the creation of a modern architecture had to come to terms with the nascent style. The principles of the style that appeared already plainly by 1922 in the projects and the executed buildings of the leaders, still control today an ever increasing group of architects throughout the world.

R. Buckminster Fuller, 1895–1983

R. Buckminster Fuller, Dymaxion House, Wichita, KS, 1946
Courtesy of the Estate of R. Buckminster Fuller

Buckminster Fuller has been described as an inventor, architect, scientist, mathematician, and poet. Indeed, he practiced in all of these fields and appears to have viewed them not as separate disciplines but as parts of a larger universal realm. After losing his first child to polio, Fuller dedicated himself to improving mankind's quality of life through technology. His efforts focused on doing more with less—designing structures and vehicles that required a minimum of energy, money, and material to construct and operate. The geodesic dome, a strong, lightweight enclosure composed of multiple self-bracing triangles, was perhaps Fuller's most famous invention. It was designed with the "more-with-less" philosophy in mind, as was his airframe dwelling, the Dymaxion House: an inexpensive, efficient, durable home to be factory produced and either delivered via airlift in one piece or assembled on site. The aluminum house used natural means for temperature control, required little external maintenance, and contained systems to recycle waste. The interior could be reconfigured easily to accommodate the occupants' needs. With the end of World War II in sight, Fuller proposed that factories previously used for wartime production manufacture his Dymaxion homes. This could preserve jobs for factory employees and provide low-cost housing for returning soldiers and their families. Fuller elaborated on these ideas in a lecture in 1946, excerpted below, given to the engineers charged with making Fuller's vision a reality. Although his Dymaxion homes never achieved a full run of production, Fuller, for the remainder of his life, continued his quest for innovative and progressive ways to raise the standard of living.

"Designing a New Industry" (1946)

. . . We have now actually met the theoretical requirements of the physical problem. We have gotten down to the proper weight. We are down, not including the bathroom and partitions, to 5,400 pounds. The copper bathroom now in the house weights 430 pounds—but in aluminum with plastic finish, as we are going to manufacture it, the bathroom will weigh around 250 pounds. The partitions, two bathrooms, kitchen, laundry, and energy unit will probably come to not more than 2,000 pounds. We will be right on our curve of the size of things man can mass produce in 1946. In other words, due to the development of the airplane industry, the house has become an extremely practical and now very real affair.

Overnight [there was] the necessity of democracy for a great number of planes to accommodate the increasing mobility of man brought about by war because man had not provided ways of developing that air technology expansion through peaceful means. This was because man was not living in a preventive pathology . . . but in a curative pathology, which has to have war to bring about the inevitable and major economic changes. *Industry* as preoccupied with the airplane overnight became *four tim*es as large as *industry* preoccupied with the automobile. People do not seem to realize it but that is what happened.

You must now realize this evolution was simply the *principle* which we have defined earlier this evening as constituting *industry* itself being comprehensively tuned up

---

Excerpt from Buckminster Fuller's Writings © The Estate of Buckminster Fuller. Originally appeared in *Designing a New Industry: A Composite of a Series of Talks by R. Buckminster Fuller, 1945–1946* (Wichita: Fuller Research Institute, 1946), 38–42. Reprinted with permission.

through its inherent self-improving advantages, which had been accumulating increment for a generation, to demonstrate dramatically a new range and degree of ability. Therefore the *airplane* industry should not be thought of as a species of industry apart, for instance, from the *automobile* industry or the *hat* industry. It should be thought of as the phenomenon industry itself, simply mobilized to its best ability or to its most recent record high in *standards of performance*.

In *industry*, as preoccupied with aircraft manufacture and maintenance during World War II, the standards and tolerances of precision that could be maintained, the size of units, the relative strength, the degree of complexity control all represent a sum total of somewhere around a ten-to-one magnitude increase in technical advantages over *industry* as we know it before this war idling along on 1917 standards.

For us now as composite proprietors, workers, and consumers, to give up the standards of industry as recently preoccupied with the technical necessities of worldwide flight of man in order to assist him to establish ultimate world-wide democracy, and to go back instead to the phase of industry as we knew it in its earlier preoccupation with exploitation of man's innate tendency to *mobilize for security* by tentative adaptation of the automobile to his paralyzed domiciling, would be to actually deflate our whole economic ability by 90%. To deflate our economic ability 90% is to decrease our potential ability 90%, which, as viewed from old-fashioned static economics simply means a 900% inflation of prices, relative to wage-hour dollars. It is an unthinkable thing. I don't think it is going to happen.

I think our house is going to have an important part in helping us to keep on upward instead of downward in historical degree of technical advantage that was developed during World War II. I don't have to talk to you much about that. You have heard about the possibility of using the aircraft plants. Last year the president of your company delivered an excellent address to the National Convention of the International

Association of Machinists. . . . It [covered] the subject of the aircraft industry's inclusion of the manufacture of *airframe dwellings*, the name we have given to that portion of dwelling machines to be manufactured by the airframe industry. Wright Field calls our dwelling machines "stationary airplanes." The power plant and electrical manufacturing and many other areas of the older industry's component parts manufacturers will provide the organic apparatus of our dwelling service.

The big fact that confronts us is that you of the aircraft industry have suddenly developed a whole new world which has recently been operating four times as much technology as was ever operated before—which happened to represent precisely the level of technology for which I had been waiting to get my house realized. We had suddenly broken through into a world where young architects who didn't have building design jobs and who couldn't find building design jobs because building technology had stalemated suddenly found the aircraft world a very good place to go. In this welcoming world of aircraft they matriculated rapidly into the performance per-pound language. They now think that way irrevocably. Everybody, throughout the whole aircraft industry thinks that way. It is no longer a *hard mental* job for us to sit down and talk, as we have talked tonight, *about how much housing weighs*, too.

Here is one more thing on the economics side I would like you to think about. Housing, as you have known it up to now, used the wood or stone or clay which was at hand. These component materials were not understood scientifically to any important degree. Wood might be considered *pretty* as oak, or pretty as maple. One was a little harder or softer to work and suited a man better than another. But it was little understood what a tree was. Despite academic study, man's understanding of trees was popularly vague. Then trees began to be used industrially by the chemical industry. It began to develop wood pulps and other by-products of wood. To some extent this began to affect the "scarcity" or "quantity" of wood relative to its availability for house building. These new industries, particularly newsprint pulp, exhausted a lot of it. Builders had to take greener and greener lumber as stock piling dwindled.

During World War II one of the most extraordinary things that happened, in its broad effects on technology and on economics, is what the Germans were forced to accomplish in wood chemistry in order to plan on how to survive during this extraordinary industrial warfare which they introduced and in which energy played such an important role. The Germans had to plan in advance on being bombed out of their oil fields. It was obvious that they could plan to use oil to a certain extent but that eventually their most vulnerable position was their oil supply. This was an "oil warfare" in a big way. Therefore the Germans set about finding other important sources of energy. They went to wood technology. The chemistry of wood developed in many directions in Germany. They suddenly discovered that here was Nature's most important trick in impounding sun energy—and in a most useful way, for therefrom you could release energy in many useful directions. They immediately brought it to the one great "Grand Central Station" of energy, in its most storable form, which was alcohol. From alcohol of various kinds you could make foods first for cattle, then for people. You could make high octane gas or synthetic rubber or plastics. The chemistry of wood began playing such an important part that the scientists in Washington were talking about it constantly. . . .

Wood technology has advanced the basic economic case for wood to such an important position in the advancing technical world that we no longer can afford to use wood in the careless way we have in the past to put it in houses for termites to eat up, or a possible fire to consume. Even if we could, world-wide technology forces our technical hand as it never has before, the rest of the world is now industrializing and is starting at the most advanced World War II levels of technology and not at our 1861 or 1890 or 1917 level. Industrial technology is born of latent knowledge and is not an inventory of obsolete machinery, so wood is in a very new historical position. How does that affect the historical wood house picture?

As children of the pioneers also came along to build a house—or their grandchildren wanted to—there was no longer much wood on the farm. They had to go increasing distances for it. Finally they went out of the state for it. Today they have to send 1,000 to 5,000 miles for most of their building wood.

They were using it simply by habit because it was originally handy and suddenly they had exhausted that supply. Long ago wood boxes disappeared from our cellars. In the war's great motion packing cases went all over the world. That broke the wood supply equilibrium altogether. World increased paper needs and the new chemistry of wood-energy conversion makes it unthinkable that wood will ever again be available in any large way for building it into houses, even into prefabs which average 70% wood. Wood is suddenly going from 'for free' as it sat stacked on the farm because it had to be cleared away, to a rapidly inflating price structure—owing not so much to its scarcity, as to its newly recognized inherent wealth.

On the other hand, there are now the many *by-products of the soil* and *by-products of the wood* which chemistry is developing, whether it is cellulose as plastics, or the metals developed from the clay, etc., which were just kicking around unrecognized on the early farm. These by-products, however, were very expensive to extract in the beginning and called for a large energy expenditure and fancy and complicated mammoth plants with giant stills and ovens such as required millions of dollars to install and develop. Few industries could afford to buy the original specialty by-products of high performance characteristic.

However in developing the aircraft industry we had to have *high performance per pound*, so for a military plane the federal government could afford to pay for special alloys of aluminum and steel. Then we suddenly called for an enormous wartime application of industry to produce those same materials and they were brought into relatively low cost brackets. They could be extremely low for they came from sands, clay, coal, air, water, etc. Producers however held up their prices during the war because of the enormous amount of inspection necessary. In order to amplify industry to the ability to mass produce planes, which meant withstanding terrific stresses with minimum of weight and bulk, it was necessary to be supercareful of the quality of the materials. So the cost of inspection, pyramided upon inspection all along the line, was reflected in the high price structure of those materials, despite quantity production.

We now have enough 24ST aluminum in war surplus and scrap to make it worthwhile to segregate 24ST scrap so that the aluminum company will say, "We will give you 24ST because we can now recirculate the scrap, and it is better scrap, actually having a little higher alloy content and preferable qualities at a much lower price than you have been paying." Just within a couple of postwar months I am beginning to see price structure of aircraft metals and other high performance materials on the way down. As you study the basic economics of the plastics or aluminum industry, you find the price structure has got to go down as we employ their mass production by our less stringent standards and large mass outlet. Why?—Because we have alternate materials for every part's design.

In the materials we are dealing with in our new airframe houses, we are in a deflating price structure, while wood of the conventional house is in a very rapidly inflating price structure.

Those are some of the really outstanding trend data for you. If you would like to have in mind before you go away some of the absolutes in the old building world, so you can see where you are situated as you enter our endeavor with us, I will read these figures. I gave you the all-time high in housing which was in 1925, when 827,000 dwelling units were built, of which 572,000 were single-family dwellings, of which 270,00 had some interior plumbing. The top wartime total of dwelling units in one year was 575,000. That was 300,000 less than 1925, despite very much larger population and despite very much increased technology in all other directions. That was 1943 and was in all classes of dwellings.

We find that during the war a lot of other kinds of dwellings or shelters were developed, in which Quonsets were among those with which to reckon. In case authorities determine that "Our standard of living will have to go down during the 1946–47–48 housing emergency, and two million G.I.s who have made the mistake of getting married and are looking for some place to live will have to live in Quonsets and prefabs," what would be the projected production of Quonset huts and other prefabs? Sixty thousand Quonsets in one year is that industry's reported top capacity. The prefabricated house industry indicated in a recent government survey that it hoped to double its production from the best prediction year during the war to a new total of 142,950 units. That is the capacity they dreamed about. Their best war capacity rate, which was never sustained, amounted to a potential 71,475 houses per year. That doesn't come anywhere near your need this coming year just for two million homeless G.I.s and their brides, paying no attention at all to the rest of the housing shortage, which is somewhere about twelve million in the United States. Those are important figures for you to have in mind to know whether you are on the right track in joining up with us here in the airframe dwelling machine industry.

I must caution you that you will be confronted constantly by the statement that mass production of houses eliminates the aspect of individuality which is so cherished by humans and without which they are afraid they will lose the identity of their personality; therefore, mass production of houses will never gain popular acceptance.

My answer to that is that reproduction or regeneration of form is a fundamental of nature and that it is neither good nor bad in itself. However, reproduction of originally inadequate or awkward forms, or poor mechanics or wasteful structures, either by the hand of man or by the regeneration of the biological species, tends to amplify the original characteristic. If the original is annoying, reproductions become increasingly annoying; if the original is highly adequate to its designed purpose, reproductions become increasingly pleasing in that confirmation of adequacy. In the latter light, we continuously admire a fine species of cultivated rose or nature's wildflowers—the more frequently repeated, the more beautiful. Conversely, the more frequently we see a maimed soldier, the more disheartening becomes the repetition. There would be even less virtue of the so-called individuality in discovery of soldiers' sons born with half a face blown away, or with three legs.

Individuality goes far deeper than these surface manifestations with which people have sought to deceive one another as to the relative importance of their status in the bitter struggle to validate one's right to live. Those who were powerful but ugly and lazy paid for fine clothes and fine surface architecture and a superstition has persisted that people who could afford to pay must be superior individuals. The powerful have whipped the weak for centuries on end to instill that superstition. As long as *might excelled over right* that superstition had to continue. Now that we propose housing to be produced by an industry in which *right makes might* at less than a pound per horsepower the superstition is obsolete.

There is no individuality in conventional houses. They are all four-square boxes with varying lengths of rotting wood Greek column nailed onto the front, every house so similar that without signboards the stranger cannot tell the difference between one American town and another, let alone detect individuality in the separate and pathetic homes.

On the other hand, it has been discovered that the more uniform and simple the surfaces with which the individual is graced, the more does the individuality, which is the abstract life, come through. Trained nurses in uniform working in a hospital are notoriously more attractive as individuals than the same girls in their street clothes when off duty.

To somebody who says, "what are your houses going to cost?" we are not yet able to say very accurately but the indications are the cost will be relatively low. "That," we say, "is very unimportant." My argument and I hope yours is going to be that costs are entirely relative. Your wage structure is going up fairly fast. If your wage structure is different your price will be different. Houses that cost $5,000 before the war are now costing $8,000. Houses reflect relative prices. Suppose we are somewhere around or below the $5,000 mark—I think that is pretty good.

What is more important, however, I think is for us all to realize the actual picture of production potential of our houses in terms of the capacity of the metals produced for the aircraft industry during this war. Not going outside of the aircraft capacity—not infringing at all on the old building world, leaving it to build as best it can we can get set up in the aircraft plants and be producing two million houses a year just as fast as we can get ready. Just as fast as you boys can get out good production drawings and complete your calculations and get this house tooled up, we can produce two million houses a year.

That is talking entirely new figures and we can amplify the aluminum capacity and amplify the aircraft capacity and get up to five million houses and approach the automobile figures. That is perfectly reasonable. There is nothing fantastic about that number of units. We are talking about something we know is really practical.

As it is practical and we really need two million houses right now for G.I.s, and need twelve million for people in substandard and crowded houses in the United States, and need thirty million houses for 100% bombed-out families in the war-torn countries, I say the cost of *not* having our houses is not only enormous, it is history's tragedy. It leads rapidly into lawlessness and ill health, to an enormous cost to society. I would ask a senatorial committee or a congressional committee asking me what houses cost, *"How much is it going to cost not to have our houses?"* That is what is important and I really look at the accumulating national debt as the accumulation of the cost of maintaining curative pathology instead of investing a few billions in establishing a preventive pathology through a scientific worldwide housing service industry. We have already come a long way downhill from the industrial peak in the face of an enormous ability to create wealth and put our environment under control. The initial cost is very important. If we can get the thing rolling we can make houses available to everyone who wants houses, and very rapidly obsolete all old standards of living. We will set up a new industry that promises to go on to rehouse the whole world and employ the whole world in the continuous wealth-making of improving living advantages.

That is clear enough as a simple a picture to the building trades. Some of the building trades people I talk to understand this, and it is very clear to mechanics that we are talking about starting up a new industry and not a new house. They are not going to be so concerned about whether the building trades are employed in erecting those houses. The building trades men tell me they have participated in the building of less than 4% of single-family dwellings. It is not a very important item to them. When you talk to them about giving them a new industry, the new industry, like the telephone, would cause a great deal of bricklaying of the individual plants, the power stations, etc. Therefore, you want to say, all of you, that you are designing an additional industry which is going to get everybody busy. Your labor man doesn't mind the idea of short man-hours, or better working conditions or steady year-round work.

Beech figures show way less than 100 man-hours per house to manufacture. Our indications are that in the field we will start with 100 man-hours and before we get through with developing the boom jig upon which we are going to hang the house as we assemble it and feed the parts off the tailboard to give a very fast assembly, we will be down to relatively few man-hours—40 man-hours or something like that—in the field. (That of course is not what we are going to do out here in the early days.)

I will prophesy however than within two years we will be down to somewhere under 100 man-hours from raw materials as delivered to the aircraft industry (that is, as sheet aluminum in rolls, steel in rods and tubes, etc.) to finished house—under 100 man-hours. So your living cost is going to be low and your standards high and rapidly rising.

Obviously, boys, the thing is now reasonably good enough to dare to put it out on the world, and the world will be reasonably tolerant enough with it to "take" all the bugs that are still in it. It is full of them. But we have harnessed out there now in our prototypes the right principles within the right weight and the right dimensions, so that's where you boys have to take over.

Thank you very much.

As co-curator with H. R. Hitchcock, Johnson participated in his first great architectural endeavor, the exhibition of Modern International Style Architecture at the New York Museum of Modern Art, before he began his formal architectural studies. Over the next few decades, Johnson established himself as a prominent figure in the field, working with a simplified, reductive architectural vocabulary of glass and steel derived from the works of Mies van der Rohe. A clear example is Johnson's own residence, the Glass House in New Canaan, Connecticut (1949), which draws upon Mies's Farnsworth House in Plano, Illinois (1946–50). From 1954 through 1958, Johnson worked with Mies on the design of the Seagram Building in New York. In the following text, originally a talk given in 1954 to students at Harvard University's Graduate School of Design, Johnson irreverently questioned the architect's reliance on certain modernist principles, or "crutches." Ultimately, he insisted that the act of creation is intensely personal and relies not on preconceived tenets, but on the architect's agency. Johnson's declaration coincided with his own architectural shift toward the postmodern playfulness expressed in his AT&T Building (New York, 1980–84).

"The Seven Crutches of Modern Architecture" (1955)

Art has nothing to do with intellectual pursuit—it shouldn't be in a university at all. Art should be practiced in the gutters—pardon me, in attics.

You can't learn architecture any more than you can learn a sense of music or of painting. You shouldn't talk about art, you should do it.

If I seem to go into words it's because there's no other way to communicate. We have to descend to the world around us if we are to battle it. We have to use words to put the "word" people back where they belong.

So I'm going to attack the seven crutches of architecture. Some of us rejoice in the crutches and pretend that we're walking and that poor other people with two feet are slightly handicapped. But we all use them at times, and especially in the schools where you have to use language. It's only natural to use language when you're teaching, because how are teachers to mark you? "Bad entrance" or "Bathrooms not backed up" or "Stairway too narrow" or "Where's head room?" "Chimney won't draw," "Kitchen too far from dining room." It is so much easier for the faculty to set up a set of rules that you can be marked against. They can't say, "That's ugly." For you can answer that for you it is good-looking, and *de gustibus non est disputandum*. Schools therefore are especially prone to using these crutches. I would certainly use them if I were teaching, because I couldn't criticize extra-aesthetic props any better than any other teacher.

The most important crutch in recent times is not valid now: the *Crutch of History*. In the old days you could always rely on books. You could say, "What do you mean you don't like my tower? There it is in Wren." Or, "They did that on the Subtreasury Building—why can't I do it?" History doesn't bother us very much now.

But the next one is still with us today although, here again, the *Crutch of Pretty Drawing* is pretty well gone. There are those of us—I am one—who have made a sort of cult of the pretty plan. It's a wonderful crutch because you can give yourself the illusion that you are creating architecture while you're making pretty drawings. Fundamentally, architecture is something you build and put together, and people walk in and they like it. But that's too hard. Pretty pictures are easier.

The next one, the third one, is the *Crutch of Utility*, of usefulness. This is where I was brought up, and I've used it myself; it was an old Harvard habit.

They say a building is good architecture if it works. This building works perfectly— if I talk loud enough. The Parthenon probably worked perfectly well for the ceremonies they used it for. In other words, merely that a building works is not sufficient. You expect that it works. You expect a kitchen hot-water faucet to run hot water these days. You expect any architect, a graduate of Harvard or not, to be able to put the kitchen in the right place. But when it's used as a crutch it impedes. It lulls you into thinking that that is architecture. The rules that we've all been brought up on—"The coat closet should be near the front door in a house," "Cross-ventilation is a necessity"—these rules are not very important for architecture. That we should have a front door to come in and a back door to carry the garbage out—pretty good, but in my house I noticed to my horror the other day that I carried the garbage out the front door. If the business of getting the house to run well takes precedence over your artistic invention the result won't be architecture at all; merely an assemblage of useful parts. You will recognize it next time you're doing a building; you'll be so satisfied when you get the banks of elevators to come out at the right floor you'll think your skyscraper is finished. I know. I'm just working on one.

That's not as bad, though as the next one: the *Crutch of Comfort*. That's a habit that we come by, the same as utility. We are all descended from John Stuart Mill in our thinking. After all, what is architecture for but the comforts of the people who live there? But when that is made into a crutch for doing architecture, environmental control starts to replace architecture. Pretty soon you'll be doing controlled environmental houses which aren't hard to do except that you may have a window on the west and you can't control the sun. There isn't an overhang in the world, there isn't a sun chart in Harvard University that will help. Because, of course, the sun is absolutely everywhere. You know what they mean by controlled environment; it is the study of "microclimatology," which is the science that tells you how to recreate a climate so that you will be comfortable. But are you? The fireplace, for example, is out of place in the controlled environment of a house. It heats up and throws off thermostats. But I like the beauty of a fireplace so I keep my thermostat way down to sixty, and then I light a big roaring fire so I can move back and forth. Now that's not controlled environment. I control the environment. It's a lot more fun.

Some people say that chairs are good-looking that are comfortable. Are they? I think that comfort is a function of whether you think the chair is good-looking or not. Just test it yourself. (Except I know you won't be honest with me.) I have had Mies van der Rohe chairs now for twenty-five years in my home wherever I go. They're not very comfortable chairs, but, if people like the looks of them they say, "Aren't these beautiful chairs," which indeed they are. Then they'll sit in them and say, "My, aren't they comfortable." If, however, they're the kind of people who think curving steel legs are an ugly way to hold up a chair they'll say, "My, what uncomfortable chairs."

The *Crutch of Cheapness*. That is one that you haven't run into as students because no one's told you to cut $10,000 off the budget, because you haven't built anything.

But that'll be your first lesson. The cheapness boys will say, "Anybody can build an expensive house. Ah, but see, my house only cost $25,000." Anybody that can build a $25,000 house has indeed reason to be proud, but is he talking about architecture or his economic ability? Is it the crutch you're talking about, or is it architecture? That economic motive, for instance, goes in New York so far that the real-estate-minded people consider it un-American to build a Lever House with no rentals on the ground floor. They find that it's an architectural sin not to fill the envelope.

Then there's another very bad crutch that you will get much later in your career. Please, please, watch out for this one: the *Crutch of Serving the Client*. You can escape all criticism if you can say, "Well, the client wanted it that way." Mr. Hood, one of our really great architects, talked exactly that way. He would put a Gothic door on a skyscraper and say, "Why shouldn't I? The client wanted a Gothic door on the modern skyscraper, and I put it on. Because what is my business? Am I not here to please my client?" As one of the boys asked me during the dinner before the lecture, where do you draw the line? When do the client's demands permit you to shoot him and when do you give in gracefully? It's got to be clear, back in your own mind, that serving the client is one thing and the art of architecture another.

Perhaps the most trouble of all is the *Crutch of Structure*. That gets awfully near home because, of course, I use it all the time myself. I'm going to go on using it. You have to use something. Like Bucky Fuller, who's going around from school to school— it's like a hurricane, you can't miss it if it's coming: he talks, you know, for five or six hours, and he ends up that all architecture is nonsense, and you have to build something like discontinuous domes. The arguments are beautiful. I have nothing against discontinuous domes, but for goodness sake, let's not call it architecture. Have you ever seen Bucky trying to put a door into one of his domed buildings? He's never succeeded, and wisely, when he does them, he doesn't put any covering on them, so they are magnificent pieces of pure sculpture. Sculpture also cannot result in architecture because architecture has problems that Bucky Fuller has not faced, like how do you get in and out. Structure is a very dangerous thing to cling to. You can be led to believe that clear structure clearly expressed will end up being architecture by itself. You say, "I don't have to design any more. All I have to do is make a clean structural order." I have believed this off and on myself. It's a very nice crutch, you see, because after all, you can't mess up a building too badly if the bays are all equal and all the windows are the same size.

Now why should we at this stage be that crutch-conscious? Why should we not step right up to it and face it: the act of creation. The act of creation, like birth and death, you have to face yourself. There aren't any rules; there is no one to tell you whether your one choice out of, say, six billion for the proportion of a window is going to be right. No one can go with you into that room where you make the final decision. You can't escape it anyhow; why fight it? Why not realize that architecture is the sum of inescapable artistic decisions that you have to make. If you're strong you can make them.

I like the thought that what we are to do on this earth is to embellish it for its greater beauty, so that oncoming generations can look back to the shapes we leave here and get the same thrill that I get in looking back at theirs—at the Parthenon, at Chartres Cathedral. That is the duty—I doubt if I get around to it in my generation—the difficulties are too many, but you can. You can if you're strong enough not to bother with the crutches, and face the fact that to create something is a direct experience.

I like Corbusier's definition of architecture. He expressed it the way I wish I could have: "L'architecture, c'est le jeu savant, correct et magnifique des formes sous la lumière"—"Architecture is the play of forms under the light, the play of forms correct, wise, and magnificent." The play of forms under the light. And, my friends, that's all it is. You can embellish architecture by putting toilets in. But there was great architecture long before the toilet was invented. I like Nietzsche's definition—that much misunderstood European—he said, "In architectural works, man's pride, man's triumph over gravitation, man's will to power assume visible form. Architecture is a veritable oratory of power made by form."

Now my position in all this is obviously not as solipsistic, not as directly intuitional as all that sounds. To get back to earth, what do we do next if we don't hang on to any of these crutches? I am a traditionalist. I believe in history. I mean by tradition the carrying out, in freedom, the development of a certain basic approach to architecture which we find upon beginning our work here. I do not believe in perpetual revolution in architecture. I do not strive for originality. As Mies once told me, "Philip, it is much better to be good than to be original." I believe that. We have very fortunately the work of our spiritual fathers to build on. We hate them, of course, as all spiritual sons hate all spiritual fathers, but we can't ignore them, nor can we deny their greatness. The men, of course, that I refer to: Walter Gropius, Le Corbusier, and Mies van der Rohe. Frank Lloyd Wright I should include—the greatest architect of the nineteenth century. Isn't it wonderful to have behind us the tradition, the work that these men have done? Can you imagine being alive at a more wonderful time? Never in history was the tradition so clearly demarked, never were the great men so great, never could we learn so much from them and go our own way, without feeling constricted by any style, and knowing that what we do is going to be the architecture of the future, and not be afraid that we wander into some little bypath, like today's romanticists where nothing can possibly evolve. In that sense I am a traditionalist.

18 Louis I. Kahn, 1901–1974

As an architect, educator, and writer, Louis Kahn occupied a unique role in the architectural realm, bridging the dogmatism of modern architecture and the introspective posmodern era that followed. Born in Estonia, Kahn emigrated to the United States with his family in 1905 and settled in Philadelphia. He proved to be a talented musician and artist and, in 1924, he graduated with a degree in architecture from the University of Pennsylvania, a program then based on the traditional Beaux-Arts model. Kahn's mature work combined this classical training with modernist concepts of social improvement and the seemingly eternal qualities of ancient ruins to create a monumental architecture characterized by solidity, mass, and the use of platonic forms. These qualities are apparent in all of his major works including the Yale University Art Gallery in New Haven, Connecticut (1951–55); the Salk Institute for Biological Sciences in La Jolla, California (1959–65); and the Kimbell Art Museum in Fort Worth, Texas (1962–72). Kahn paid particular attention to the inherent nature of the materials—often brick and concrete—with which he worked, and spoke about architecture in almost mystical terms: Thought and Feeling, the measurable and the unmeasurable, the "existence will" of architectural spaces, and the realization of "what a thing wants to be." The comments below, originally titled "Structure and Form," were first presented as a radio broadcast in the Voices of America series on architecture. Through such lectures and as an educator at various institutions, primarily Yale and the University of Pennsylvania, Kahn influenced numerous architects with his humane and spiritual approach to design.

"Form and Design" (1961)

A young architect came to ask a question. "I dream of spaces full of wonder. Spaces that rise and envelop flowingly without beginning, without end, of a jointless material white and gold. When I place the first line on paper to capture the dream, the dream becomes less."

This is a good question. I once learned that a good question is greater than the most brilliant answer.

This is a question of the unmeasurable and the measurable. Nature, physical nature, is measurable.

Feeling and dream has no measure, has no language, and everyone's dream is singular.

Everything that is made however obeys the laws of nature. The man is always greater than his works because he can never fully express his aspirations. For to express oneself in music or architecture is by the measurable means of composition or design. The first line on paper is already a measure of what cannot be expressed fully. The first line on paper is less.

"Then," said the young architect, "what should be the discipline, what should be the

Louis I. Kahn, "Form and Design," in Vincent Scully, *Louis I. Kahn* (New York: George Braziller, Inc., 1962), 114–21. Reprinted with permission from the Louis I. Kahn Archive at the University of Pennsylvania. After the radio broadcast, the lecture was published as "A Statement by Louis Kahn" in *Arts and Architecture* (February 1961), and as "Form and Design" in *Architectural Design* (April 1961).

ritual that brings one closer to the psyche. For in the aura of no material and no language, I feel man truly is."

Turn to Feeling and away from Thought. In Feeling is the Psyche. Thought is Feeling and presence of Order. Order, the maker of all existence, has No Existence Will. I choose the word Order instead of knowledge because personal knowledge is too little to express Thought abstractly. This Will is the Psyche.

All that we desire to create has its beginning in feeling alone. This is true for the scientist. It is true for the artist. But I warned that to remain in Feeling away from Thought means to make nothing.

Said the young architect: "To live and make nothing is intolerable. The dream has in it already the *will to be* and the desire to express this *will*. Thought is inseparable from Feeling. In what way then can Thought enter creation so that this psychic will can be more closely expressed? This is my next question."

When personal feeling transcends into Religion (not a religion but the essence religion) and Thought leads to Philosophy, the mind opens to realizations. Realization of what may be the *existence will* of, let us say, particular architectural spaces. Realization is the merging of Thought and Feeling at the closest rapport of the mind with the Psyche, the source of *what a thing wants to be*.

It is the beginning of Form. Form encompasses a harmony of systems, a sense of Order and that which characterizes one existence from another. Form has no shape or dimension. For example, in the differentiation of a spoon from spoon, spoon characterizes a form having two inseparable parts, the handle and the bowl. A spoon implies a specific design made of silver or wood, big or little, shallow or deep, Form is "what." Design is "how." Form is impersonal, Design belongs to the designer. Design is a circumstantial act, how much money there is available, the site, the client, the extent of knowledge. Form has nothing to do with circumstantial conditions. In architecture, it characterizes a harmony of spaces good for a certain activity of man.

Reflect then on what characterizes abstractly House, a house, home. House is the abstract characteristic of spaces good to live in. House is the form, in the mind of wonder it should be there without shape or dimension. *A* house is a conditional interpretation of these spaces. This is design. In my opinion the greatness of the architect depends on his powers of realization of that which is House, rather than his design of *a* house which is a circumstantial act. Home is the house and the occupants. Home becomes different with each occupant.

The client for whom a house is designed states the areas he needs. The architect creates spaces out of those required areas. It may also be said that this house created for the particular family must have the character of being good for another. The design in this way reflects its trueness to Form. . . .

I want to talk about the difference between form and design, about realization, about the measurable and the unmeasurable aspects of our work and about the limits of our work.

Giotto was a great painter because he painted the skies black for the daytime and he painted birds that couldn't fly and dogs that couldn't run and he made men bigger than doorways because he was a painter. A painter has this prerogative. He doesn't have to answer to the problems of gravity, nor to the images as we know them in real life. As a painter he expresses a reaction to nature and he teaches us through his eyes and his reactions to the nature of man. A sculptor is one who modifies space with the objects expressive again of his reactions to nature. He does not create space. He modifies space. An architect creates space.

Architecture has limits.

When we touch the invisible walls of its limits then we know more about what is contained in them. A painter can paint square wheels on a cannon to express the futility of war. A sculptor can carve the same square wheels. But an architect must use round wheels. Though painting and sculpture play a beautiful role in the realm of architecture as architecture plays a beautiful role in the realms of painting and sculpture, one does not have the same discipline as the other.

One may say that architecture is the thoughtful making of spaces. It is, note, the filling of areas prescribed by the client. It is the creating of spaces that evoke a feeling of appropriate use.

To the musician a sheet of music is seeing from what he hears. A plan of a building should reach like a harmony of spaces in light.

Even a space intended to be dark should have just enough light from some mysterious opening to tell us how dark it really is. Each space must be defined by its structure and the character of its natural light. Of course I am not speaking about minor areas which serve the major spaces. An architectural space must reveal the evidence of its making by the space itself. It cannot be a space when carved out of a greater structure meant for a greater space because the choice of a structure is synonymous with the light and which gives image to that space. Artificial light is a single tiny static moment in light and is the light of night and never can equal the nuances of mood created by the time of day and the wonder of the seasons.

A great building, in my opinion, must begin with the unmeasurable, must go through measurable means when it is being designed and in the end must be unmeasurable. The design, the making of things is a measurable act. In fact at that point, you are like physical nature itself because in physical nature everything is measurable, even that which is yet unmeasured, like the most distant stars which we can assume will be eventually measured.

But what is unmeasurable is the psychic spirit. The psyche is expressed by feeling and also thought and I believe will always be unmeasurable. I sense that the psychic Existence Will calls on nature to make what it wants to be. I think a rose wants to be a rose. Existence Will, *man*, becomes existence, through nature's law and evolution. The results are always less than the spirit of existence.

In the same way a building has to start in the unmeasurable aura and go through the measurable to be accomplished. It is the only way you can build, the only way you can get it into being is through the measurable. You must follow the laws but in the end when the building becomes part of living it evokes unmeasurable qualities. The design involving quantities of brick, method of construction, engineering is over and the spirit of its existence takes over. . . .

From all I have said I do not mean to imply a system of thought and work leading to realization from Form to Design.

Designs could just as well lead to realizations in Form.

This interplay is the constant excitement of Architecture.

19 ALDO VAN EYCK, 1918–1999

In his role as a designer, educator, and editor, the Dutch architect Aldo van Eyck campaigned against the notion of functionalism entrenched in the practice of modern architecture. In Van Eyck's opinion, the preoccupation with functional principles produced homogenous, vacuous spaces that failed to address humanist concerns such as man's desire for variety, specificity, and comfort. Van Eyck cited the need for "place and occasion" over "space and time"; the latter are abstract and theoretical, as opposed to "place and occasion," which imply an identifiable locale and a memorable experience. Van Eyck designed with these principles in mind, as is evident in his Amsterdam Orphanage of 1955–60. He organized this large building as he would a city, with spacious areas for communal interaction and smaller nodes tailored to the specific occupants. The children of the orphanage, both male and female, ranged in age, so Van Eyck crafted each place accordingly. The following comments address both architecture and urbanism, and were written shortly after the completion of the orphanage. They express Van Eyck's sentiments as a member of Team 10, a group of architects opposed to modernist functionalism and dedicated to the creation of a more humane built environment based on the physical, social, and psychological needs of man.

Untitled Thoughts on Place and Occasion (1962)

Space has no room, time not a moment for man. He is excluded.

In order to "include" him—help his homecoming—he must be gathered into their meaning. (Man is the subject as well as the object of architecture).

Whatever space and time mean, place and occasion mean more.

For space in the image of man is place, and time in the image of man is occasion.

Today, space and what it should coincide with in order to become "space"—man at home with himself—are lost. Both search for the same place, but cannot find it.

Provide that space, articulate the inbetween.

Is man able to penetrate the material he organizes into hard shape between one man and another, between what is here and what is there, between this and a following moment? Is he able to find the right place for the right occasion?

Aldo van Eyck, Untitled Thoughts on Place and Occasion, in *Team 10 Primer*, ed. Alison Smithson (Cambridge, MA: MIT Press, 1968), 101. Reprinted with permission from the publisher.

No—So start with this: make a welcome of each door and a countenance of each window.

Make of each place, a bunch of places of each house and each city, for a house is a tiny city, a city a huge house. Get closer to the shifting centre of human reality and build its counterform—for each man and all men, since they no longer do it themselves.

Whoever attempts to solve the riddle of space in the abstract, will construct the outline of emptiness and call it space.

Whoever attempts to meet man in the abstract will speak with his echo and call this a dialogue.

Man still breathes both in and out. When is architecture going to do the same?

Peter Cook, b. 1936, and Warren Chalk, 1927–1987

The term "Archigram"—an amalgamation of "architecture" and "telegram"—refers to both an irreverent, experimental magazine and the group of six young British architects associated with that publication. From 1961 through 1974, *Archigram* featured a collage of thoughts, cartoons, projects, and fantastic proposals by Peter Cook, Warren Chalk, and the four other members of the group. Their basic message involved issues of change and obsolescence. Archigram embraced new possibilities afforded by technology that modern architecture failed to make a reality. Impermanence, expendability, flexibility, growth—these qualities informed their projects to varying degrees. Peter Cook's Plug-in City (1964), for example, was a new expandable urban development comprised of building components, movable by crane and replaceable when outdated, that would plug into the larger infrastructural framework of the city. The group's Instant City (late 1960s) was a "traveling metropolis" conceived to jumpstart the cultural growth of nonurban areas. The city would descend on a small town by balloon and, over the course of a few days, expose the inhabitants to cosmopolitan excitement and vitality. In general, Archigram's designs extended beyond available technology and thus were not then possible to construct. Nevertheless, through their projects, publications, and exhibitions, Archigram had a considerable impact on the architectural community in England and elsewhere. They challenged the true modernity of modern architecture and the accepted notions of buildings as fixed and permanent. Archigram thus prompted a reconsideration of architecture as both an object and a discipline.

Editorial from *Archigram* 3 (1963)

Peter Cook

More and more

Almost without realizing it, we have absorbed into our lives the first generation of expendables . . . foodbags, paper tissue, polythene wrappers, ballpens, E.P.s . . . so many things about which we don't have to think. We throw them away almost as soon as we acquire them.

Also with us are the items that are bigger and last longer, but are nevertheless planned for obsolescence . . . the motor car . . . and its unit-built garage.

Now the second generation is upon us—paper furniture is a reality in the States, paper sheets are a reality in British hospital beds, the Greater London Council is putting up limited life-span houses.

Through and through

With every level of society and with every level of commodity, the unchanging scene is being replaced by the increase in change of our user-habits—and thereby, eventually, our user-habitats.

We are becoming much more used to the idea of changing a piece of clothing year by year, rather than expecting to hang on to it for several years. Similarly, the idea

Peter Cook and Warren Chalk, "Editorial from *Archigram* 3," in *Archigram*, ed. Peter Cook et al. (New York: Princeton Architectural Press,1999), 16–17. Reprinted with permission.

of keeping a piece of furniture long enough to be able to hand it on to our children is becoming increasingly ridiculous. In this situation we should not be surprised if such articles wear out within their 'welcome-life' span, rather than their traditional life span.

The attitude of mind that accepts such a situation is creeping into our society at about the rate that expendable goods become available. We must recognize this as a healthy and altogether positive sign. It is the product of a sophisticated consumer society, rather than a stagnant (and in the end, declining) society.

Our collective mental blockage occurs between the land of the small-scale consumer-products and the objects which make our environment. Perhaps it will not be until such things as housing, amenity-place and workplace become recognized as consumer products that can be 'bought off the peg'—with all that this implies in terms of expendability (foremost), industrialization, up-to-date-ness, customer choice, and basic product-design—that we can begin to make an environment that is really part of a developing human culture.

Why is there an indefinable resistance to planned obsolescence for a kitchen, which in twelve years will be highly inefficient (by the standards of the day) and in twenty years will be intolerable, yet there are no qualms about four-year obsolescence for cars?

This idea of an expendable environment is still somehow regarded as akin to anarchy . . . as if, in order to make it work, we would bulldoze Westminster Abbey. . . .

We shall not bulldoze Westminster Abbey
Added to this, the idea of a non-permanent building has overtones of economy, auster-

ity, economy. Architects are the first to deny the great potential of expendability as the built reflection of the second half of the twentieth century. Most of the buildings that exist that are technically expendable have the fact skillfully hidden . . . they masquerade as permanent buildings—monuments to the past.

Housing as a consumer product
Warren Chalk

One of the most flagrant misconceptions held about us is that we are not ultimately concerned with people. This probably arises directly from the type of imagery we use. A section through, say, something like City Interchange, appears to predict some automated wasteland inhabited only by computers and robots. How much this is justified is difficult to assess, but if our work is studied closely there will be found traces of a very real concern for people and the way in which they might be liberated from the restrictions imposed on them by the existing chaotic situation, in the home, at work and in the total built environment.

Human situations are as concerned with environmental changes and activity within the city, as with the definition of places. Important in this is the precept of situation as an ideas generator in creating a truly living city. Cities should generate, reflect and activate life, their structure organized to precipitate life and movement. Situation, the happenings within spaces in the city, the transient throwaway world of people, the passing presence of cars, etc., are as important, possibly more important than the built environment, the built demarcation of space. Situation can be caused by a single individual, by groups or a crowd, their particular purpose, occupation, movement and direction.

This is in fact a follow-on from thinking related to the South Bank scheme where the original basic concept was to produce an anonymous pile, subservient to a series of pedestrian walkways, a sort of Mappin Terrace for people instead of goats.

So once again the pedestrian, the gregarious nature of people and their movement is upper-most in our minds and the built demarcation of space used to channel and direct pedestrian patterns of movement.

In an attempt to get closer to the general public, to study their attitudes and behavior, we have extended ourselves beyond the narrow boundaries of conventional architectural thought, causing the misconceptions about what we are trying to do. We must extend the conventional barriers and find people without any formal architectural training, producing concepts showing a marked intuitive grasp of current attitudes related to city images and the rest. In the world of science fiction we dig out prophetic information regarding geodesic nets, pneumatic tubes and plastic domes and bubbles.

If we turn to the back pages of the popular press we find ads for do-it-yourself living-room extensions, or instant garage kits. Let's face it, we can no longer turn away from the hard fact that everyone in the community has latent creative instincts and that our role will eventually be to direct these into some tangible and acceptable form. The present gulf between people, between the community and the designer may well be eventually bridged by the do-it-yourself interchangeable kit of parts.

In a technological society more people will play an active part in determining their own individual environment, in self-determining a way of life. We cannot expect to take this fundamental right out of their hands and go on treating them as cultural and creative morons. We must tackle it from the other end in a positive way. The inherent qualities of mass-production for a consumer orientated society and those of repetition and standardization, but parts can be changeable or interchangeable depending on individual needs and preferences and, given a world market, could also be economically feasible.

In the States one can select a car consisting of a whole series of interchangeable options, as Reyner Banham has pointed out (in his article on Clip-on Architecture). Chevrolet [produces] a choice of seventeen bodies and five different engines.

The current success of pop music is to an extent due to the importance of audience participation; the 'Frug' and the 'Jerk' are self-expressive and free-forming. The pop groups themselves are closer in dress and habits, including musical dexterity, to the audience. Despite pop music becoming a vast industry its success depends on its ability to keep up with the pace of its consumer taste.

Of course the idea of mass-produced expendable component dwellings is not new. We are all familiar with Le Corbusier's efforts in collaboration with Prouvé and with Prouvé's own bits and pieces, with Buckminister Fuller's Dymaxion house, the Phelps Dodge Dymaxion bathroom and the Dymaxion deployment unit, Alison and Peter Smithson's House of the Future at the Ideal Home Exhibition of 1955, Ionel Schien's pre-fabricated hotel units and the Monsanto Plastic House in Disneyland; there has also been work done by the Metabolist Group in Japan and Arthur Quarmby in England.

The Plug-in Capsule Home is an attempt to sustain the idea in the hope that some brave soul might eventually be persuaded to finance research and development.

The techniques of mass-production and automation are a reality, yet we see the research that goes into, and the products that come out of today's building and are dismayed.

The Plug-in Capsule attempts to set new standards and find an appropriate image for an assembly-line product. The order of its design criteria are in correct order to consumer requirements. First, a better consumer product, offering something better than, and different from, traditional housing, more closely related to the design of cars and refrigerators, than placing itself in direct competition with tradition.

21 | ROBERT VENTURI, B. 1925

Robert Venturi with John Rauch, Vanna Venturi House, Chestnut Hill, PA, 1962
Photo from R. Venturi and Denise Scott Brown, *A View from the Campidoglio: Selected Essays 1953–1984*
ed. P. Arnell, T. Bickford and C. Bergart (New York: Harper & Row, Publishers, 1984), 75
Photograph by Rollin R. La France
Courtesy of Venturi, Scott Brown and Associates, Inc.

Despite a number of constructed works, Venturi is perhaps best known as the author of *Complexity and Contradiction in Architecture*. This text appeared in 1966 as a challenge to the position held by many modern architects in which form—and hence meaning—theoretically derived from function, not from other sources such as history, tradition, or culture. In contrast, Venturi advocated an inclusive approach toward design that embraced multiplicity of meaning and form. To support this argument and to counter the perceived rift between modern and historical architecture, Venturi cited works from antiquity through the present. This view of architectural continuity placed the architecture of the past on a par with that of the present.

Demonstrating the ways in which revered modern architects learned from the past, Venturi encouraged his colleagues to accept both historical architecture and the "messy vitality" of contemporary life as valid sources of inspiration. This concept appears in Venturi's own architecture as well; for example, the design for his mother's house (the Vanna Venturi House, 1962) incorporates abstracted elements from classical architecture (the applied arch over the front door); modern architecture (the strip or ribbon window of Le Corbusier); and traditional and vernacular homes (the square window with mullions, the pitched roof, and the prominent chimney). To Venturi's dismay, many interpreted his message as a call for a revived classicism or stylistic eclecticism, practices which led in part to postmodernism, an architectural movement often characterized by irony and pastiche.

In 1967, Venturi married architect and urban planner Denise Scott Brown. Since then, they have been partners in design, have cotaught architectural studios, and have coauthored several texts including *Learning from Las Vegas* (1972), written in conjunction with Steven Izenour.

Complexity and Contradiction in Architecture (1966)

1. Nonstraightforward Architecture: A Gentle Manifesto

I like complexity and contradiction in architecture. I do not like the incoherence or arbitrariness of incompetent architecture nor the precious intricacies of picturesqueness or expressionism. Instead, I speak of a complex and contradictory architecture based on the riches and ambiguity of modern experience, including that experience which is inherent in art. Everywhere, except in architecture, complexity and contradiction have been acknowledged, from Gödel's proof of ultimate inconsistency in mathematics to T. S. Eliot's analysis of "difficult" poetry and Joseph Albers' definition of the paradoxical quality of painting.

But architecture is necessarily complex and contradictory in its very inclusion of the traditional Vitruvian elements of commodity, firmness, and delight. And today the wants of program, structure, mechanical equipment, and expression, even in single buildings in simple contexts, are diverse and conflicting in ways previously unimaginable. The increasing dimension and scale of architecture in urban and regional planning add to the difficulties. I welcome the problems and exploit the uncertainties. By embracing contradiction as well as complexity, I aim for vitality as well as validity.

Architects can no longer afford to be intimidated by the puritanically moral language of orthodox Modern architecture. I like elements which are hybrid rather than "pure,"

Robert Venturi, *Complexity and Contradiction in Architecture,* 2nd ed. (1966; New York: Museum of Modern Art, 1977, 16–19. © The Museum of Modern Art, New York, 1966, 1977). Reprinted with permission from the publisher.

compromising rather than "clean," distorted rather than "straightforward," ambiguous rather than "articulated," perverse as well as impersonal, boring as well as "interesting," conventional rather than "designed," accommodating rather than excluding, redundant rather than simple, vestigial as well as innovating, inconsistent and equivocal rather than direct and clear. I am for messy vitality over obvious unity. I include the non sequitur and proclaim the duality.

I am for richness of meaning rather than clarity of meaning; for the implicit function as well as the explicit function. I prefer "both-and" to "either-or," black and white, and sometimes gray, to black or white. A valid architecture evokes many levels of meaning and combinations of focus; its space and its elements become readable and workable in several ways at once.

But an architecture of complexity and contradiction has a special obligation toward the whole: its truth must be in its totality or its implications of totality. It must embody the difficult unity of inclusion rather than the easy unity of exclusion. More is not less.

2. Complexity and Contradiction vs. Simplification or Picturesqueness

Orthodox Modern architects have tended to recognize complexity insufficiently or inconsistently. In their attempt to break with tradition and start all over again, they idealized the primitive and elementary at the expense of the diverse and the sophisticated. As participants in a revolutionary movement, they acclaimed the newness of modern functions, ignoring their complications. In their role as reformers, they puritanically advocated the separation and exclusion of elements, rather than the inclusion of various requirements and their juxtapositions. As a forerunner of the Modern movement, Frank Lloyd Wright, who grew up with the motto "Truth against the World," wrote: "Visions of simplicity so broad and far-reaching would open to me and such building harmonies appear that . . . would change and deepen the thinking and culture of the modern world. So I believed."[1] And Le Corbusier, co-founder of Purism, spoke of the "great primary forms" which, he proclaimed, were "distinct . . . and without ambiguity."[2] Modern architects with few exceptions eschewed ambiguity.

But now our position is different: "At the same time that the problems increase in quantity, complexity, and difficulty they also change faster than before,"[3] and require an attitude more like that described by August Heckscher: "The movement from a view of life as essentially simple and orderly to a view of life as complex and ironic is what every individual passes through in becoming mature. But certain epochs encourage this development; in them the paradoxical or dramatic outlook colors the whole intellectual scene. . . . Amid simplicity and order rationalism is born, but rationalism proves inadequate in any period of upheaval. Then equilibrium must be created out of opposites. Such inner peace as men gain must represent a tension among contradictions and uncertainties. . . . A feeling for paradox allows seemingly dissimilar things to exist side by side, their very incongruity suggesting a kind of truth."[4]

Rationalizations for simplification are still current, however, though subtler than the early arguments. They are expansions of Mies van der Rohe's magnificent paradox, "less is more." Paul Rudolph has clearly stated the implications of Mies' point of view: "All problems can never be solved. . . . Indeed it is a characteristic of the twen-

---

[1] Frank Lloyd Wright, in *An American Architecture,* ed. Edgar Kaufmann (New York: Horizon Press, 1955), 207.

[2] Le Corbusier, *Towards a New Architecture* (London: The Architectural Press, 1927), 31.

[3] Christopher Alexander, *Notes on the Synthesis of Form* (Cambridge, MA: Harvard University Press, 1964), 4.

[4] August Heckscher, *The Public Happiness* (New York: Atheneum Publishers, 1962), 102.

tieth century that architects are highly selective in determining which problems they want to solve. Mies, for instance makes wonderful buildings only because he ignores many aspects of a building. If he solved more problems, his buildings would be far less potent."[5]

The doctrine "less is more" bemoans complexity and justifies exclusion for expressive purposes. It does, indeed, permit the architect to be "highly selective in determining which problems [he wants] to solve." But if the architect must be "committed to his particular way of seeing the universe,"[6] such a commitment surely means that the architect determines how problems should be solved, not that he can determine which of the problems he will solve. He can exclude important considerations only at the risk of separating architecture from the experience of life and the needs of society. If some problems prove insoluble, he can express this: in an inclusive rather than exclusive kind of architecture there is room for the fragment, for contradiction, for improvisation, and for the tensions these produce. Mies' exquisite pavilions have had valuable implications for architecture, but their selectiveness of content and language is their limitation as well as their strength.

I question the relevance of analogies between Japanese pavilions and recent domestic architecture. They ignore the real complexity and contradiction inherent in the domestic program—the spatial and technological possibilities as well as the need for variety in visual experience. Forced simplicity results in oversimplification. In the Wiley House, for instance, in contrast to his glass house, Philip Johnson attempted to go beyond the simplicities of the elegant pavilion. He explicitly separated and

---

[5] Paul Rudolph, in *Perspecta 7, The Yale Architectural Journal* (New Haven: Yale University Press, 1961), 51.
[6] Kenneth Burke, *Permanence and Change* (Los Altos, CA: Hermes Publications, 1954), 107.

articulated the enclosed "private functions" of living on a ground floor pedestal, thus separating them from the open social functions in the modular pavilion above. But even here the building becomes a diagram of an oversimplified program for living—an abstract theory of either-or. Where simplicity cannot work, simpleness results. Blatant simplification means bland architecture. Less is a bore.

The recognition of complexity in architecture does not negate what Louis Kahn has called "the desire for simplicity." But aesthetic simplicity which is a satisfaction to the mind derives, when valid and profound, from inner complexity. The Doric temple's simplicity to the eye is achieved through the famous subtleties and precision of its distorted geometry and the contradictions and tensions inherent in its order. The Doric temple could achieve apparent simplicity through real complexity. When complexity disappeared, as in the late temples, blandness replaced simplicity.

Nor does complexity deny the valid simplification which is part of the process of analysis, and even a method of achieving complex architecture itself. "We oversimplify a given event when we characterize it from the standpoint of a given interest."[7] But this kind of simplification is a method in the analytical process of achieving a complex art. It should not be mistaken for a goal.

An architecture of complexity and contradiction, however, does not mean picturesqueness or subjective expressionism. A false complexity has recently countered the false simplicity of an earlier Modern architecture. It promotes an architecture of symmetrical picturesqueness—which Minoru Yamasaki calls "serene"—but it represents a new

---

[7] T.S. Eliot, *Selected Essays, 1917–1932* (New York: Harcourt, Brace and Co., 1932), 96.

formalism as unconnected with experience as the former cult of simplicity. Its intricate forms do not reflect genuinely complex programs, and its intricate ornament, though dependent on industrial techniques for execution, is dryly reminiscent of forms originally created by handicraft techniques. Gothic tracery and Rococo rocaille were not only expressively valid in relation to the whole, but came from a valid showing-off of hand skills and expressed a vitality derived from the immediacy and individuality of the method. This kind of complexity through exuberance, perhaps impossible today, is the antithesis of "serene" architecture, despite the superficial resemblance between them. But if exuberance is not characteristic of our art, it is tension, rather than "serenity" that would appear to be so.

The best twentieth-century architects have usually rejected simplification—that is, simplicity through reduction—in order to promote complexity within the whole. The works of Alvar Aalto and Le Corbusier (who often disregards his polemical writings) are examples. But the characteristics of complexity and contradiction in their work are often ignored or misunderstood. Critics of Aalto, for instances, have liked him mostly for his sensitivity to natural materials and his fine detailing, and have considered his whole composition willful picturesqueness. I do not consider Aalto's Imatra church picturesque. By repeating in the massing the genuine complexity of the triple-divided plan and the acoustical ceiling pattern, this church represents a justifiable expressionism different from the willful picturesqueness of the haphazard structure and spaces of Giovanni Michelucci's recent church for the Autostrada.[8] Aalto's complexity is part of the program and structure of the whole rather than a

---

[8] *Venturi added the following note in the 2nd edition (1977):* "I have visited Giovanni Michelucci's Church of the Autostrada since writing these words, and I now realize it is an extremely beautiful and effective building. I am therefore sorry I made this unsympathetic comparison."

device justified only by the desire for expression. Though we no longer argue over the primacy of form or function (which follows which?), we cannot ignore their interdependence.

The desire for a complex architecture, with its attendant contradictions, is not only a reaction to the banality or prettiness of current architecture. It is an attitude common in the Mannerist periods: the sixteenth century in Italy or the Hellenistic period in Classical art, and is also a continuous strain seen in such diverse architects as Michelangelo, Palladio, Borromini, Vanbrugh, Hawksmoor, Soane, Ledoux, Butterfield, some architects of the Shingle Style, Furness, Sullivan, Lutyens, and recently, Le Corbusier, Aalto, Kahn, and others.

Today this attitude is again relevant to both the medium of architecture and the problem in architecture.

First, the medium of architecture must be re-examined if the increased scope of our architecture as well as the complexity of its goals is to be expressed. Simplified or superficially complex forms will not work. Instead the variety inherent in the ambiguity of visual perception must once more be acknowledged and exploited.

Second, the growing complexities of our functional problems must be acknowledged. I refer, of course, to those programs, unique in our time, which are complex because of their scope, such as research laboratories, hospitals, and particularly the enormous projects at the scale of city and regional planning. But even the house, simple in scope, is complex in purpose if the ambiguities of contemporary experience are expressed. This contrast between the means and the goals of a program is significant. Although the means involved in the program of a rocket to get to the moon, for instance, are almost infinitely complex, the goal is simple and contains few contradictions; although the means involved in the program and structure of buildings are far simpler and less sophisticated technologically than almost any engineering project, the purpose is more complex and often inherently ambiguous.

22 ALDO ROSSI, 1931–1997

Aldo Rossi, *La Fabbrica della Città*, 1978
Photo Credit: Digital Image © The Museum of Modern Art
Licensed by SCALA/Art Resource
NY Courtesy of the Foundazione Aldo Rossi

In 1966, the Italian architect and educator Aldo Rossi published *L'architettura della città*, or *The Architecture of the City*, which examined the European city as a source of architectural knowledge. Within the fabric of the city, Rossi identified "urban artifacts" that, while changing function as the city evolved, retained their basic forms. This concept posed a challenge to the modernist dictum that "form follows function,"—that a building's particular form should derive from its intended purpose—because Rossi showed that, over time, multiple functions had indeed been accommodated within a single form. He thus shifted focus from function to a quasi-scientific investigation of type, as he believed type to be the essence of architectural and urban elements. His architectural analysis reflected the work of sociologists concerned with the relationship between personal recollection and collective memory.

Rossi's own architecture incorporated aspects of his theoretical discoveries; for example, his vocabulary included forms that he recognized as recurrent and timeless, such as the square window and linear housing block. He found support in Boullée's recognition of immutable architectural principles; yet, where Boullée's point of reference was nature, Rossi's was architecture, as manifest in the historical city. In Italy, Rossi's architecture and theoretical work were seen as related enterprises, often associated with the development of the Tendenza—a group of like-minded architects who viewed the European city as a source of architectural inspiration—and a new Rational Architecture that found a basis for architecture within architecture itself. This was not the case in the United States, where Rossi's haunting, De Chirico-esque drawings appeared in the mid-1970s, essentially without his critical writings. These enigmatic images proved quite influential, but the American understanding of Rossi was largely incomplete until the arrival of his theoretical texts in the early 1980s.

The Architecture of the City (1966)

Introduction: Urban Artifacts and a Theory of the City

The city, which is the subject of this book, is to be understood here as architecture. By architecture I mean not only the visible image of the city and the sum of its different architectures, but architecture as construction, the construction of the city over time. I believe that this point of view, objectively speaking, constitutes the most comprehensive way of analyzing the city; it addresses the ultimate and definitive fact in the life of the collective, the creation of the environment in which it lives.

I use the term architecture in a positive and pragmatic sense, as a creation inseparable from civilized life and the society in which it is manifested. By nature it is collective. As the first men built houses to provide more favorable surroundings for their life, fashioning an artificial climate for themselves, so they built with aesthetic intention. Architecture came into being along with the first traces of the city; it is deeply rooted in the formation of civilization and is a permanent, universal, and necessary artifact.

Aesthetic intention and the creation of better surroundings for life are the two permanent characteristics of architecture. These aspects emerge from any significant attempt to explain the city as a human creation. But because architecture gives concrete form to society and is intimately connected with it and with nature, it differs fundamentally from every other art and science. This is the basis for an empirical study of the city as it has evolved from the earliest settlements. With time, the city grows upon itself;

Aldo Rossi, *The Architecture of the City*, trans. Joan Ockman and Diane Ghirardo (Cambridge, MA: MIT Press, 1982) 21, 35, 40–41. © 1982 by the Institute for Architecture and Urban Studies and the Massachusetts Institute of Technology. Reprinted with permission from the publisher. [*The Architecture of the City* appeared in 1982 in English, following the 1981 publication of *A Scientific Autobiography*, essentially Rossi's collected notes from the previous ten years.]

it acquires a consciousness and memory. In the course of its construction, its original themes persist, but at the same time it modifies and renders these themes of its own development more specific. Thus, while Florence is a real city, its memory and form come to have values that also are true and representative of other experiences. At the same time, the universality of these experiences is not sufficient to explain the precise form, the type of object which is Florence.

The contrast between particular and universal, between individual and collective, emerges from the city and from its construction, its architecture. This contrast is one of the principal viewpoints from which the city will be studied in this book. It manifests itself in different ways: in the relationship between the public and private sphere, between public and private buildings, between the rational design of urban architecture and the values of *locus* or place. . . .

Chapter 1. The Structure of Urban Artifacts

. . .

The Urban Artifact as a Work of Art

. . . We believe . . . that the whole is more important than the single parts, and that only the urban artifact in its totality, from street system and urban topography down to the things that can be perceived in strolling up and down a street, constitutes this totality. Naturally we must examine this total architecture in terms of its parts. . . .

Typological Questions

The city as above all else a human thing is constituted of its architecture and of all those works that constitute the true means of transforming nature. Bronze Age men adapted the landscape to social needs by constructing artificial islands of brick, by digging wells, drainage canals, and watercourses. The first houses sheltered their inhabitants from the external environment and furnished a climate that man could begin to control; the development of an urban nucleus expanded this type of control to the creation and extension of a microclimate. Neolithic villages already offered the first transformations of the world according to man's needs. The "artificial homeland" is as old as man.

In precisely this sense of transformation the first forms and types of habitation, as well as temples and more complex buildings, were constituted. The *type* developed according to both needs and aspirations to beauty; a particular type was associated with a form and a way of life, although its specific shape varied widely from society to society. The concept of type thus became the basis of architecture, a fact attested to both by practice and by the treatises.

It therefore seems clear that typological questions are important. They have always entered into the history of architecture, and arise naturally whenever urban problems are confronted. Theoreticians such as Francesco Milizia never defined type as such, but statements like the following seem to be anticipatory: "The comfort of any building consists of three principal items: its site, its form, "and the organization of its parts."[1] I would define the concept of type as something that is permanent and complex, a logical principle that is prior to form and that constitutes it.

One of the major theoreticians of architecture, Quatremère de Quincy, understood the importance of these problems and gave a masterly definition of type and model: "The word 'type' represents not so much the image of a thing to be copied or perfectly imitated as the idea of an element that must itself serve as a rule for the model. . . . The model, understood in terms of the practical execution of art, is an object that must be repeated such as it is; type, on the contrary, is an object according to which one

---

[1] Francesco Milizia, *Principi di Architettura Civile*, ed. Giovanni Antolini (Milan, 1832); 2nd ed., ed. L. Masieri, S. Majocchi (Milan: 1847); reprinted with "Riproduzione anastatica conforme all'originale" (Milan: Gabrielle Mazzotta, 1972). The phrase quoted is from the beginning of the second part, "Della comodità," 221.

can conceive works that do not resemble one another at all. Everything is precise and given in the model; everything is more or less vague in the type. Thus we see that the imitation of types involves nothing that feelings or spirit cannot recognize. . . .

"We also see that all inventions, notwithstanding subsequent changes, always retain their elementary principle in a way that is clear and manifest to the senses and to reason. It is similar to a kind of nucleus around which the developments and variations of forms to which the object was susceptible gather and mesh. Therefore a thousand things of every kind have come down to us, and one of the principal tasks of science and philosophy is to seek their origins and primary causes so as to grasp their purposes. Here is what must be called 'type' in architecture, as in every other branch of human inventions and institutions. . . . We have engaged in this discussion in order to render the value of the word *type*—taken metaphorically in a great number of works—clearly comprehensible, and to show the error of those who either disregard it because it is not a model, or misrepresent it by imposing on it the rigor of a model that would imply the conditions of an identical copy."[2]

In the first part of this passage, the author rejects the possibility of type as something to be imitated or copied because in this case there would be, as he asserts in the second part, no "creation of the model"—that is, there would be no making of architecture. The second part states that in architecture (whether model or form) there is an element that plays its own role, not something to which the architectonic object conforms but something that is nevertheless present in the model. This is the *rule*, the structuring principle of architecture.

---

[2] Antoine Chrysostôme Quatremère de Quincy, *Dictionnaire historique d'architecture comprenant dans son plan les notions historiques, descriptives, archaeologiques, biographiques, théoriques, didactiques et pratiques de cet art*, 2 vols. (Paris, 1832). The passage quoted is from volume 2, the section on "Type". . . [Note: For more information on this concept, see note 11 on page 182 of Ockman and Ghirardo's translation of Rossi.]

In fact, it can be said that this principle is a constant. Such an argument presupposes that the architectural artifact is conceived as a structure and that this structure is revealed and can be recognized in the artifact itself. As a constant, this principle, which we can call the typical element, or simply the type, is to be found in all architectural artifacts. It is also then a cultural element and as such can be investigated in different architectural artifacts; typology becomes in this way the analytical moment of architecture, and it becomes readily identifiable at the level of urban artifacts.

Thus typology presents itself as the study of types of elements that cannot be further reduced, elements of a city as well as of an architecture. The question of monocentric cities or of buildings that are or are not centralized, for example, is specifically typological; no type can be identified with only one form, even if all architectural forms are reducible to types. The process of reduction is a necessary, logical operation, and it is impossible to talk about problems of form without this presupposition. In this sense all architectural theories are also theories of typology, and in an actual design it is difficult to distinguish the two moments.

Type is thus a constant and manifests itself with a character of necessity; but even though it is predetermined, it reacts dialectically with technique, function, and style, as well as with both the collective character and the individual moment of the architectural artifact. It is clear, for example, that the central plan is a fixed and constant type in religious architecture; but even so, each time a central plan is chosen, dialectical themes are put into play with the architecture of the church, with its functions, with its constructional technique, and with the collective that participates in the life of that church. I tend to believe that housing types have not changed from antiquity up to today, but this is not to say that the actual way of living has not changed, nor that new ways of living are not always possible. The house with a loggia is an old scheme; a corridor that gives access to rooms is necessary in plan and present in any number of urban houses. But there are a great many variations on this theme among individual houses at different times.

Ultimately, we can say that type is the very idea of architecture, that which is closest to its essence. In spite of changes, it has always imposed itself on the "feelings and reason" as the principle of architecture and of the city.

While the problem of typology has never been treated in a systematic way and with the necessary breadth, today its study is beginning to emerge in architecture schools and seems quite promising. I am convinced that architects themselves, if they wish to enlarge and establish their own work, must again be concerned with arguments of this nature.[3] Typology is an element that plays its own role in constituting form; it is a constant. The problem is to discern the modalities within which it operates and, moreover, its effective value.

Certainly, of the many past studies in this field, with a few exceptions and save for some honest attempts to redress the omission, few have addressed this problem with much attention. They have always avoided or displaced it, suddenly pursuing something else—namely *function*. Since this problem of function is of absolutely primary importance in the domain of our inquiry, I will try to see how it emerges in studies of the city and urban artifacts in general and how it has evolved. Let us say immediately that the problem can be addressed only when we have first considered the related problems of description and classification. For the most part, existing classifications have failed to go beyond the problem of function.

---

[3] Among the new aspects of the research by architects on the problems of typology, the lectures given by Carlo Aymonino at the Istituto di Architettura di Venezia are particularly interesting. . . . Aymonino's lectures are found in two volumes published by the Istituto Universaitario di Architettura di Venezia, *Aspetti e problemi della tipologia edilizia. Documenti del corso di caratteri distributivi degli edifici. Anno accademico 1963–1964* (Venice, 1964); and *La formazione del concetto di tipologia edilizia. Atti corso di carotteri distributivo degli edifici. Anno accademico 1964–1965* (Venice, 1965). Some of these lectures are also republished with revisions in *Carlo Aymonino, Il significato della città* (Bari: Editori Laterza, 1975).

23 DENISE SCOTT BROWN, B. 1931

Las Vegas Strip, Nevada, ca. 1968. Photograph from R. Venturi, D. Scott Brown, and S. Izenour, *Learning from Las Vegas*, rev. ed. (Cambridge, MA: MIT Press, 1977), 126
Photograph by Denise Scott Brown. Courtesy of Venturi, Scott Brown and Associates, Inc.

An architect and an urban planner, Denise Scott Brown asserts that architects have the responsibility to learn from the existing, often "unarchitected" environment, be it Main Street or the Las Vegas Strip. She does not advocate the wholesale acceptance of these environments; rather, she urges architects to learn what appeals to the public, to understand "what people want." This has been a central theme in Scott Brown's career, a message she has disseminated as a practitioner, educator, and author of writings such as *Learning from Las Vegas* (1972), coauthored with Steven Izenour and her husband Robert Venturi.

Robert Venturi, Duck and Decorated Shed, from R. Venturi, D. Scott Brown, and S. Izenour, *Learning from Las Vegas*, rev. ed. (Cambridge, MA: MIT Press, 1977), 88–89. Courtesy of Venturi, Scott Brown and Associates, Inc.

Learning from Las Vegas grew from a 1968 Yale studio held by Venturi, Scott Brown, and Izenour with the intent of analyzing the form and symbolism of a unique popular environment that appealed to common, working class people. Both versions convey Venturi, Scott Brown, and Izenour's intent—to analyze the form and symbolism of a unique popular environment that appealed to common, working class people. The subsequent publication documented this process and proposed a controversial assessment: in the contemporary era, the authors declared, architecture was increasingly concerned with the *communication across* space as opposed to the *creation of* space. This concept linked to Scott Brown's and Venturi's notion of the "decorated shed." In place of the modernist "duck," a building whose external form reflects its purpose, Scott Brown and Venturi proposed the "decorated shed," a boxlike structure accompanied by a sign that communicates its purpose. The essential argument was that, as a building's use changed, it was far easier to replace the external decoration or sign than to alter the form. Not surprisingly, the "decorated shed" theory as well as *Learning from Las Vegas* drew heavy criticism. The debates hinged on issues of populism, social responsibility, and the role of the architect—themes that pervade architectural discourse to the current day.

The article reprinted below, "Learning from Pop" (1971), addresses more concisely the issues that characterize *Learning from Las Vegas*. These two writings, along with numerous others by Scott Brown, helped direct the attention of practitioners and theorists toward a previously ignored aspect of the American environment and forged a path for the reconsideration of the everyday landscape.

"Learning From Pop" (1971)

Las Vegas, Los Angeles, Levittown, the swinging singles on the Westheimer Strip, golf resorts, boating communities, Co-op City, the residential backgrounds to soap operas, TV commercials and mass mag ads, billboards, and Route 66 are sources for a changing architectural sensibility. New sources are sought when the old forms go stale and the way out is not clear; then a Classical heritage, an art movement, or industrial engineers' and primitives' "architecture without architects" may help to sweep out the flowery remains of the old revolution as practiced by its originators' conservative descendants. In America in the sixties an extra ingredient was added to this recipe for artistic change: social revolution. Urban renewal, supplier of work for architects for two decades and major focus of the soft remains of the Modern movement, was not merely artistically stale, it was socially harmful. The urgency of the social situation, and the social critique of urban renewal and of the architect as server of a rich narrow spectrum of the population—in particular the criticism of Herbert Gans—have been as important as the Pop artists in steering us toward the existing American city and its builders. If high-style architects are not producing what people want or need, who is, and what can we learn from them?

Needs, plural
Sensitivity to needs is a first reason for going to the existing city. Once there, the first lesson for architects is the pluralism of need. No builder-developer in his right mind would announce: I am building for Man. He is building for a market, for a group of people defined by income range, age, family composition, and life style. Levittowns,

---

Denise Scott Brown, "Learning from Pop," *Casabella*, 359/60 (December 1971), 15–23. Reprinted with permission of the author.

Leisureworlds, Georgian-styled town houses grow from someone's estimation of the needs of the groups who will be their markets. The city can be seen as the built artifacts of a set of subcultures. At the moment, those subcultures which willingly resort to architects are few.

Of course learning from what's there is subject to the caveats and limitations of all behavioristic analysis—one is surveying behavior which is constrained, it is not what people might do in other conditions. The poor do not willingly live in tenements and maybe the middle classes don't willingly live in Levittowns; perhaps the Georgian-styling is less pertinent to the townhouse resident than is the rent. In times of housing shortage this is a particularly forceful argument against architectural behaviorism since people can't vote against a particular offering by staying away if there is no alternative. To counteract this danger one must search for comparison environments where for some reason the constraints do not hold. There are environments which suggest what economically constrained groups' tastes might be if they were less constrained. They are the nouveau riche environments: Hollywood for a former era, Las Vegas for today, and the homes of film stars, sportsmen, and other groups where upward mobility may resemble vertical takeoff, yet where maintenance of previous value systems is encouraged.

Another source is physical backgrounds in the mass media, movies, soap operas, pickle and furniture polish ads. Here the aim is not to sell houses but something else, and the background represents someone's (Madison Avenue's?) idea of what pickle buyers or soap opera watchers want in a house. Now the Madison Avenue observer's view may be as biased as the architect's, and it should be studied in the light of what it is trying to sell—must pickle architecture look homey like my house or elegant like yours if it is to sell me pickles? But at least it's another bias, an alternative to the architectural navel contemplation we so often do for research, i.e., ask: What did Le Corbusier do? Both Madison Avenue and the builder, although they can tell us little of the needs of the very poor, cover a broader range of the population and pass a stiffer market test than does the architect in urban renewal or public housing, and if we learn no more from these sources than that architecture must differ for different groups, that is a great deal. But an alternative to both is to examine what people do to buildings—in Levittowns, Society Hills, gray areas and slums—once they are in them. Here, costs and availability are less constraining forces since the enterprise is smaller. Also, changes tend often to be symbolic rather than structural, and aspirations can perhaps be more easily inferred from symbols than from structures.

Attention to built sources for information on need does not imply that asking people what they want is not extremely necessary as well. This is an important topic, as is the relation between the two types of survey, asking and looking; but it is not the subject of this enquiry, which is on what can be learned from the artifacts of pop culture.

Formal analysis as design research

A second reason for looking to pop culture is to find formal vocabularies for today which are more relevant to people's diverse needs and more tolerant of the untidiness of urban life than the "rationalist," Cartesian formal orders of latter-day Modern architecture. How much low-income housing and nineteenth-century architecture has been cleared so some tidy purist architect or planner could start with a clean slate?

Modern architects can now admit that whatever forces, processes, and technologies determine architectural form, ideas about form determine it as well; that a formal vocabulary is as much a part of architecture as are bricks and mortar (plastics and systems, for futurists); that form does not, cannot, arise from function alone, newborn and innocent as Venus from her shell, but rather that form follows, *inter alia*, function, forces, and form. Formal biases, if they are consciously recognized, need not tyrannize as they have done in urban renewal; and formal vocabularies, given their place in architecture, can be studied and improved to suit functional requirements, rather than accepted unconsciously and unsuitably—an old hand-me-down from some irrelevant master. The forms of the pop landscape are as relevant to us now as were the forms of antique Rome to the Beaux-Arts, Cubism and Machine Architecture to the early Moderns, and the industrial midlands and the Dogon to Team 10, which is to say extremely relevant, and more so than the latest bathysphere, launch pad, or systems hospital (or even, *pace* Banham, the Santa Monica pier). Unlike these, they speak to our condition not only aesthetically, but on many levels of necessity, from the social necessity to rehouse the poor without destroying them to the architectural necessity to produce buildings and environments that others will need and like. The pop landscape differs from the earlier models in that it is also the place where we build; it is our context. And it is one of the few contemporary sources of data on the symbolic and communicative aspects of architecture, since it was untouched by the Modern movement's purist reduction of architecture to space and structure only. But formal analysis presents a problem. First, since form has for so long been an illegitimate topic, we have lost the tradition of analyzing it, and second, the forms we are dealing with are new and don't relate easily to traditional architectural or planning techniques of analysis and communications. Orthographic projection hardly conveys the essence of the Stardust sign, and, although this sign is a block long and has an overpowering visual impact "in situ," it doesn't show well on a land use map. Suburban space, being automobile space, is not defined by enclosing walls and floors and is therefore difficult to portray graphically using systems devised for the description of buildings. In fact, space is not the most important constituent of suburban form. Communication across space is more important, and it requires a symbolic and a time element in its descriptive systems which are only slowly being devised.

New analytic techniques must use film and videotape to convey the dynamism of sign architecture and the sequential experience of vast landscapes; and computers are needed to aggregate mass repeated data into comprehensible patterns. Valuable traditional techniques should also be resuscitated by their application to new phenomena;

for example, when Nolli's mid-eighteenth-century technique for mapping Rome is adapted to include parking lots, it throws considerable light on Las Vegas. It could also lend itself fairly easily to computer techniques.

Formal analysis should be comparative, linking the new forms, by comparison, to the rest of the formal tradition of architecture thereby incorporating them into the architectural discipline and helping us to understand our new experience in light of our formal training. By suggesting that form should be analyzed, I do not imply that function (the program), technologies, or forces (urban social processes or land economics) are not vital to architecture, nor indeed, that they too can't serve as sources of artistic inspiration to the architect. All are necessary and they work in combination. The others are merely not the subject of this particular enquiry.

The soup can and the establishment

There is an irony in the fact that the "popular" culture and the "popular" landscape are not popular with those who make the decisions to renew the city and rehouse the poor. Here is John Kenneth Galbraith, an important and influential liberal, quoted in *Life* magazine:

> For the average citizen there are some simple tests which will tell him when we have passed from incantation to practical action on the environment. Restriction of auto use in the large cities will be one. Another will be when the billboards, the worst and most nearly useless excrescence of industrial civilization, are removed from the highways. Yet another will be when telephone and electric wires everywhere in the cities go underground and we accept the added charge on our bills.
>
> My own personal test, for what it may be worth, concerns the gasoline service station. This is the most repellent piece of architecture of the past two thou-

sand years. There are far more of them than are needed. Usually they are filthy. Their merchandise is hideously packaged and garishly displayed. They are uncontrollably addicted to great strings of ragged little flags. Protecting them is an ominous coalition of small businessmen and large. The stations should be excluded entirely from most streets and highways. Where allowed, they should be franchised to limit the number, and there should be stern requirements as to architecture, appearance and general reticence. When we begin on this (and similar roadside commerce), I will think that we are serious.[1]

He does not even mention the need for low-income housing as an urgent environmental problem, and in my opinion he should stick to economics. But the conventional wisdom which Galbraith expounds is shared by his colleagues, the elderly architectural radicals who man American's fine arts commissions, the "design" departments of HUD and the planning and redevelopment agencies, who plan and build for the larger public and private corporations and have the ear of the city markers. If the public is to be well served by their decisions, these members of the architectural establishment must learn to separate out for a different type of scrutiny their aesthetic preoccupations from other concerns with "environmental pollution." Fouled water and billboards are not of the same magnitude or order of problem. The first cannot be done well, but the second can; particularly if we are given the opportunity to study them for a while, nonjudgmentally.

When "blighted" neighborhoods are swept away together with billboards and gasoline stations in the name of avoidance of "visual pollution," the social harm can be irreparable. However, an old aesthetic formula, even though it is shown to be obstructive,

---

[1] John Kenneth Galbraith, "To my new friends in the affluent society—greetings," *Life*, 27 Mar. 1970

will not be relinquished until it is replaced by a new one, since, as we have seen, form depends on form for its making. And, for the architectural establishment, the new vocabulary must have a respectable lineage. Hence, if the popular environment is to provide that vocabulary, it must be filtered through the proper processes for its acceptance. It must become a part of the high-art tradition; it must be last year's avant-garde. This is another reason to submit the new landscape to traditional architectural analysis: for the sake of its acceptance by the establishment. They can't learn from pop until Pop hangs in the academy.

Hop on pop
I have recommended an investigation of the forms of the new, existing city on both social and aesthetic grounds for architects who hope to hone their skills to a sharp new edge. High art has followed low art before and vice versa; in fact, where did the McDonald's parabola and the split-level rancher come from in the first place?

In the movement from low art to high art lies an element of the deferral of judgment. Judgment is withheld in the interest of understanding and receptivity. This is an exciting heuristic technique but also a dangerous one since liking the whole of pop culture is as irrational as hating the whole of it, and it calls forth the vision of a general and indiscriminate hopping on the pop bandwagon, where everything is good and judgment is abandoned rather than deferred. Yet artists, architects, actors, must judge, albeit, one hopes, with a sigh. After a decent interval, suitable criteria must grow out of the new source. Judgment is merely deferred to make subsequent judgment more sensitive.

Hassan Fathy, 1899–1989

The Egyptian architect, educator, and writer Hassan Fathy sought to improve rural living conditions in developing countries through an emphasis on vernacular architecture and building techniques. Fathy recognized the problematic nature of many housing proposals for these poorer regions; too often those in charge neglected the specifics of climate and topography in favor of modernist concepts that relied on materials too expensive and training too specialized. Aside from the practical issue of cost, Fathy believed that modernist tendencies threatened local building flavor and traditions that, in many cases, had persisted for centuries. These thoughts conditioned Fathy's approach to his most emblematic project, the design for New Gourna (1945–53), a village near Luxor intended to accommodate seven thousand Egyptian peasants displaced by archaeological excavations. Under Fathy's leadership, the plan for New Gourna incorporated time-honored architectural forms, such as domes, vaults, and the courtyard house, particularly suited to hot, arid climates. The village's primary method of construction involved mud brick, an infinitely available sun-baked mixture of straw and clay that was easily fabricated and worked by villagers. As is chronicled in *Architecture for the Poor* (first published in an abbreviated form in 1969 and then in its current form in 1973), Fathy's design for New Gourna was both an architectural and social experiment that, due to difficulties ranging from the sponsoring government to the villagers' resistance to change, did not turn out as planned. Nevertheless, Fathy's interest in the vernacular presented an alternative to universalizing modernist inclinations of the mid-twentieth century.

Architecture for the Poor (1973)

2. Chorale: Man, Society, And Technology

Architectural Character

Every people that has produced architecture has evolved its own favorite forms, as peculiar to that people as its language, its dress, or its folklore. Until the collapse of cultural frontiers in the last century, there were all over the world distinctive local shapes and details in architecture, and the buildings of any locality were the beautiful children of a happy marriage between the imagination of the people and the demands of their countryside. I do not propose to speculate upon the real springs of national idiosyncrasy, nor could I with any authority. I like to suppose simply that certain shapes take a people's fancy, and that they make use of them in a great variety of contexts, perhaps rejecting the unsuitable applications, but evolving a colorful and emphatic visual language of their own that suits perfectly their character and their homeland. No one could mistake the curve of a Persian dome and arch for the curve of a Syrian one, or a Moorish one, or an Egyptian one. No one can fail to recognize the same curve, the same signature, in dome and jar and turban from the same district. It follows, too, that no one can look with complacency upon buildings transplanted to an alien environment.

Yet in modern Egypt there is no indigenous style. The signature is missing; the houses of rich and poor alike are without character, without an Egyptian accent. The tradition is lost, and we have been cut off from our past even since Mohammed Ali cut the throat of the last Mameluke. This gap in continuity of Egyptian tradition has been

Hassan Fathy, *Architecture for the Poor* (New York and London: University of Chicago Press, 1973), 19–20, 23–26. © 1973 by The University of Chicago. Reprinted with permission from the publisher.

felt by many people, and all sorts of remedies have been proposed. There was, in fact, a kind of jealousy between those who regarded the Copts as the true lineal descendants of the Ancient Egyptians, and those who believed that the Arab style should provide the pattern for a new Egyptian architecture. Indeed, there was one statesmanlike attempt to reconcile these two factions, when Osman Moharam Pasha, the Minister of Public Works, suggested that Egypt be divided into two, rather as Solomon suggested dividing the baby, and that Upper Egypt be delivered to the Copts, where a traditional Pharaonic style could be developed, while Lower Egypt should go to the Moslems, who would make its architecture truly Arab!

This story goes to show two things. One is the encouraging fact that people do recognize and wish to remedy the cultural confusion in our architecture. The other—not so encouraging—is that this confusion is seen as a problem of style, and style is looked upon as some sort of surface finish that can be applied to any building and even scraped off and changed if necessary. The modern Egyptian architect believes that Ancient Egyptian architecture is represented by the temple with its pylons and cavetto cornice, and Arab by clustered stalactites, whereas Ancient Egyptian domestic architecture was quite unlike temple architecture, and Arab domestic architecture quite different from mosque architecture. Ancient Egyptian secular buildings like houses were light constructions, simple, with the clean lines of the best modern houses. But in the architectural schools they make no study of the history of domestic buildings, and learn architectural periods by the accidents of style, the obvious features like the pylon and the stalactite. Thus the graduate architect believes this to be all there is in "style," and imagines a building can change its style as a man changes clothes. It was thinking like this that led some architect to ruin the entrance to the classrooms at Gourna school by transforming the original archway into an Ancient Egyptian-style temple doorway complete with cavetto cornice. It is not yet understood that real architecture cannot exist except in a living tradition. . . .

The Process of Decision Making

. . . The world at any moment is a blank page awaiting our pencil; an open space may hold a cathedral or a slagheap.

Because no two men make the same decisions in similar circumstances, we say that men's characters differ. Decision making, choosing, is another word for self-expression—or, perhaps better, is the necessary prelude to all self-expression.

A conscious decision may be reached either by consulting tradition or by logical reasoning and scientific analysis. Both processes should yield the same result, for tradition embodies the conclusions of many generations' practical experiment with the same problem, while scientific analysis is simply the organized observation of the phenomena of the problem. . . .

Tradition's Role

It may be that what we call modern is nothing but what is not worthy of remaining to become old.

Dante Alighieri

Tradition is the social analogy of personal habit, and in art has the same effect, of releasing the artist from distracting and inessential decisions so that he can give his whole attention to the vital ones. Once an artistic decision has been made, no matter when or by whom, it cannot profitably be made again; better that it should pass into the common store of habit and not bother us further.

Tradition is not necessarily old-fashioned and is not synonymous with stagnation. Furthermore, a tradition need not date from long ago but may have begun quite recently. As soon as a workman meets a new problem and decides how to overcome it, the first step has been taken in the establishment of a tradition. When another workman has decided to adopt the same solution, the tradition is moving, and by the time a third man has followed the first two and added his contribution, the tradition is fairly established. Some problems are easy to solve; a man may decide in a few minutes what to do. Others need time, perhaps a day, perhaps a year, perhaps a whole lifetime; in each case the solution may be the work of one man.

Yet other solutions may not be worked out fully before many generations have passed, and this is where tradition has a creative role to play, for it is only by tradition, by respecting and building on the work of earlier generations, that each new generation may make some positive progress toward the solution of the problem. When tradition has solved its problem and ceased developing, we may say that a cycle has been completed. However, in architecture as in other human activities and in natural processes, there are cycles just beginning, others that have been completed, and others at all stages of development in between, that exist simultaneously in the same society. There are, too, traditions that go back to the beginning of human society, yet which are still living and which will exist perhaps as long as human society does: in bread making for example, and in brick making.

There are, on the other hand, traditions which, although they have appeared only recently and ought to be in an early phase of their cycle, were in fact born dead. Modernity does not necessarily mean liveliness, and change is not always for the better. On the other hand there are situations that call for innovation. My point is that innovation must be a completely thought-out response to a change in circumstances, and not indulged in for its own sake. Nobody asks that an airport control tower be built in some peasant idiom, and an industrial structure like a nuclear power station may force a new tradition upon the designer.

Once a particular tradition is established and accepted, the individual artist's duty is to keep this tradition going, with his own invention and insight to give it that additional momentum that will save it from coming to a standstill, until it will have reached the end of its cycle and completed its full development. He will be relieved of many decisions by the tradition, but will be obliged to make others equally demanding to stop the tradition dying on his hands. In fact, the further a tradition has developed, the more effort the artist must expend to make each step forward in it. . . .

Architecture is still one of the most traditional arts. A work of architecture is meant to be used, its form is largely determined by precedent, and it is set before the public where they must look at it every day. The architect should respect the work of his predecessors and the public sensibility by not using his architecture as a medium of personal advertisement. Indeed, no architect can avoid using the work of earlier architects; however hard he strains after originality, by far the larger part of his work will be in some tradition or other. Why then should he despise the tradition of his own country or district, why should he drag alien traditions into an artificial and uncomfortable synthesis, why should he be so rude to earlier architects as to distort and misapply their ideas? This happens when an architectural element, evolved over many years to a perfect size, shape, and function, is used upside down or enlarged beyond recognition till it no longer even works properly, simply to gratify the architect's own selfish appetite for fame.

For example, it has taken men very many years to arrive at the right size for a window in various architectural traditions; if an architect now commits the gross error of enlarging the window till it takes up a whole wall, he is at once confronted with a problem: his glass wall lets in ten times a much radiation as did the solid wall. If now to shade the window he adds a brise-soleil, which is nothing more than an enlarged Venetian blind, the room will still receive 300 percent more radiation than one with a solid wall. Furthermore, when the architect enlarges the width of the slats of the Venetian blind from 4 centimeters to 40, so as not to upset the scale of the glass wall, what is the result? Instead of admitting a gentle diffused light, as a shutter or Venetian blind does, it dazzles the eye of anyone in the room with a pattern of broad black bars against a brilliant glare of light.

Not only that, but the view, the securing of which was the initial object of the glass wall, is permanently spoiled by these large bars cutting it up; the brise-soleil has not even the virtue of folding away, as have the shutter and the Venetian blind. Even in a cool climate like that of Paris, the glass wall can prove to be an unmanageable extravagance; during the hot summer of 1959 the temperature inside the UNESCO building, due to the "greenhouse effect" of its glass walls, and despite the labors of the air conditioning machinery, rose so high that many of the employees fainted. Superfluous then, to comment on the introduction of glass walls and brise-soleils in tropical countries; yet it is hard to find an example of modern tropical architecture that does not employ these features.

If the architect walks soberly in the tradition of his culture, then he must not suppose that his artistry will be stifled. Far from it; it will express itself in relevant contributions to the tradition and contribute to the advance of his society's culture.

25 PETER EISENMAN, B. 1932

Peter Eisenman, House II (Falk House), Hardwick, VT, 1969–70. © Norman McGrath

Since the 1967 formation of the Institute of Architecture and Urban Studies (IAUS) in New York, an architectural think tank largely responsible for introducing European philosophical thought into the American architectural realm, Peter Eisenman has earned a reputation as an intensely theoretical practitioner. Eisenman's early work was dedicated to the establishment of an autonomous or purely self-referential architecture. The abstracted forms of his Cardboard House series directly reflected this search; through a sequence of moves—superimposing, shifting, shearing, rotating the basic cubic volumes with which he began—Eisenman attempted to remove all normative meaning from architectural elements, an ambitious and ultimately impossible goal. He continued this line of thought in "Post-Functionalism," an editorial that appeared in *Oppositions*, the journal affiliated with the IAUS. Eisenman asserted that the path to true autonomy, already achieved by the other modern arts, demanded the displacement of man as the focus of these disciplines. Yet, due to modern architecture's fixation on anthropocentric functionalism, architecture had failed to become autonomous and thus truly modern. Eisenman's position was controversial for many reasons. Perhaps the most disturbing aspect of his postfunctionalist concept was that it countered accepted notions of architecture's purpose, questioning the fundamental nature of architecture as a creation of and for man. In the past few decades, initially in connection with theories of deconstruction, Eisenman has continued to challenge conventional architectural expectations concerning the realms of form, structure, and meaning.

"Post-Functionalism" (1976)

The critical establishment within architecture has told us that we have entered the era of "post-modernism." The tone with which this news is delivered is invariably one of relief, similar to that which accompanies the advice that one is no longer an adolescent. Two indices of this supposed change are the quite different manifestations of the "Architettura Razionale" exhibition at the Milan Triennale of 1973, and the "Ecole Des Beaux Arts" exhibition at The Museum of Modern Art in 1975. The former, going on the assumption that modern architecture was an outmoded functionalism, declared that architecture can be generated only through a return to itself as an autonomous or pure discipline. The latter, seeing modern architecture as an obsessional formalism, made itself into an implicit statement that the future lies paradoxically in the past, within the peculiar response to function that characterized the nineteenth century's eclectic command of historical styles.

What is interesting is not the mutually exclusive character of these two diagnoses and hence of their solutions, but rather the fact that both of these views enclose the very project of architecture within the same definition: one by which the terms continue to be function (or program) and form (or type). In so doing, an attitude toward architecture is maintained that differs in no significant way from the 500-year-old tradition of humanism.

The various theories of architecture which properly can be called "humanist" are characterized by a dialectical opposition: an oscillation between a concern for internal

Peter Eisenman, "Post-Functionalism," originally in *Oppositions* 6 (1976); reprinted in Peter Eisenman, *Eisenman Inside Out, Selected Writings, 1963–1988* (New Haven: Yale University Press, 2004), 83–87. © 2004 by Yale University. Reprinted with permission from the publisher.

accommodation—the program and the way it is materialized—and a concern for articulation of ideal themes in form—for example, as manifested in the configurational significance of the plan. These concerns were understood as two poles of a single, continuous experience. Within pre-industrial, humanist practice, a balance between them could be maintained because both type and function were invested with idealist views of man's relationship to his object world. In a comparison first suggested by Colin Rowe, of a French Parisian hotel and an English country house, both buildings from the early-nineteenth century, one sees this opposition manifested in the interplay between a concern for expression of an ideal type and a concern for programmatic statement, although the concerns in each case are differently weighted. The French hotel displays rooms of an elaborate sequence and a spatial variety born of internal necessity, masked by a rigorous, well-proportioned external facade. The English country house has a formal internal arrangement of rooms which gives way to a picturesque external massing of elements. The former bows to program on the interior and type on the façade; the latter reverses these considerations.

With the rise of industrialization, this balance seems to have been fundamentally disrupted. In that it had of necessity to come to terms with problems of a more complex functional nature, particularly with respect to the accommodation of a mass client, architecture became increasingly a social or programmatic art. And as the functions became more complex, the ability to manifest the pure type-form eroded. One has only to compare William Kent's competition entry for the houses of Parliament, where the form of a Palladian Villa does not sustain the intricate program, with Charles Barry's solution where the type-form defers to program and where one sees an early example of what was to become known as the *promenade architecturale*. Thus, in the nineteenth century, and continuing on into the twentieth, as the program grew in complexity, the type-form became diminished as a realizable concern, and the balance thought to be fundamental to all theory was weakened. (Perhaps only Le Corbusier in recent history has successfully combined an ideal grid with the architectural promenade as an embodiment of the original interaction.)

This shift in balance has produced a situation whereby, for the past fifty years, architects have understood design as the product of some oversimplified form-follows-function formula. This situation even persisted during the years immediately following World War II, when one might have expected it would be radically altered. And as late as the end of the 1960s, it was still thought that the polemics and theories of the early Modern Movement could sustain architecture. The major thesis of this attitude was articulated in what could be called the English Revisionist Functionalism of Reyner Banham, Cedric Price, and Archigram. This neo-functionalist attitude, with its idealization of technology, was invested with the same ethical positivism and aesthetic neutrality of the prewar polemic. However, the continued substitution of moral criteria for those of a more formal nature produced a situation which now can be seen to have created a functionalist predicament, precisely because the primary theoretical justification given to formal arrangements was a *moral* imperative that is no longer operative within contemporary experience. This sense of displaced positivism characterizes certain current perceptions of the failure of humanism within a broader cultural context.

There is also another, more complex, aspect to this predicament. Not only can functionalism indeed be recognized as a species of positivism, but like positivism, it now can be seen to issue from within the terms of an idealist view of reality. For functionalism, no matter what its pretense, continued the idealist ambition of creating architecture as a kind of ethically constituted form-giving. But because it clothed this idealist ambition in the radically stripped forms of technological production, it has seemed to represent a break with the pre-industrial past. But, in fact, functionalism is really no more than a late phase of humanism, rather than an alternative to it. And in this sense, it cannot continue to be taken as a direct manifestation of that which has been called "the modernist sensibility."

Both the Triennale and the Beaux Arts exhibitions suggest, however, that the problem is thought to be somewhere else—not so much with functionalism *per se*, as with the nature of this so-called modernist sensibility. Hence, the implied revival of neo-classicism and Beaux Arts academicism as replacements for a continuing, if poorly understood, modernism. It is true that sometime in the nineteenth century, there was indeed a crucial shift within Western consciousness: one which can be characterized as a shift from humanism to modernism. But, for the most part, architecture, in its dogged adherence to the principles of function, did not participate in or understand the fundamental aspects of that change. It is the potential difference in the nature of modernist and humanist theory that seems to have gone unnoticed by those people who today speak of eclecticism, post-modernism, or neo-functionalism. And they have failed to notice it precisely because they conceive of modernism as merely a stylistic manifestation of functionalism, and functionalism itself as a basic theoretical proposition in architecture. In fact, the idea of modernism has driven a wedge into these attitudes. It has revealed that the dialectic form and function is culturally based.

In brief, the modernist sensibility has to do with a changed mental attitude toward the artifacts of the physical world. This change has not only been manifested aesthetically, but also socially, philosophically, and technologically—in sum, it has been manifested in a new cultural attitude. This shift away from the dominant attitudes of humanism, that were pervasive in Western societies for some four hundred years, took place at various times in the nineteenth century in such disparate disciplines as mathematics, music, painting, literature, film, and photography. It is displayed in the non-objective abstract painting of Malevich and Mondrian; in the non-narrative, atemporal writing of Joyce and Apollinaire; the atonal and polytonal compositions of Schönberg and Webern; in the non-narrative films of Richter and Eggeling.

Abstraction, atonality, and atemporality, however, are merely stylistic manifestations of modernism, not its essential nature. Although this is not the place to elaborate a theory of modernism, or indeed to represent those aspects of such a theory which have already found their way into the literature of the other humanist disciplines, it can simply be said that the symptoms to which one has just pointed suggest a displacement of man away from the center of his world. He is no longer viewed as an *originating agent*. Objects are seen as ideas independent of man. In this context, man is a discursive function among complex and already-formed systems of language, which he witnesses but does not constitute. As Levi-Strauss has said, "Language, an unreflecting totalization, is human reason which has its reason and of which man knows nothing." It is this condition of displacement which gives rise to design in which authorship can no longer either account for a linear development which has a 'beginning' and an 'end'—hence the rise of the atemporal—or account for the invention of form—hence the abstract as a mediation between pre-existent sign systems.

Modernism, as a sensibility based on the fundamental displacement of man, represents what Michel Foucault would specify as a new *épistème*. Deriving from a non-humanistic attitude toward the relationship of an individual to his physical environment, it breaks with the historical past, both with the ways of viewing man as subject and, as we have said, with the ethical positivism of form and function. Thus, it cannot be related to functionalism. It is probably for this reason that modernism has not up to now been elaborated in architecture.

But there is clearly a present need for a theoretical investigation of the basic implications of modernism (as opposed to modern style) in architecture. In his editorial "Neo-Functionalism," in *Oppositions* 5, Mario Gandelsonas acknowledges such a need. However, he says merely that the "complex contradictions" inherent in functionalism—such as neo-realism and neo-rationalism—make a form of neo-functionalism necessary to any new theoretical dialectic. This proposition continues to refuse to recognize that the form/function opposition is not necessarily inherent to any architectural theory and so fails to recognize the crucial difference between modernism and humanism. In contrast, what is being called post-functionalism begins as an attitude which recognizes modernism as a new and distinct sensibility. It can best be understood in architecture in terms of a theoretical base that is concerned with what might be called a modernist *dialectic*, as opposed to the old humanist (i.e., functionalist) opposition of form and function.

This new theoretical base changes the humanist balance of form/function to a dialectical relationship within the evolution of form itself. The dialectic can best be described as the potential co-existence within any form of two non-corroborating and non-sequential tendencies. One tendency is to presume architectural form to be a recognizable transformation from some pre-existent geometric or platonic solid. In this case, form is usually understood through a series of registrations designed to recall a more simple geometric condition. This tendency is certainly a relic of humanist theory. However, to this is added a second tendency that sees architectural form in an atemporal, decompositional mode, as something simplified from some pre-existent set of non-specific spatial entities. Here, form is understood as a series of fragments—signs without meaning dependent upon, and without reference to, a more basic condition. The former tendency, when taken by itself, is a reductivist attitude and assumes some primary unity as both an ethical and an aesthetic basis for all creation. The latter, by itself, assumes a basic condition of fragmentation and multiplicity from which the resultant form is a state of simplification. Both tendencies, however, when taken together, constitute the essence of this new, modern dialectic. They begin to define the inherent nature of the object in and of itself and its capacity to be represented. They begin to suggest that the theoretical assumptions of functionalism are in fact cultural rather than universal.

Post-functionalism, thus, is a term of absence. In its negation of functionalism it suggests certain positive theoretical alternatives—existing fragments of thought which, when examined, might serve as a framework for the development of a larger theoretical structure—but it does not, in and of itself, propose to supply a label for such a new consciousness in architecture which I believe is potentially upon us.

26 CHARLES JENCKS, B. 1939

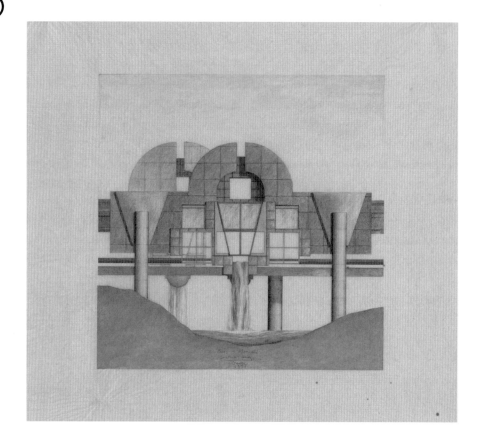

Michael Graves, Fargo-Moorhead Cultural Center Bridge project
Fargo, North Dakota and Moorhead, Minnesota, 1978. Drawing of south elevation
Photo Credit: Digital Image © The Museum of Modern Art/Licensed by SCALA/Art Resource, NY
Image courtesy of Michael Graves and Associates

While trained as an architect, the American architectural historian Charles Jencks is best known for his critical writings on postmodern architecture. He did not invent the term "Post-Modernism," but is generally credited with its introduction to architecture through his 1977 publication, *The Language of Post-Modern Architecture.*[*] In this text, Jencks theorized architecture of the 1960s and 70s that deviated from modernist tendencies of the time. As the main point of departure for postmodern architecture he identified "dual-coding," the ability to communicate on at least two levels simultaneously. Jencks suggested that double-coded architecture contains differing and sometimes contradictory meanings that exist in tension with one another; this plurality of meaning stood in marked opposition to doctrinaire modern architecture that sought to convey messages based on function. In theory, multiple meanings rendered postmodern architecture accessible to both architects and laymen. Some praised the eclecticism, historical quotation, and playfulness of works such as Graves's project for the Fargo-Moorhead Bridge (Fargo, North Dakota, and Moorhead, Minnesota, 1978) as witty and ironic while others criticized them as kitschy and superficial. Yet, despite their dichotomous views, both positions generally situated postmodern architecture as a response to and an expression of the complexity of contemporary life.

---

[*] Throughout the 1980s, Jencks frequently updated *The Language of Post-Modern Architecture*, first published in 1977 in London by Academy Editions and in New York by Rizzoli International Publications. The text is currently in its sixth edition (John Wiley & Sons and Academy Editions, 1991).

"Why Post-Modernism?" (1978)

The notion of Post-Modernism has had an unusual history which requires a little explanation. A situation has been developing over the past 20 years which is now in the process of focusing very quickly into a new style and approach. It has grown out of Modern architecture in much the way Mannerist architecture grew out of the High Renaissance—as a partial inversion and modification of the former language of architecture. This development is now generally being called Post-Modern architecture because the term is wide enough to encompass the variety of departures, and yet still indicate its derivation from Modernism. Like its progenitor the movement is committed to engaging current issues, to changing the present, but unlike the avant-garde it does away with the notion of continual innovation or incessant revolution.

A Post-Modern building is, if a short definition is needed, one which speaks on at least two levels at once: to other architects and a concerned minority who care about specifically architectural meanings, and to the public at large, or the local inhabitants, who care about other issues concerned with comfort, traditional building and a way of life. Thus Post-Modern architecture looks hybrid and, if visual definition is needed, rather like the front of a Classical Greek temple. The latter is a pure white architecture of elegantly fluted columns below, and a riotous billboard of struggling giants above, a pediment painted in deep reds and blues. The architects can read the subtle metaphors and subtle meanings of the column drums, whereas the public can respond to the explicit metaphors and messages of the sculptors. Of course everyone responds somewhat to both codes of meaning, as they do in a Post-Modern building,

Charles Jencks, "Why Post-Modernism?" *Architectural Design* 48, no. 1 (1978), 13–14. © John Wiley & Sons Limited. Reproduced with permission.

but certainly with different intensity and understanding, and it is this discontinuity in taste and cultures which creates both the theoretical base and 'dual coding' of Post-Modernism. The dual image of the Classical temple is a helpful visual formula to keep in mind as the unifying factor while different departures from Modernism are presented here. The buildings most characteristic of Post-Modernism show a marked duality, a conscious schizophrenia.

. . . [The] term 'Post-Modern' has to be clarified and used . . . precisely to cover, in general, only those designers who are aware of architecture as a *language*—hence one part of the title of my book: *The Language of Post-Modern Architecture.* Paul Goldberger and a few American critics have used the term this way and focused on other important qualities, its attention to historical memory and local context. These aspects are significant, but as history shows, they are only part of the story. For Post-Modern architecture also takes a positive approach toward metaphorical buildings, the vernacular, and a new, ambiguous kind of space. Hence only a plural definition will capture its many heads, something I have tried to clarify with the evolutionary chart. . . . For the same reason, there is no one architect who altogether combines these various strands, or one building which summarizes them. If forced to point at an entirely convincing Post-Modernist I would instance Antonio Gaudi, obviously not a possibility, as reviewers of my book have been quick to point out, because he was a Pre-Modernist. I still regard Gaudi as *the* touchstone for Post-Modernism, a model with which to compare any recent buildings to see if they are really metaphorical, 'contextual' and rich in a precise way, but I have confined my examples to the present.

The ambiguity of the prefix 'Post' has its amusing and powerful aspects, which partly explain why it has become current. People are naturally exhilarated at the prospect of being 'Post-Present.' In the middle 60s Daniel Bell wrote on the Post-Industrial Society, with the implication that some fortunate Westerners could escape laborious toil altogether. There was the short-lived 'Post-Painterly Abstraction,' a movement of opposition as it states, and more recently President Carter has come out in favor of a new foreign policy based on the 'Post-War' world. Very convenient this slippery word, it simply states where you've left, not arrived.

But the mind rebels at all this linguistic paradox: how can we be beyond the modern age if we are still alive? Have we banished the present tense like the Futurists and located Elysium in a perpetual state of tomorrow (or yesterday)? If so we might look forward to a 'Post-Natal,' or is it 'Post-Coital' depression, as we reap the benefits of evading the present.

Such thoughts made me consider Post-Modern architecture as a temporary label when I first used it in 1975, but now I've changed my mind. Partly this is due to overtones of 'modern' which are still kept in the hybrid title; its power and contemporaneity. Architects, artists, people in general want to keep up to date, even if they don't want to relinquish their cultural past as the avant-garde has often done. We can see in the Renaissance an instructive parallel when the word 'modern' was first put into currency.

At that time they had debates, and confusions, similar and relevant to our own. Filarete, for instance, claimed he "used to like modern ([namely] Gothic) buildings" until the time "when I began to appreciate classical ones, I came to be disgusted with the former. . . ." But then as the renaissance of antiquity proceeded, the Gothic style became old-fashioned and, finally, with Vasari, the equation was reversed: the older, classical style was perfected, that is to say *improved* (or so they thought) as the new 'good modern style" (*buona maniera moderna*). Thus Renaissance writers were confused over the use of this term, *moderna* was applied to the Gothic, the classical Roman and its revival—three different modes. No matter how committed to the past the architects were they still called it 'modern' as if the term had (and still has?) an unchallengeable hold on the present tense—on being 'now.' Only after Giorgio Vasari systematically and consciously used *moderna* to mean revival style did his usage become common and accepted.

The battle of the 'Ancients and the Moderns' has been fought many times since then with equal confusion over usage, and in a sense we are again in such a predicament with the adversaries not only disagreeing, but also using their basic words differently. This is not the place to analyze the differing versions of 'the modern,' an analysis which I am sure will occur as the attacks and counter-attacks mount in vehemence. But it is the point to emphasize that the word 'modern' still has an ambiguous power, as it did for Vasari, because it refers to a contemporaneous, growing climate of opinion, and it has this power even for those who would deny, refute, or criticize it. Post-*Modernism* thus gains some of these overtones even while it attacks the concept of the avant-garde and the *Zeitgeist*.

Secondly, and more importantly, the label describes the *duality* of the present situation quite well. Most, if not all, the architects of the movement have been trained in Modernism yet have moved beyond or counter to this training. They have not yet arrived at a new synthetic goal, nor have they given up entirely their Modernist sensibility, but rather they are at a half-way house, half Modern, half Post. If we look at Venturi, Stern, or Moore's work—three of the hard-core PMs—we can see all the quotes from Le Corbusier, Kahn, the 20s *and* all the references to Palladio, Lutyens, and Route 66. There is no doubt such work is schizophrenically coded, something you'd expect *after* a movement has broken down and the architects have moved on. For we are talking here of an evolution out of or away from a shared position, not a revolutionary schism with the immediate past, and so one of the really surprising, even defining, characteristics of Post-Modernism emerges: it includes Modernist style and iconography as a potential approach, to be used where this is appropriate (on factories, hospitals, and a few offices). Whereas Modernism like Mies van der Rohe was exclusivist, PM is so totally inclusive as to allow even its purist opposite a place when this is justifiable. Put another way, Post-Modernism is finding a rationale for 20s revivalism, in an era when all revivals are possible and each depends on an argument from *plausibility*, since it certainly can't be proved as necessity.

27 DEMETRI PORPHYRIOS, B. 1949

The Greek architect and educator Demetri Porphyrios studied architectural design, history, and theory at Princeton University, earning his Master of Architecture degree in 1974 and his doctorate in 1980. Since then, Porphyrios has become one of the foremost proponents of a traditional architectural vocabulary. In the following passage from the 1982 essay "Classicism Is Not a Style," Porphyrios posited classical architecture as a model for contemporary practice, arguing that classicism should not be viewed as a mere dressing or style, but as a theoretical system that describes the nature of architecture through reference to both the practical and representational aspects of building. He explained that classicism derives from basic universal tenets of construction that were first manifest in regional or vernacular architecture and then adopted by classical architecture. In his opinion, these constructional principles—the need for load-bearing, enclosing, and demarcating elements—give rise to architectural forms that convey pragmatic and symbolic information about structural and mythical functions. Porphyrios asserted that a contemporary architecture based on this classical system offers a meaningful alternative to the perceived architectural poverty of consumer culture.

As the principal of the London-based firm Porphyrios Associates, Porphyrios has continued to cultivate a present-day role for the classicism by which his work abides. His recent design of Princeton University's Whitman Residential College (fall 2007) in a collegiate Gothic idiom supports his belief that classicism is indeed not a style. Rather, as Porphyrios has emphasized, the principles of classicism offer a foundation for all architectural design.

"Classicism Is Not a Style" (1983)

The predicament of contemporary architecture . . . stems from our twofold inheritance: on the one hand, the symbolically mute elements of industrial production inherited from Modernism, and on the other the expendable historicist and high-tech signs of industrial kitsch inherited from Modern Eclecticism. This raises, in my opinion, the crucial problem we face today: if there is an opposition between the economic priorities of mass industrial society and the yearning for an authentic culture that would sustain individual freedom in public life, under what qualifications is it possible to practise architecture at all? Paradoxically, the only possible critical stance for architecture today is to build an alliance between building construction and symbolic representation. To construct, that is, a tectonic discourse which, while addressing the pragmatics of shelter, could at the same time represent its own tectonics in a symbolic way.

It is from such a perspective that classicism should be re-evaluated today: not as a borrowed stylistic finery but as an ontology of building. Classicism is not a style. Its lesson lies in the way by which it raises construction and shelter to the realm of the symbol.

The Constructional Logic of Vernacular

Despite the superficial associations with rusticity and nature that the word 'vernacular' brings to mind its essential meaning is different. The idea of vernacular has nothing to

Demetri Porphyrios, "Classicism Is Not a Style," *Demetri Porphyrios: Selected Buildings and Writings*, Architectural Monograph no. 25 (London: Academy Editions, 1993) 125–27. © John Wiley & Sons Limited. Reproduced with permission. A version of this essay first appeared in *Architecural Design* 5–6 (1982), 51–57 do with stylistics. It rather points to the universal ethos of constructing shelter under the conditions of scarcity of materials and operative constructional techniques.

By involving vernacular, one does not seek the primitivism of pre-industrial cultures. The temptation to turn one's back on contemporary industrial society in order to return to the security and institutions of some pre-industrial order, when pursued, leaves us suspended amid the reverberations of Plato's ghost: 'what then?' Instead, the essential meaning of vernacular refers to straightforward construction, to the rudimentary building of shelter, an activity that exhibits reason, efficiency, economy, durability and pleasure. Certainly, varying materials and techniques attribute regionalist characteristics to vernacular. But beyond appearances, all vernacular is marked by a number of constructional *a prioris* which are universal and essentially phenomenological.

To begin with, building—by its very nature—involves the experiences of load-bearing and load-borne, the primary manifestations of which are the column and the lintel. Secondly, it involves the experience of horizontal and vertical enclosure, the primary manifestations of which are the roof and the wall. The floor, since it repeats the original ground, is flat for it is meant to be walked upon; whereas the roof is inclined since, in addition to its shedding off water, it marks the terminus and should appear as such. Finally, since all construction is construction by means of finite elements, the act of building involves necessarily the experience of demarcating, the primary manifestations of which are the beginning and ending.

When applied to the making of shelter, these constructional a *prioris* give rise to a set of constructional forms: as for example the gable which marks the sectional termination of the roof and thus points to the primary experience of entry; or the engaged pilaster, which manifests the confluent experiences of load-bearing and enclosure; or the window and door, which manifest the experience of suspending enclosure locally for purposes of passage; or the colonnade, which demarcates the experience of boundary; and so on.

Classicism: The Symbolic Elaboration of Vernacular

Such constructional *a prioris* and their ensuing constructional corollaries can be identi-fied—it would appear—beyond fear of interpretative dispute and could serve as the core of a common architectural knowledge.

Yet architecture cannot remain at this 'starting point.' Its vocation is to lift itself above the contingencies of building by commemorating those very contingencies from which it sprung in the first place. What distinguishes a shed from a temple is the mythopoeic power the temple possesses: it is a power that transgresses the boundaries of contingent reality and raises construction and shelter to the realm of the symbol.

This is the sense in which we can say that classicism is not a style. The classical natu-ralises the constructional *a prioris* of shelter by turning them into myth: the demarca-tions of beginning and ending are commemorated as base and capital; the experience of load-bearing is made perceptible through the entasis in the shaft of the column; the chief beam, binding the columns together and imposing on them a common load, becomes the architrave; the syncopation of the transversal beams resting on the ar-chitrave is rendered visible in the figures of the triglyphs and metopes of the frieze; the projecting rafters of the roof, supported by the frieze, appear in the form of the cornice; finally—and most significantly—the whole tectonic assemblage of column, architrave, frieze and cornice become the ultimate object of classical contemplation in the ideal of the Order.

The Order sets form over the necessities of shelter; it sets the myth of the tectonic over the contingencies of construction. The power of mythical fiction presides. It is the possibility of such an act of mythical fiction that constitutes the prime aesthetic subject-matter of classical thought. Classical architecture constructs a tectonic fiction out of the productive level of building. The artifice of constructing this fictitious world is seen as analogous to the artifice of constructing the human world. In its turn, myth allows for a convergence of the real and the fictive so that the real is redeemed. By rendering construction mythically fictive, classical thought posits reality in a contemplative state, wins over the depredations of petty life and, in a moment of rare disinterestedness, rejoices in the power it has over contingent life and nature.

Mythical thinking, of course, is not necessarily primitive or prelogical as common opinion might maintain today. It is true thinking for it reduces the world to order. Its truth is no less than that experimentally verified by science. Today, if it appears that the mythopoeic mind cannot achieve objectivity (and should therefore be doomed as an irrationality that can never attain consensus) this is not because it is incapable of dealing with the world, but rather because contemporary industrial life is dominated by vulgar positivism. That is why architecture today is systematically denied its mythopoeic power. The vulgarity lies not in the search for objectivity but in the immanence with which consumer culture boasts of being the mere extension of production.

28

In *The Architecture of Humanism* (1914), Geoffrey Scott discussed the power of architecture to elicit an emotional response from its occupants. Relying on the concept of empathy, he declared that "[we transcribe] ourselves into terms of architecture . . . [and] . . . transcribe architecture into terms of ourselves."[*] Seventy-one years later, the Finnish architect Juhani Pallasmaa addressed a similar line of thought in "The Geometry of Feeling: The Phenomenology of Architecture," an exegesis on the human experience of architectural form. Yet, while Scott countered what he perceived to be the progressive decline in taste since the fifteenth century, Pallasmaa described his contemporaries as obsessed with formal manipulation at the expense of "the artistic essence of architecture," namely, "the experiential and mental dimensions of architecture." Pallasmaa argued that architectural form derives meaning only from the images with which the form is connected. Form alone means nothing; it is the human interaction with and interpretation of that form that gives a form meaning.

Pallasmaa's humanism stems from the Finnish legacy exemplified by Alvar Aalto, an architect known for his careful attention to the tactile and material qualities of his design and concern for the ways in which his works would be inhabited. As an architect, professor, and author, Pallasmaa continues these phenomenological interests, offering a model of thought and design grounded in the realities of human experience and emotive possibility.

---

[*] Geoffrey Scott, *The Architecture of Humanism*, p. 119–20 in this collection.

"Geometry of Feeling: The Phenomenology of Architecture" (1985)

Why do so few modern buildings appeal to our emotions, when an anonymous house in an old town, or an unpretentious farm building, will give us a sense of familiarity and pleasure? Why is it that the stone foundations we discover in an overgrown meadow, or a dilapidated barn, or an abandoned boathouse can arouse our imagination, while our own houses seem to stifle and smother our day dreams? The buildings of our own time may arouse our curiosity with their daring or inventiveness, but they give us little sense of the meaning of our world or our own existence.

Efforts are being made to revitalize the debilitated language of architecture, through both a richer idiom and by reviving historical themes. But despite their effusive diversity, such avant-garde works are just as bereft of meaning as the coldly technical approach to building against which they rebel.

Architecture's impoverished inner meaning has also been considered in numerous recent writings on architectural theory. Some writers think our architecture is too poor in terms of form, others contend that its form is too abstract or intellectual. Philosophically, our culture of hedonistic materialism seems to be losing any meaningful dimension that might in general be worthy of perpetuation in stone. As Ludwig Wittgenstein argues, "Architecture glorifies and eternalizes something. When there is nothing to glorify there is no architecture."[1]

Juhani Pallasmaa, "The Geometry of Feeling: The Phenomenology of Architecture," *Encounters, Architectural Essays*, ed. Peter MacKeith (Helsinki: Rakennustieto Oy, 2005), 87–91, 93–96. Initially published in *Arkkitehti, The Finnish Review* 3 (Mar. 1985). Reprinted with permission of the author and publisher.

[1] Ludwig Wittgenstein, *Culture and Value*, ed. George Henrik von Wright, in collaboration with Heikki Nyman (Oxford: Blackwell, 1998), 74e.

Architecture as Play with Form

. . . [Proof] exits to demonstrate architecture's detachment from its proper background and purpose. I consider one viewpoint here: the relationship between architectural form and how architecture is experienced. Design has become so intensively a kind of game with form that the reality of how a building is experienced has been overlooked. We make the mistake of thinking of, and assessing, a building as a formal composition, no longer understanding that it is a metaphor, let alone experiencing the other reality that lies behind the metaphor. . . .

The Architecture of Imagery

The artistic dimension of a work of art does not lie in the actual physical thing; it exists only in the consciousness of the person experiencing that object. The analysis of a work of art is, at its most genuine level, an introspection by the consciousness subjected to it. The work of art's meaning lies not in its forms, but in the images transmitted by the forms and the emotional force that they carry. Form only affects our feelings through what it represents.

As long as teaching and criticism do not strive to clarify the experiential and mental dimensions of architecture, they will have little to do with the artistic essence of architecture. Current efforts to restore the richness of the architectural idiom through a greater diversity of form are based on a lack of understanding of the essence of art. The richness of a work of art lies in the vitality of the images it arouses, and—paradoxically—the simplest, most archetypal forms arouse the images open to the most interpretations. Post-Modernism's (superficial) return to ancient themes lacks emotive power precisely because these collages of architectural motifs are no longer linked with phenomenologically authentic feelings true to architecture. . . .

The Eidos of Architecture

As architects, we do not design buildings primarily as physical objects: we design with regard to the images and emotions of the people who live in them. . . . [The] effect of architecture stems from more or less shared images and basic emotions connected with building.

Phenomenology analyzes such basic responses, and its method has become a more common means of examining architecture, too, in the last few years. A philosophical approach initially attached most closely to the names of philosophers in nature, in contrast to the postivist's standpoint's desire for objectivity. Phenomenology strives to depict phenomena appealing directly to the consciousness as such, without any theories and categories taken from the natural sciences or psychology. Phenomenology thus means examining a phenomenon of the consciousness in its own dimension of consciousness. That, using Husserl's concept, means a "pure looking at" the phenomenon, or "viewing its essence."[2] Phenomenology is a purely theoretical approach to research in the original sense of the Greek word *theoria*, which means precisely "a looking at."

The phenomenology of architecture is thus "looking at" architecture from within the consciousness experiencing it, through architectural feeling, in contrast to the analysis of the physical proportions and properties of the building or a stylistic frame of reference. The phenomenology of architecture seeks the inner language of building. . . .

The Primary Emotions of Architecture
I have said that architecture cannot be a mere play with form. This view does not spring from the self-evident fact that architecture is tied to its practical purpose and many other external conditions. But if a building does not fulfill its basic phenomenological

---

[2] Edmund Husserl, *The Crisis of European Sciences and Transcendental Phenomenology* (Evanston, IL: Northwestern University Press, 1970); Edmund Husserl, *Phenomenology and the Crisis of Philosophy* (New York: Harper & Row, 1965).

conditions as a metaphor of human existence, it is unable to influence the emotions linked in our souls with the images a building creates. An architectural effect is based on a number of what we could call primary emotions. These emotions form the genuine "basic vocabulary" of architecture and it is by working through them that a work becomes architecture and not, for instance, a large-scale sculpture or scenography.

Architecture is a direct expression of existence, of human presence in the world, in the sense that architecture is largely based on a language of the body—of which neither the creator of the work nor the person experiencing the work is aware. . . .

Architecture exists in another reality from our everyday life and pursuits. The emotional force of the ruins of an abandoned house or of rejected objects, stems from the fact that these artifacts make us imagine and share the fate of their owners. They seduce our imagination into wandering away from the world of everyday realities. The quality of architecture does not lie in the sense of reality that it expresses, but in quite the reverse, in architecture's capacity for awakening our imagination.

Architecture is always inhabited by spirits. People known to us may well live in the building, but they are only understudy actors in a waking dream. In reality, architecture is always the home of spirits, the dwelling place of metaphysical beings. . . .

28 BERNARD TSCHUMI, B. 1944

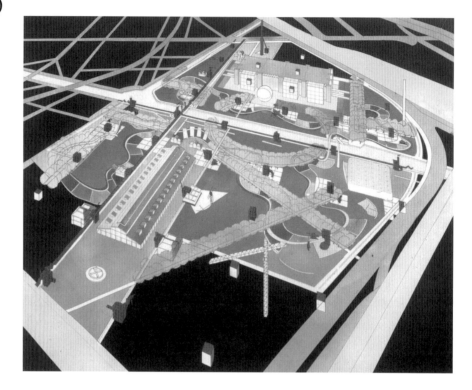

Bernard Tschumi, Parc de la Villette Paris, 1982, axonometric site plan
Courtesy of Bernard Tschumi Architects

Since the 1970s, the work of the Swiss architect, educator, and theorist Bernard Tschumi has challenged accepted ideas of space and program. Through text and design, Tschumi has proposed a novel view of architecture that embraces the "disjunction between use, form and social values." Space, Tschumi has contended, is neutral; the events that take place in a space, the use to which a space is put, are what generate meaning. One implication of this concept is that the correlation between form and function is neither exclusive nor direct, if it exists at all. Tschumi explored this idea in his *folies*, a series of small buildings based on variations of the cube. The *folies* appear at regular intervals throughout the Parisian Parc de la Villette (1982), Tschumi's first major public work, and are designed for no specific purpose. Rather, they can hold whatever programmatic event is deemed appropriate. These *folies* respond to the notion that the architect can never foresee what events actually will occur in a given space, for example, "pole vaulting in the chapel."* Variability and unpredictability give rise to unexpected and perhaps unprecedented meanings, interactions, and events. Another version of this idea appears in the text below, "De-, Dis-, Ex-," originally a lecture Tschumi presented in 1987 in which he discussed the de-regulated, dis-integrated, ex-centric nature of late-twentieth-century society.

---

* Bernard Tschumi, "Spaces and Events," in *Architecture and Disjunction* (Cambridge, MA: MIT Press, 1996), 146.

"De-, Dis-, Ex-" (1989)

Cities today have no visible limits. In America, they never had. In Europe, however, the concepts of "city" once implied a closed and finite entity. The old city had walls and gates. But these have long ceased to function. Are there other types of gates, new gates to replace the gates of the past? Are the new gates those electronic warning systems installed in airports, screening passengers for weapons? Have electronics and, more generally, technology replaced the boundaries, the guarded borders of the past? The walls surrounding the city have disappeared and, with them, the rules that made the distinction between inside and outside, despite politicians' and planners' guidelines, despite geographical and administrative boundaries. In *"L'Espace Critique,"* Paul Virilio develops a challenging argument for anyone concerned with the making of urban society: Cities have become *deregulated*. This deregulation is reinforced by the fact that much of the city does not belong to the realm of the visible anymore. What was once called urban design has been replaced by a composite of invisible systems. Why should architects still talk about monuments? Monuments are invisible now. They are *disproportionate*—so large (at the scale of the world) that they cannot be seen. Or so small (at the scale of computer chips) that they cannot be seen either.

Remember: architecture was first the art of measure, of proportions. It once allowed whole civilizations to measure time and space. But speed and the telecommunications of images have altered that old role of architecture. *Speed* expands time by contracting space; it negates the notion of physical dimension.

Bernard Tschumi, "De-, Dis-, Ex-," in *Architecture and Disjunction* (Cambridge, MA: MIT Press, 1996) 215–226. First published in Barbara Kruger and Phil Mariani, eds., *Remaking History* (Seattle: Bay Press, 1989). Originally delivered as a lecture at the Dia Foundation (New York, fall 1987). Reprinted with permission of the author and MIT Press.

Of course, physical environment still exists. But, as Virilio suggests, the appearance of permanence (buildings as solid, made of steel, concrete, glass) is constantly challenged by the immaterial representation of abstract systems, from television to electronic surveillance, and so on. Architecture is constantly subject to reinterpretation. In no way can architecture today claim permanence of meaning. Churches are turned into movie houses, banks into yuppie restaurants, hat factories into artists' studios, subway terminals into nightclubs, and sometimes nightclubs into churches. The supposed cause-and-effect relationship between function and form ("form follows function") is forever condemned the day function becomes almost as transient as those magazines and mass media images in which architecture now appears as such a fashionable object.

History, memory, and tradition, once called to the rescue by architectural ideologists, become nothing but modes of disguise, fake regulations, so as to avoid the question of transience and temporality.

When the philosopher Jean-Francois Lyotard speaks about the crisis of the grand narratives of modernity ("progress," the "liberation of humanity," etc.), it only prefigures the crisis of any narrative, any discourse, any mode of representation. The crisis of these grand narratives, their coherent totality, is also the crisis of limits. As with the contemporary city, there are no more boundaries delineating a coherent and homogenous whole. On the contrary, we inhabit a fractured space, made of accidents, where figures are disintegrated, *dis*-integrated. From a sensibility developed during centuries around the "appearance of a stable image" ("balance," "equilibrium," "harmony"), today we favor a sensibility of the disappearance of unstable images: first movies (twenty-four images per second), then television, then computer-generated images, and recently (among a few architects) disjunctions, dislocations, deconstructions. Virilio argues that the abolition of permanence—through the collapse of the notion of distance as a time factor—confuses reality. First deregulation of airlines, then deregulation of Wall

Street, finally deregulation of appearances: it all belongs to the same inexorable logic. Some unexpected consequences, some interesting distortions of long-celebrated icons are to be foreseen. The city and its architecture lose their symbols—no more monuments, no more axes, no more anthropomorphic symmetries, but instead fragmentation, parcellization, atomization, as well as the random superimposition of images that bear no relationship to one another, except through their collision. No wonder that some architectural projects sublimate the idea of *explosion*. A few architects do it in the form of drawings in which floor plans, beams, and walls seem to disintegrate in the darkness of outer space. Some even succeed in building those explosions and other accidents (by giving them the appearance of control—clients want control—but it's only a "simulation").

Hence the fascination for cinematic analogies: on the one hand, moving cranes and expressways and, on the other, montage techniques borrowed from film and video—frames and sequences, lap dissolves, fade-ins and fade-outs, jump cuts, and so forth. One must remember that, initially, the sciences were about substance, about foundation: geology, physiology, physics, and gravity. And architecture was very much part of that concern, with its focus on solidity, firmness, structure, and hierarchy. Those foundations began to crumble in the twentieth century. Relativity, quantum theory, the uncertainty principle: this shakeup occurred not only in physics, as we know, but also in philosophy, the social sciences, and economics.

How then can architecture maintain some solidity, some degree of certainty? It seems impossible today—unless one decides that the accident or the explosion is to be called the rule, the new regulation, through a sort of philosophical inversion that considers the accident the norm and the continuity the exception.

No more certainties, no more continuities. We hear that energy, as well as matter, is a discontinuous structure of points: punctum, quantum. Question: could the only certainty be the *point*?

The crises of determinism, or cause-and-effect relationships, and of continuity completely challenge recent architectural thought. Here, bear with me if I go through a rather tedious but quick recapitulation of "meaning" in architecture—without entering into a detailed discussion of Ferdinand de Saussure or Émile Benveniste. Ethnologists tell us that, in traditional symbolic relations, things have meanings. Quite often the symbolic value is separated from the utilitarian one. The Bauhaus attempted to institute a "universal semanticization of the environment in which everything became the object of function and of signification" (Jean Baudrillard). This functionality, this synthesis of form and function, tried to turn the whole world into a homogenous signifier, objectified as an element of signification: for every form, every signifier, there is an objective signified, a function. By focusing on denotation, it eliminated connotation.

Of course, this dominant discourse of rationality was bound to be attacked. At that time, it was by the surrealists, whose transgressions often relied on the ethics of functionalism, *a contrario*. In fact, some fixed, almost functionalist expectations were necessary to surrealists, for they could only be unsettled through confrontation: the surreal set combining "the sewing machine and the umbrella on the dissecting table" only works because each of these objects represents a precise and unequivocal function.

The transgressed order of functionality that resulted reintroduced the order of the symbolic, now distorted and turned into a poetic phantasm. It liberated the object from its function, denounced the gap between subject and object, and encouraged free association. But such transgressions generally acted upon singular objects, while the world was becoming an environment of ever-increasing complex and abstract systems.

The abstraction of the following years—whether expressionist or geometric—had its architectural equivalent. The endlessly repeated grids of skyscrapers were associated with a new zero-degree of meaning: perfect functionalism.

Fashion upset all that. It had always addressed issues of connotation: against fashion's unstable and ever-disappearing image, the stable and universal denotation of functionalism appeared particular and restrictive.

Partly fascinated by such connotation, partly longing for some long-lost traditional forms, architectural postmodernism in the seventies attempted to combine—to quote Charles Jencks—"modern techniques with traditional building, in order to communicate both with the public *and* with an elite" (hence "double-coding"). It was above all concerned with *codes*, with communicating some *message*, some *signifier* (perhaps characterized by irony, parody, eclecticism). Architectural postmodernism was totally in line with the mission of architecture according to dominant history, which has been to invest shelter with a given meaning.

Ten years later, the illusion was already vanishing. The Doric orders made of painted plywood had begun to warp and peel. The instability, the ephemerality of both signifier and signified, form and function, form and meaning, could only stress the obvious, what Jacques Lacan had pointed out years before: that there is no cause-and-effect relationship between signifier and signified, between word and intended concept. The signifier does not have to answer for its existence in the name of some hypothetical signification. As in literature and psychoanalysis, the architectural signifier does not represent the signified. Doric columns and neon pediments suggest too many interpretations to justify any single one. Again, there is no cause-and-effect relationship between an architectural sign and its possible interpretation. Between signifier and signified stands a barrier: the barrier of actual use. Never mind if this very room was once a fire station, then a furniture storage room, then a ritualistic dance hall, and now a lecture hall (it has been all of these). Each time, these uses distorted both signifier and signified. Not only are linguistic signs arbitrary (as de Saussure showed us long ago), but interpretation is itself open to constant questioning. Every interpretation can be the object of interpretation, and that new interpretation can in turn be interpreted, until every interpretation erases the previous one. The dominant history of architecture, which is a history of the signified, has to be revised, at a time when there is no longer a normative rule, a cause-and-effect relationship between a form and a function, between a signifier and its signified: only a deregulation of meaning.

The deregulation of architecture began long ago, at the end of the nineteenth century, with the world fairs of London and Paris, where light metallic structures radically changed the appearance of architectural solids. Suddenly, architecture was merely scaffolding supporting glass, and it was discredited as the "solid," symbolic character of masonry and stone. Human scale ceased to be an issue, as the logic of industrial construction took over. Human proportions from the ages of classicism and humanism were rapidly replaced by grids and modular systems, a superimposition of light and materials that were becoming increasingly immaterial—another form of deconstruction.

In the mid-seventies, nostalgic architects, longing for meaning and tradition, applied sheetrock and plywood cutouts to those scaffoldings, but the images they were trying to provide were weak in comparison to the new scaffoldings of our time: the mediatized images of ephemeral representations.

"To represent construction or to construct representation" (Virilio): this is the new question of our time. As Albert Einstein said, "There is no scientific truth, only temporary representations, ever-accelerating sequences of representation." In fact, we are forced to

253

go through a complete reconsideration of all concepts of figuration and representation: the constant storm of images (whether drawings, graphs, photographs, films, television, or computer-generated images) increasingly negates any attempt to restore the Renaissance ideal of the unity of reality and its representation. The concept of double-coding was the last and futile attempt to keep some of that ideal intact by establishing a new relation between communication and tradition. It is the word "tradition" that misled much of the architectural scene in the late seventies and made some aspects of architectural postmodernism what I think will soon appear as a short-lived avatar of history: a form of contextual eclecticism that has been recurrent throughout architectural history, with and without irony, allegory, and other parodies.

In any case, the problem is not a problem of images: gables and classical orders, however silly, are free to be consumed by whoever wishes to do so. But to pretend that these images could suggest new rules and regulations in architecture and urbanism by transcending modernism is simply misplaced.

There are no more rules and regulations. The current metropolitan deregulation caused by the dis-industrialization of European and American cities, by the collapse of zoning strategies, contradicts any attempt to develop new sets of regulating forces, however desirable it may be for some. The 1987 Wall Street "crash" and its relation to the economic deregulation that immediately preceded it is another illustration that an important change has taken place. Let me go back to Virilio's argument. In the Middle Ages, society was self-regulated, auto-regulated. Regulation took place at its center. The prince of the city was the ruler; there was a direct cause-and-effect relationship between rules and everyday life, between the weight of masonry and the way that buildings were built.

In the industrial era, societies became artificially regulated. The power of economic and industrial forces took over by establishing a coherent structure throughout the whole territory: control was defined at the limits, at the edges of society. The relation between rules and everyday life ceased to be clear, and so large bureaucracies and administrators took over. Regulation was not at the center anymore but at the periphery. Abstract architecture used grids on its sheds International-style, before it discovered that one could decorate the same shed Multinational-style—regardless of what happened in them. Function, form, and meaning ceased to have any relationship to one another.

Today we have entered the age of deregulation, where control takes place *outside* of society, as in those computer programs that feed on one another endlessly in a form of autonomy, recalling the autonomy of language described by Michel Foucault. We witness the separation of people and language, the decentering of the subject. Or, we might say, the complete *decentering of society*.

Ex-centric, dis-integrated, dis-located, dis-juncted, deconstructed, dismantled, disassociated, discontinuous, deregulated . . . de-, dis-, ex-. These are the prefixes of today. Not post-, neo-, or pre-.

29 REM KOOLHAAS, B. 1944

Office for Metropolitan Architects and LMN Architects, Seattle Central Library, Seattle, WA, 1999–2004
View from the corner of Madison Street and Fourth Avenue
Photo courtesy of the Seattle Public Library

In 1978, a Dutch journalist/screenwriter-turned-architect published *Delirious New York*. This engrossing book analyzed what the author termed the "culture of congestion" that characterized densely populated lower Manhattan. The author, Rem Koolhaas, welcomed the chaos of this metropolitan realm in which the skyscraper, with wildly disparate programs on each floor, was the ultimate "Social Condenser: a machine to generate and intensify desirable forms of human intercourse."[*] Where else could one discover the promise of new interactions and experiences such as "Eating oysters with boxing gloves, naked on the nth floor?"[†] Embedded in this explication of the skyscraper was a related yet distinct topic Koolhaas would later address: Bigness. Aptly, Koolhaas's meditations on this subject, "Bigness, or the Problem of the Large," appeared in *S, M, L, XL*, a hefty publication of 1995. In a discipline so fond of theorizing, Bigness, Koolhaas announced, has yet to be theorized. This "absence," he continued, "is architecture's most debilitating weakness," precisely because "only Bigness instigates the *regime of complexity* that mobilizes the full intelligence of architecture and its related fields." With this in mind, Koolhaas discussed the particular architectural qualities engendered by Bigness, issues he has no doubt encountered in his many design projects. Thus "Bigness, or the Problem of the Large" can be understood both as Koolhaas's attempt to conceptualize this neglected subject and to set forth thoughts conceived in the process of Big design.

---

[*] Rem Koolhaas, *Delirious New York* (1978; New York: Monacelli Press, 1994), 152.

[†] Ibid., 155.

"Bigness, or the Problem of Large" (1993)

Species

Beyond a certain scale, architecture acquires the properties of BIGNESS. The best reason to broach BIGNESS is the one given by climbers of Mount Everest: "because it is there." BIGNESS is the ultimate architecture.

It seems incredible that the size of a building alone embodies an ideological problem, independent of the will of its architects.

Of all possible categories, BIGNESS does not seem to deserve a manifesto; discredited as an intellectual problem, it is apparently on its way to extinction—like the dinosaur—through clumsiness, slowness, inflexibility, difficulty. But in fact, only BIGNESS instigates the *regime of complexity* that mobilizes the full intelligence of architecture and its related fields.

One hundred years ago, a generation of conceptual breakthroughs and supporting technologies unleashed an architectural BIG BANG. By randomizing circulation, short-circuiting distance, artificializing interiors, reducing mass, stretching dimensions, and accelerating construction, the elevator, electricity, air-conditioning, steel, and finally, the new infrastructures formed a cluster of mutations that induced another *species* of architecture. The combined effects of these inventions were structures taller and deeper—BIGGER—than ever before conceived, with a parallel potential for the reorganization of the social world—a vastly richer programmation.

Rem Koolhaas, "Bigness, or the Problem of the Large," OMA, Rem Koolhaas, and Bruce Man, *S, M, L, XL* (New York: Monacelli Press, 1995), 494–516. © 1994 by Rem Koolhaas and the Monacelli Press, Inc. Reprinted with permission of author and publisher.

Theorems

Fuelled initially by the thoughtless energy of the purely quantitative, BIGNESS has been, for nearly a century, a condition almost without thinkers, a revolution without program.

Delirious New York implied a latent "Theory of BIGNESS" based on five theorems:

1. Beyond a certain critical mass, a building becomes a BIG Building. Such a mass can no longer be controlled by a singular architectural gesture, or even by any combination of architectural gestures. The impossibility triggers the autonomy of its parts, which is different from fragmentation: the parts remain committed to the whole.

2. The elevator—with its potential to establish mechanical rather than architectural connections—and its family of related inventions render null and void the classical repertoire of architecture. Issues of composition, scale, proportion, detail are now moot. The 'art' of architecture is useless in BIGNESS.

3. In BIGNESS, the distance between core and envelope increases to the point where the façade can no longer reveal what happens inside. The humanist expectation of 'honesty' is doomed; interior and exterior architectures become separate projects, one dealing with the instability of programmatic and iconographic needs, the other—agent of disinformation—offering the city the apparent stability of an object. Where architecture reveals, BIGNESS perplexes; BIGNESS transforms the city from a summation of certainties into an accumulation of mysteries. What you see is no longer what you get.

4. Through size alone, such buildings enter an amoral domain, beyond good and bad. Their impact is independent of their quality.

5. Together, all these breaks—with scale, with architectural composition, with tradi-

tion, with transparency, with ethics—imply the final, most radical break: BIGNESS is no longer part of any tissue. It exists; at most, it coexists. Its subtext is *fuck* context.

Maximum
. . . The absence of a theory of BIGNESS—what is the maximum architecture can do?—is architecture's most debilitating weakness. Without a theory of BIGNESS, architects are in the position of Frankenstein's creators: instigators of a partly successful experiment whose results are running amok and are therefore discredited.

Because there is no theory of BIGNESS, we don't know what to do with it, we don't know where to put it, we don't know when to use it, we don't know how to plan it.

Big mistakes are our only connection to BIGNESS. But in spite of its dumb name, BIGNESS is a theoretical domain at this fin de siècle: in a landscape of disarray, disassembly, dissociation, disclamation, the attraction of BIGNESS is its potential to reconstruct the whole, resurrect the real, reinvent the collective, reclaim maximum possibility.

Only through BIGNESS can architecture dissociate itself from the exhausted ideological and artistic movements of modernism and formalism to regain its instrumentality as a vehicle of modernization.

BIGNESS recognizes that architecture as we know it is in difficulty, but it does not overcompensate through regurgitations of even more architecture. It proposes a new economy in which "all is architecture" no longer, but in which a strategic position is regained through retreat and concentration, yielding the rest of a contested territory to enemy forces.

Beginning
BIGNESS destroys, but it is also a new beginning. It can reassemble what it breaks.

A paradox of BIGNESS is that in spite of the calculation that goes into its planning—in fact, through its very rigidities—it is the one architecture that engineers the unpredictable. Instead of enforcing coexistence, BIGNESS depends on regimes of freedoms, the assembly of maximum difference.

Only BIGNESS can sustain a promiscuous proliferation of events in a single container. It develops strategies to organize both their independence and interdependence within the larger entity in a symbiosis that exacerbates rather than compromises specificity.

Through contamination rather than purity and quantity rather than quality, only BIGNESS can support genuinely new relationships between functional entities that expand rather than limit their identities. The artificiality and complexity of BIGNESS release function from its defensive armor to allow a kind of liquefaction; programmatic elements react with each other to create new events—BIGNESS returns to a model of programmatic alchemy.

At first sight, the activities amassed in the structure of BIGNESS *demand* to interact, but BIGNESS also keeps them apart. Like plutonium rods that, more or less immersed, dampen or promote nuclear reaction, BIGNESS regulates the intensities of programmatic coexistence.

Although BIGNESS is a blueprint for a perpetual performance, it also offers degrees of serenity and even blandness. It is simply impossible to animate its entire mass with intention. Its vastness exhausts architecture's compulsion to decide and determine. Zones will be left out, free from architecture.

Team

BIGNESS is where architecture becomes both most and least architectural: most because of the enormity of the object; least through the loss of autonomy—it becomes instrument of other forces, it *depends*. BIGNESS is impersonal: the architect is no longer condemned to stardom.

Beyond signature, BIGNESS means surrender to technologies; to engineers, contractors, manufacturers; to others. It promises architecture a kind of post-heroic status—a realignment with neutrality.

Even as BIGNESS enters the stratosphere of architectural ambition—the pure chill of megalomania—it can be achieved only at the price of giving up control, of transmogrification. It implies a web of umbilical cords to other disciplines whose performance is at critical as the architect's: like mountain climbers tied together by life-saving ropes, the makers of BIGNESS are a team (a word not mentioned in the last forty years of architectural polemic).

Bastion
If BIGNESS transforms architecture, its accumulation generates a new kind of city.

The exterior of the city is no longer a collective theater where 'it' happens; there's no collective 'it' left. The street has become residue, organizational device, mere segment of the continuous metropolitan plane where the remnants of the past face the equipments of the new in an uneasy standoff. BIGNESS can exist *anywhere* in that plane.

Not only is BIGNESS incapable of establishing relationships with the classical city—*at most, it coexists*—but in the quantity and complexity of the facilities it offers, it is itself urban. BIGNESS no longer needs the city: it competes with the city; it preempts the city; or better still, it *is* the city. If urbanism generated potential and architecture exploits it, BIGNESS enlists the generosity of urbanism against the meanness of architecture. BIGNESS = urbanism vs. architecture.

BIGNESS, through its very independence of context, is the one architecture than can survive, even exploit, the now-global condition of the tabula rasa: it does not take its inspiration from givens too often squeezed for the last drop of meaning; it gravitates opportunistically to locations of maximum infrastructural promise; it is, finally, its own *raison d'être*.

In spite of its size, it is modest. Not all architecture, not all program, not all events will be swallowed by BIGNESS. There are many 'needs' too unfocused, too weak, too unrespectable, too defiant, too secret, too subversive, too weak, too 'nothing' to be part of the constellations of BIGNESS.

BIGNESS is the last bastion of architecture—a contraction, a hyperarchitecture. The containers of BIGNESS will be landmarks in a postarchitectural landscape—a world scraped of architecture in the way Richter's paintings are scraped of paint: inflexible, immutable, definitive, forever there, generated through superhuman effort. BIGNESS surrenders the field to after-architecture.

30 DANIEL LIBESKIND, B. 1946

In the 1988 Deconstructivist Architecture exhibition at the New York Museum of Modern Art, the work of the Polish-American architect Daniel Libeskind was featured alongside those of Rem Koolhaas, Frank Gehry, Bernard Tschumi, Peter Eisenman, Zaha Hadid, and Coop-Himmelblau. What united these architects, according to the show's cocurator Mark Wigley, was their "ability to disturb our thinking about form."[*] Indeed, their works in general are characterized by fractured, skewed, abstracted elements. But that is where the similarities end; indeed, the divergence between their design philosophies is striking. Libeskind speaks most openly of the spiritual nature of architecture—spiritual in an emotive, experiential, and humanistic sense. This approach is conveyed in his architecture, whether it be his first large public commission, the Jewish Museum in Berlin (1989–99, opened 2001), or his most famous recent project, the Master Plan for the World Trade Center in New York (awarded 2003). The mystical nature of things present but not seen and the potential strength of architecture as a communicative device come through quite clearly in Libeskind's writings, including the comments below, originally issued in 1997 as his acceptance speech for an honorary degree from Humboldt University in Berlin.

---

[*] Mark Wigley, *Deconstructivist Architecture* (New York: Museum of Modern Art, 1988). Wigley curated the exhibition with Philip Johnson.

"Proof of Things Invisible" (1997)

As I was thinking about what to say today I realized how difficult it is for an architect to speak about his work without the usual paraphernalia of slide projectors and images. Architecture, which is evoked only by words, makes one almost feel 'at home' in language. By surrounding oneself with language one almost comes to believe that one has escaped from the opacity of space and that what remains 'out there' is only an empty stage set. That is perhaps why most intelligent people apply their intelligence and analytic powers to everything but architecture; why architecture is given over to technicians and specialists, and why one is resigned to it as an inevitable and anonymous force which will shape the cities without one's personal participation.

The experience of alienation from architecture, as a dimension of culture, should be contrasted with the stark and astonished encounter with IT—crowned-out, spewed-out into night—resistant to theorization. For then, one might see that architecture—something static and unfeeling, as all that's turned into a coming—can be interpreted, but itself continues to remain oblivious to the interpretation. It continues to live its own existence whether we share it or not.

Perhaps language and its meaning [are] grounded in the spaces of architecture, and not vice-versa. Consider the functions of foundation, circumcision, territorialization, openness and closure. These are all experiences of space—and of a certain kind of architecture—which provide a symbolic model and understanding of life itself. Is archi-

Daniel Libeskind, "Proof of Things Invisible," http://www.daniel-libeskind.com/words. Acceptance speech for an honorary doctorate awarded by Humbolt University, Berlin, in 1997. Reprinted with permission from the author.

tecture not the quintessential 'taken for granted,' the unthinkable, the monstrous, the gender-less, the repressed, the other? Perhaps this is the point of its madness, perhaps it is your conscience: the knot of life in which what is recognized is untied. And what thinking person does not want a fire-place, a home, a Utopia, 'the way it is,' 'the way it was'? What thoughtful person is not grateful for the beams of clear lines directed by this silent ray?

What ineffable—immeasurable power of building in the city! The epiphany of the constructible is the strange sucking of the earth's axis. In the realm of architecture, ideas having stared at Medusa turn to stone. Here it is matter which carries the aura of ideas—ideas which metastasize into crystalline sleep-shapes assumed in the language shadow. Wasps, buildings, antennae sting the air, driving the sting to pass through the world of dream and death in order to sense this axis: The Earth's Axis.

All this is accomplished through technique such as drawing wherein an exiled line falls to the ground. Two parallel lines signify a wall; precisely the wall which is between the lines and is not a line. Whether this wall imprisons and releases depends on whether one is a saint or a prisoner. It is doubly illegible; twice over. In attempting to surmount the inner poles of this contradiction, architecture becomes like the plow, turning time up, revealing its invisible layers on the surface.

The power of building is certainly more than meets the eye. It is the non-thematized, the twilight, the marginal, event. But architecture forming this background is a surplus beyond obvious need: that which itself has no legitimacy in a proper foundation. This has led some to ask whether the true and the real need to be embodied at all. Whether one needs architecture or just a simulation mechanism. Whether architecture can flutter nearby like a spirit, the bell or the Internet. It cannot.

In its opacity and resistance, architecture rebels and communicates that only the superfluous, the transcendent, the ineffable is allied to us: the sky, the stars, the gods. I would like to confess my fascination for this strange activity, quite distant from the obsessive technologism, globalized marketing and withered modernism progressively eradicating spiritual life.

I would like to share with you something about the nature of the approach to architecture which I am following, through buildings which not only house exhibitions within them but as architectural works 'exhibit' the world; are indeed the 'production' of the earth. Together they delineate a trajectory which musters the letters, mortal-immortal; show the Aleph as coming after the Beit; the alphabet after the House. Henry Adams considered the Virgin as the mobilizing form of medieval times and compared her to the dynamo, the mechanism of industrialization. Were he to write today, he would perhaps add to the Virgin and the dynamo—the Museum—as the catalyst and conveyor of reality, since this institution is seen today as a force able to regenerate areas of experience, revive histories, transform images and create a new identity.

Throughout my projects I have followed a certain path which one could name as the search for the Irreplaceable, that which was known by the pagans as the genus loci. I am interested in the unique portrayal of architecture and space of provinces, mountains, maps, ships, horoscopes, fish, instruments, rooms, stars, horses, texts, people. In this labyrinth of places, one can discover the uniqueness of a human face and of a particular hand as a figure of architecture and of the city.

Lines of history and of events; lines of experience and of the look; lines of drawing and of construction. These vectors form a patterned course towards 'the unsubsided' which paradoxically grows more heavy as it becomes more light. I think of it as that which cannot be buried: that which cannot be extinguished: Call it Architecture if you want. . . .

Architecture's reality is as old as the substance of the things hoped for. It is the proof of things invisible. Contrary to public opinion the flesh of architecture is not cladding, insulation and structure, but the substance of the individual in society and history; a figuration of the inorganic and organic, the body and the soul, and that which is visible beyond.

Some would deny this substance and as a result might themselves vanish into the emptiness of "facts" which as indices of power are only the illusory ghosts of a virtual world. One must reject the emptiness of ideologies, the nihilistic obsession with the return of the same, the vacuity of systems which base the whole on its part. The road to authentic construction, just like a smile, cannot be faked for it remains insubordinate, not slave. . . .

The Spiritual in architecture is urgent, though it seems to have become an embarrassment, a rumor on the street. The spiritual, appropriated by the fundamentalist right, has been expropriated from culture and history, eliminated from discourse through which it should be reclaimed. One should attempt to retrieve the spirit of architecture, to recall its Humanity, even within a situation in which the goal and the way have been eclipsed. The erasure of history and its carriers, the obliviousness of the market economy to the degradation and ongoing genocide of human beings must be countered with a deeper awareness and action.

Architecture is and remains the ethical, the true, the good and the beautiful, no matter what those who know the price of everything and the value of nothing may say.

Contemporary architecture is split bitterness/sweetness, strictly, the ends of its smile go off into the anarchy of life, opening a paradoxical freedom.

Greg Lynn's meditations and architectural projects have stimulated and contributed to the discipline's growing interest in computer-aided design. As an architect and philosopher, Lynn has reconceptualized the traditional practice of architecture, challenging the notion of the architectural object as static and fixed and the accepted method of "paper" design. Relying on the computer as a design tool, not solely a representational device, Lynn incorporates environmental and programmatic factors into the formation of his structures, creating an architecture that, in its form and organization, reflects the conditions of its site and intended use. The resulting work, rarely rectilinear, conveys a sense of fluidity and motion that suggest the forces that act on it. A former member of Peter Eisenman's architectural firm, Lynn's abstraction stems not from an attempt to strip architecture of external meaning, but rather reflects his desire to integrate an array of information into the process of architectural production.

Animate Form (1999)

Animation is a term which differs from, but is often confused with, motion. While motion implies movement and action, animation implies evolution of a form and its shaping forces; it suggests animalism, animism, growth, actuation, vitality and virtuality.[1] In its manifold implications, animation touches on many of architecture's most deeply embedded assumptions about its structure. What makes animation so problematic for architects is that they have maintained an ethics of statics in their discipline. Because of its dedication to permanence, architecture is one of the last modes of thought based on the inert. More than even its traditional role of providing shelter, architects are expected to provide culture with stasis. This desire for timelessness is intimately linked with interest in formal purity and autonomy. Challenging these assumptions by introducing architecture to models of organization that are not inert will not threaten the essence of the discipline, but will advance it. Just as the development of calculus drew upon the historical mathematical developments that preceded it, so too will an animate approach to architecture subsume traditional models of statics into a more advanced system of dynamic organizations. Traditionally, in architecture, the abstract space of design is conceived as an environment of force and motion rather than as a neutral vacuum. In naval design, for example, the abstract space of design is imbued with the properties of flow, turbulence, viscosity, and drag so that the form of

Greg Lynn, *Animate Form* (New York: Princeton Architectural Press, 1999), 9–11, 13–16, 41. Reproduced with permission from the publisher. All terms in bold face were treated as such by Lynn in his original text.

[1] For varied and rigorous discussions of the animal as the surrogate, model and metaphor for architecture in history, theory and design, see the chapter "Donkey Urbanism" in Catherine Ingraham's book *Architecture and the Burdens of Linearity* (New Haven: Yale University Press, 1998), as well as her essay, "Animals 2: The Problem of Distinction (Insects, For Example)" in *Assemblage* 14 (Cambridge, MA: MIT Press, 1991),25–29.

a hull can be conceived in motion through water. Although the form of a boat hull is designed to anticipate motion, there is no expectation that its shape will change. An ethics of motion neither implies nor precludes literal motion. Form can be shaped by the collaboration between an envelope and the active context in which it is situated. While physical form can be defined in terms of static coordinates, the visual force of the environment in which it is designed contributes to its shape. The particular form of a hull stores multiple vectors of motion and flow from the space in which it was designed. A sailboat hull, for example, is designed as a planing surface. For sailing into the wind, the hull is designed to heal, presenting a greater surface area to the water. A boat hull does not change its shape when it changes direction, obviously, but variable points of sail are incorporated into its surface. In this way, topology allows for not just the incorporation of a single moment but rather a multiplicity of vectors, and therefore, a multiplicity of times, in a single continuous surface.

Likewise, the forms of a dynamically conceived architecture may be shaped in association with virtual motion and force, but again, this does not mandate that the architecture change its shape. Actual movement often involves a mechanical paradigm of multiple discrete positions,whereas virtual movement allows form to occupy a multiplicity of possible positions continuously with the same form.

The term **virtual** has recently been so debased that it often simply refers to the digital space of computer-aided design. It is often used interchangeably with the term simulation. Simulation, unlike virtuality, is not intended as a diagram for future possible concrete assemblage but is instead a visual substitute. "Virtual reality" might describe architectural design but as it is used to describe a simulated environment it would be better replaced by "simulated reality" or "substitute reality." Thus, use of the term virtual here refers to an abstract scheme that has the possibility of becoming actualized, often in a variety of possible configurations. Since architects produce drawings of buildings and not buildings themselves, architecture, more than any other discipline, is involved with the production of virtual descriptions.

There is one aspect of virtuality that architects have neglected, however, and that is the principle of virtual force and the differential variation it implies. Architectural form is conventionally conceived in a dimensional space of idealized stasis, defined by Cartesian fixed-point coordinates. An object defined as a vector whose trajectory is relative to other objects, forces, fields and flows, defines form within an active space of force and motion. This shift from a passive space of static coordinates to an active space of interactions implies a move from autonomous purity to contextual specificity.[2]

Contemporary animation and special-effects software are just now being introduced as tools for design rather than as devices for rendering, visualization and imaging.[3]

The dominant mode for discussing architecture has been the cinematic model, where the multiplication and sequencing of static snap-shots simulates movement. The problem with the motion-picture analogy is that architecture occupies the role of static frame through which motion progresses. Force and motion are eliminated from form only to be reintroduced, after the fact of design, through concepts and techniques of optical procession.

---

[2] It is important to any discussion of parameter-based design that there be both the unfolding of an internal system and the unfolding of contextual information fields. This issue of contextualism is discussed more extensively in my essay "Architectural Curvilinearity: The Folded, the Pliant and the Supple," in *Architectural Design* 102, *Folding in Architecture* (London, 1993) where in the same volume it is also criticized by Jeffrey Kipnis in his essay "Towards a New Architecture."

[3] There are two instances of architectural theorists and designers crossing over from models of cinema to models of animation. The first is Brian Boigon's "The Cartoon Regulators" in *Assemblage* 19 (Cambridge, MA: MIT Press, 1992), 66–71. The second is Mark Rakatansky's discussions of the writing and animation of Chuck Jones regarding theories of mobility, action, and gesture in *Any Magazine* 23 (New York, 1998).

In contrast, animate design is defined by the co-presence of motion and force at the moment of formal conception. Force is an initial condition, the cause of both motion and the particular inflections of a form. For example, in what is called *"inverse kinematic"* animation, the motion and shape of a form is defined by multiple interacting vectors that unfold in time perpetually and openly. With these techniques, entities are given vectorial properties before they are released into a space differentiated by gradients of force. Instead of a neutral, abstract space for design, the context for design becomes an active abstract space that directs form within a current of forces that can be stored as information in the shape of the form. Rather than as a frame through which time and space pass, architecture can be modeled as a participant immersed within dynamic flows. In addition to the special-effects and animation industries, many other disciplines such as aeronautical design, naval design, and automobile design employ this animate approach to modeling form in a space that is a medium of movement and force. . . .

Stasis is a concept which has been intimately linked with architecture in at least five important ways, including 1) permanence, 2) usefulness, 3) typology, 4) procession, and 5) verticality. However, statics does not hold an essential grip on architectural thinking as much as it is a lazy habit or default that architects either choose to reinforce or contradict for lack of a better model. Each of these assumptions can be transformed once the virtual space in which architecture is conceptualized is mobilized with both time and force. With the example of permanence, the dominant cultural expectation is that buildings must be built for eternity when in fact most buildings are built to persist for only a short time. Rather than designing for permanence, techniques for obsolescence, dismantling, ruination, recycling and abandonment through time warrant exploration. Another characteristic of static models is that of functional fixity. Buildings are often assumed to have a particular and fixed relationship to their programs, whether they are intersected, combined or even flexibly programmed. Typological fixity, of the kind promoted by Colin Rowe for instance, depends on a closed static order to underlie a family of continuous variations. This concept of a discrete, ideal, and fixed prototype can be subsumed by the model of the numerically controlled multi-type that is flexible, mutable, and differential. This multi-type, or **performance envelope**, does not privilege a fixed type but instead models a series of relationships or expressions between a range of potentials. Similarly, independent interacting variables can be linked to influence one another through logical expressions defining the size, position, rotation, direction, or speed of an object by looking to other objects for their characteristics. This concept of an envelope of potential from which either a single or a series of **instances** can be taken, is radically different from the idea of a fixed prototype that can be varied.

Finally, static models underwrite the retrograde understanding of gravity as a simple, unchanging, vertical force. Architecture remains as the last refuge for members of the flat-earth society. The relationships of structure to force and gravity are by definition multiple and interrelated, yet architects tend to reduce these issues to what is still held as a central truth: that buildings stand up vertically. In fact, there are multiple interacting structural pressures exerted on buildings from many directions, including lateral wind loads, uplift, shear, and earthquakes, to name a few of the non-vertical conditions. Any one of these **live** loads could easily exceed the relative weight of the building and its vertical **dead** loads. The naive understanding of structure as primarily a problem of the vertical transfer of dead gravity loads to the ground excludes, for instance, the fact that lighter buildings have a tendency to uplift; the main structural concern in these cases is how to tether the roof. Of course architects and structural engineers do not ignore these other structural factors, but the primary perception of structure has always been that it should be vertical. A reconceptualization of ground and verticality in light of complex vectors and movements might not change the expediency and need for level floors, but it would open up possibilities for structure and support that take into account orientations other than the simply vertical.

These concerns are not merely technical as architecture presently expresses also the cultural diagrams of stasis. Despite the popular conception among architects that gravity is a fact, the contemporary debates about theories of gravity could inform present discussions of architecture in the same spirit that they have done in the past. The history of theories of gravity are extremely nuanced, fascinating and unresolved. Since the time of Sir Isaac Newton, gravity has been accepted as the mutual relative attraction of masses in space. Given a constant mass, stability is achieved through orbits rather than stasis. This distinction between stasis and orbital or dynamic stability is important. In the case of a single, simple gravity, **stasis** is the ordering system through the unchanging constant force of a ground point. In the case of a more complex concept of gravity, mutual attraction generates motion; **stability** is the ordering of motion into rhythmic phases. In the simple, static model of gravity, motion is eliminated at the beginning. In the complex, stable model of gravity, motion is an ordering principle. Likewise, discreteness, timelessness, and fixity are characteristics of stasis; multiplicity, change, and development are characteristics of stability. . . .

If architecture is to approach this more complex concept of gravity, its design technologies should also incorporate factors of time and motion. Throughout the history of architecture, descriptive techniques have impacted the way in which architectural design and construction has been practiced. . . . Events such as the advent of perspective, stereometric projection, and other geometric techniques have extended the descriptive repertoire of architectural designers. In our present age, the virtual space within which architecture is conceived is now being rethought by the introduction of advanced motion tools and a constellation of new diagrams based on the computer. . . .

The availability and rapid colonization of architecture design by computer-aided techniques presents the discipline with yet another opportunity to both retool and rethink itself as it did with the advent of stereometric projection and perspective. If there is a single concept that must be engaged due to the proliferation of topological shapes and computer-aided tools, it is that in their structure as abstract machines, these technologies are animate.

32 Norman Foster, b. 1935

Foster and Partners, Hearst Tower, New York City, NY, 2000–06
Photo courtesy of Nigel Young and Foster and Partners

Throughout his career, the British architect Norman Foster has relied on technological experimentation to create user-friendly and environmentally sensitive architecture. His relationship with Buckminster Fuller, with whom he collaborated on various projects during the 1970s and early 1980s, contributed to Foster's focus on his buildings' occupants and ecological concerns. Foster's first major work, the Willis Faber Dumas Building (1975) in Ipswich, England, took both issues into account. To provide a pleasant atmosphere for the company's workers, Foster's design incorporated amenities such as an open-air rooftop garden and restaurant and an indoor swimming pool. Innovative structural and mechanical systems allowed for flowing, flexible interior space infused with natural light. This hi-tech, glass-sheathed edifice was a precursor for many of Foster's later works, including the recently completed Hearst Tower in New York City (2000–06). This office tower utilizes recycled building materials, innovative steel structural bracing, a rainwater collection and rehabilitation system, and sensors to regulate energy use. A percentage of the harnessed rainwater contributes to a three-story "Icefall," a sculptural installation that helps cool, humidify, and animate the atrium of the Hearst Tower. Workers also benefit from maximum natural illumination afforded by the building's extensive glass skin. These inventive technological features attest to Foster's interest in user comfort and environmentally responsible design. As Foster conveys in the essay below, such issues will continue to guide his work.

"The Architecture of the Future" (1999)

The architecture of the future will, by necessity, be one that addresses the world's increasing ecological crisis. Architecture can contribute to dealing with the crisis to a degree that few other activities can. Buildings use half of the energy consumed in the developed world, yet virtually every building could be designed to run on a fraction of current energy levels.

Why do we rely so heavily upon artificial lighting when we can easily design buildings that are filled with daylight? Why do we continue to rely upon wasteful air-conditioning systems in locations where we could simply open a window? A holistic approach to architecture—one that sees buildings as the sum of all the systems at work within them—is the start of the solution to our problems. Structure, form and materials each have their part to play in this. Natural lighting and ventilation, recycled rainwater, and heat recycled from lights, computers and people, for example, can all contribute to reducing a building's energy demands.

Applying these methods in the Reichstag, in Berlin, we were able to reduce the building's energy requirements to such an extent that it creates more energy than it consumes. Our integrated energy strategy has also allowed us to reduce pollution; the Reichstag burns renewable vegetable oil, rather than dwindling fossil fuels, which has led to a dramatic reduction in the building's carbon dioxide emissions. If a nineteenth-century building can be transformed from an energy guzzler into a building so efficient that it is now a net provider of energy—literally a power station for its neighborhood—how much

---

Norman Foster, "The Architecture of the Future," in *On Foster, Foster On* (Munich: Prestel Publishing, 2000). © 2000, Foster and Partners, London and Prestel Verlag, Munich-London-New York. Reprinted with permission from the author and publisher.

easier is it to design new buildings that make responsible use of precious resources?

However, individual buildings cannot be viewed in isolation. They must be seen in the context of our ever expanding cities and their infrastructures. Unchecked urban sprawl is one of the chief problems facing the world today. One example will serve to illustrate this phenomenon. In the period 1970–1990 the population of greater Chicago increased by a mere 4 percent, yet its physical area grew by 50 percent. Moreover, the peripheral growth of cities is rarely accompanied by integrated public transport networks or other services. Instead, people are forced to travel greater distances by car, creating congestion and pollution.

Higher urban densities provide one solution to this problem—it is surprising to discover that the world's two most densely populated areas, Monaco and Macao, are at opposite ends of the economic spectrum. High density—or high rise—does not automatically mean overcrowding or economic hardship; it can also lead to an improved quality of life, where housing, work and leisure facilities are all close by.

The Millennium Tower that we have proposed in Tokyo takes a traditional horizontal city quarter—housing, shops, restaurants, cinemas, museums, sporting facilities, green spaces and public transport networks—and turns it on its side to create a supertall building with a multiplicity of uses. It would be over 800 metres high with 170 storeys—twice the height of anything so far built—and would house a community of up to 60,000 people. This is 20,000 more than the population of Monaco and yet the building would occupy only 0.013 square kilometres of land in comparison to Monaco's 1.95 square kilometres. It would create a virtually self-sufficient, fully self-sustaining community in the sky.

This sounds like future fantasy. But we now have all the means at our disposal to create such buildings. There are no technological barriers to a sustainable architecture, only ones of political will. The architecture of the future could be the architecture of today.

33   SAMUEL MOCKBEE, 1944–2001

In the early 1990s, Samuel Mockbee left his well-established private practice and dedicated his attention to the creation of a socially responsible architecture. Mockbee's mission was two-fold: to create dignified, low-budget architecture for the impoverished and to cultivate a new generation of culturally aware architects. He accomplished these goals with the Rural Studio, a philanthropic initiative run through Auburn University. After immersing themselves in the community and determining the clients' needs, students under Mockbee's leadership designed and constructed small-scale sustainable structures such as housing and recreational centers for the underprivileged inhabitants of Hale Country, Alabama. The works often utilized unconventional materials such as hay bales, discarded license plates, and salvaged items to devise inexpensive contemporary structures based on local vernacular forms. Since Mockbee's death in 2001, the Rural Studio has continued to thrive, existing as a model for an innovative, socially conscious alternative to traditional methods of architectural practice.

"The Hero of Hale County" (2001)

This is the eighth year that Samuel Mockbee and his architecture students at Auburn University have been designing and building striking houses and community buildings for impoverished residents of Alabama's Hale County. In some ways, the place has changed little since James Agee and Walker Evans went there in 1936 to document the lives of poor white sharecroppers. The 1990 Census shows per capita income still averaging no more than $8,164 and 1,700 families still living in substandard houses. Most of the Rural Studio's clients are African-Americans, "left behind by Reconstruction," as Mockbee says. Many live in unheated, leaky shacks without plumbing in Masons Bend, a little settlement of about 150 people tucked into a bend of Black Warrior River at the end of a winding dirt road about 10 miles from Greensboro, the county seat.

In addition to being a social welfare venture, the Rural Studio—Taliesin South, it's been called—it also an education experiment and a prod to the architectural profession to act on its finest instincts. In June, Mockbee learned he had been awarded a MacArthur "genius grant." Not long afterward, speaking in the deep drawl of his region, the burly, bearded sixth-generation Mississippian had the following conversation with contributing editor Andrea Oppenheimer Dean:

ARCHITECTURAL RECORD: *What Will You Do With $500,000?*
SAM MOCKBEE: It'll allow me to take care of my family and get way out on the edge in my work and maybe do something that most people would think I was crazy to do, follow my instincts, let a project evolve, and concentrate on it. More than likely it'll be for the Rural Studio.

Samuel Mockbee, "The Hero of Hale County," interview by Andrea Oppenheimer Dean, *Architectural Record* 189, n. 2, (February 2001) 76–82. Reprinted with permission from the publisher, McGraw-Hill.

AR: *Any ideas what the project might be?*

SM: You know the profession's IDP internship development program? It is a well-intended program, but most interns dread it. I would like to offer architecture graduates an opportunity to come down to the Rural Studio as intern architects, under my stamp.

One idea is to also ask something of the premier architects in America, the Frank Gehrys, the I. M. Peis, the Richard Meiers, and Michael Rotondis. I'd like to ask each to design a cottage for a family that's living down here in a cardboard shack. I'd take their sketch and get four intern architects to build the house. Masons Bend, Alabama, would become like Seaside, Florida, but I'd be doing this for the poorest one percent of Americans.

I'd find the money to build these houses—we build them for $30,000—and make sure the workmanship is up to par. That's the sort of thing I'm thinking about.

AR: *You've stayed close to your Southern roots. Can you get an appropriate design from an architect who isn't rooted in place?*

SM: I'm not going to say that someone like Frank Gehry can't build something beautiful in a culture and place he doesn't know well. For the rest of us mere mortals, the best way to make real architecture is by letting a building evolve out of the culture and place.

I don't want to be pigeonholed as a regionalist, yet I am, and I certainly don't want to get marked as a local colorist. I pay attention to my region; I keep my eyes open. Then I see how I can take that and, using modern technology, reinterpret certain principles that are going to be true 200 years from now. I want the work to be looked at as contemporary American architecture, and in that sense, it has to have a certain honesty to it. That's what's wonderful about the really great American architecture, its honesty.

AR: *What do you mean by dishonesty in architecture?*

SM: There's a gluttonous affluence around, stage-set design that's way beyond the appropriateness for the client, the program, and it's all because a client or a developer has the money to build it. Alberti talked about choosing between fortune and virtue. The profession is becoming more a part of the corporate world while corporations (citizens of no place or anyplace) are more and more resembling nation-states. Every piece of architecture should express some moral. If it has moral merit, it deserves the title of 'architecture.' For me, the professional challenge, whether I am an architect in the rural American South or the American West, is how to avoid becoming so stunned by the power of modern technology and economic affluence that I lose focus on the fact that people and place matter.

These small projects designed by students at the Rural Studio remind us of what it means to have an American architecture without pretense. They remind us that we can be awed by the simple as much as by the complex, and if we pay attention, they will offer us a simple glimpse into what is essential to the future of American architecture . . . its honesty.

AR: *You say you've been cursed and blessed to be a Southerner. How so?*

SM: I grew up in a segregated South, in a very humanly warm environment, and had a wonderful education. But looking back on it, I know it was probably at the expense of the black community. I realize some of the things I'd been taught are wrong. The blessed part is that as an artist or an architect I have the opportunity to address wrongs and try to correct them.

AR: *So the Rural Studio is your way to redress wrongs?*

SM: We're excluding a whole army of people who've been excluded forever. These people down here are left over from Reconstruction; we need to reinstitute Reconstruction. W. E. B. Dubois said it 100 years ago: Reconstruction was prematurely stopped. He said that would be the big challenge of the 20th century; now we're in the 21st and we still have the problem and we're still ignoring it and they're still invisible.

AR: *What about the profession? What's happened to its social conscience?*
SM: Everyone's too busy trying to make a living. We have to be more than a house pet to the rich; we need to get out of that role.

AR: *Have your students had any problems learning to work with poor clients?*
SM: No. However, most of our students come from affluent families. For the most part, they haven't experienced this sort of poverty. They've seen it, but they haven't crossed over into that world, smelled it, felt it, experienced it. They come with abstract opinions that are fairly quickly reconsidered once they meet the families and realize that they're really no different from other American families. It's good to see these white middle-class students working hard all day trying to win the respect of people they wouldn't even acknowledge on the street before.

AR: *How important is the building process as an education tool?*
SM: It's valuable but not totally necessary. What's important is that students understand the process. It's the same regardless of whether they're building a little bitty studio for a basket weaver or a large building. We do preliminary sketches, schematic designs and foundation designs and then we go out and start digging the foundations. Everything then happens on-site. It's how architects worked 100 years ago.

What's important is that for young architects this experience takes it out of the theoretical and makes it real. They start to understand the power that architecture has and the responsibility they have to the creative process and how that manifests itself in something physical. That's what architecture is. It's not paper architecture. No one loves to draw and paint more than I do. But it's important that students learn that drawing on paper and building models is not architecture.

AR: *This is the Rural Studio's eighth year, and it has built more than 13 projects. Why haven't other schools adapted the model for their own use?*

SM: I don't think the 100-plus architecture schools across the country realize how alike each program is, how interchangeable their curricula and faculty are. I've spoken at most of them. The faculty are usually all dressed in black. They all seem to say the same things. It's all become redundant and very stale, unimaginative. What's ironic is that you hear professors talk about how out of the box we need to be, how risk-taking is part of being an architect, yet the faculty is often guilty of sitting on their hands. If architecture is going to nudge, cajole, and inspire a community or to challenge the status quo into making responsible environmental and social-structural changes now and in the future, it will take the "subversive leadership" of academics and practitioners to keep reminding the students of architecture that theory and practice are not only interwoven with one's culture but have a responsibility for shaping the environment, breaking up social complacency, and challenging the power of the status quo.

The Rural Studio is not an easy curriculum to run. It's a 24/7 obligation. During the week, I'm in Newbern living with students in a house built in 1890. If you're going to do this you gotta pack your bags, kiss your wife good-bye, and go to war. If you're not willing to do that, at least get out of the way and let the rest of us march on through.

AR: *It's unusual to really integrate teaching with practice as you've done.*

SM: I'm not an academician, but I am an educator. I'm an architect and I'm also a painter. It's all part of the creative act. That is my passion—to be responsible to the creative process. I enjoy certain technical ability, natural ability, and I get to use it. It's what all architects have and want to use. We're living the myth. I was willing to take the jump in the dark, as I like to say, and it's not going to be fatal.

34 WILLIAM MCDONOUGH, B. 1951, AND MICHAEL BRAUNGART, 1958

Over the past three decades, the American architect William McDonough has dedicated his attention to the development of sustainable and environmentally friendly architecture. Early in his career, he discovered that such architecture depended on more than sensitive design; it required ecologically sound construction materials that simply did not exist. He later began collaboration with the German chemist Michael Braungart, eventually founding the firm MBDC (McDonough Braungart Design Chemistry, 1995) and issuing their manifesto, *Cradle to Cradle: Remaking the Way We Make Things* (2002). The phrase "cradle to cradle" describes a system or material that, throughout its lifecycle, produces no waste and can ultimately become "nutrients" for other processes. The inorganic "paper" of McDonough and Braungart's text, composed of plastic resins and synthetic fibers, is one such product.

Architecturally, McDonough relies on manmade and organic materials to create structures beneficial to both the environment and the client. McDonough's design for the Ford Rouge Truck Plant in Dearborn, Michigan (completed in 2004) is an example of such a work. This low-rise industrial structure is crowned by a 10-acre "living" grass roof that helps insulate the building and collects rainwater to be used in manufacturing processes. These aspects are intended to reduce heating, cooling, and production costs. In addition, the living roof provides a home for insects and birds displaced by the complex. Such innovative and considerate design corresponds to McDonough's broader interest in sustainability that encompasses, yet extends beyond, architectural production.

"**This Book Is Not a Tree**" (2002)

At last. You have finally found the time to sink into your favorite armchair, relax, and pick up a book. Your daughter uses a computer in the next room while the baby crawls on the carpet and plays with a pile of colorful plastic toys. It certainly feels, at this moment, as if all is well. Could there be a more compelling picture of peace, comfort and safety?

Let's take a closer look. First, that comfortable chair you are sitting on. Did you know that the fabric contains mutagenic materials, heavy metals, dangerous chemicals, and dyes that are often labeled hazardous by regulators—except when they are presented and sold to a customer? As you shift in your seat, particles of the fabric abrade and are taken up by your nose, mouth and lungs, hazardous materials and all. Were they on the menu when you ordered that chair?

That computer your child is using—did you know that it contains more than a thousand different kinds of materials, including toxic gases, toxic metals (such as cadmium, lead, and mercury), acids, plastics, chlorinated and brominated substances, and other additives? The dust from some printer toner cartridges has been found to contain nickel, cobalt, and mercury, substances harmful to humans that your child may be inhaling as you read. Is this sensible? Is it necessary? Obviously, some of those thousand materials are essential to the functioning of the computer itself. What will happen to them when your family outgrows the computer in a few years? You will have little other choice but to dispose of it, and both its valuable and its hazardous

William McDonough and Michael Braungart, "This Book Is Not a Tree," *Cradle to Cradle* (New York: North Point Press, 2002), 3–7, 13–16. Reprinted with permission from the author and publisher.

materials will be thrown "away." You wanted to use a computer, but somehow you have unwittingly become party to a process of waste and destruction.

But wait a minute—you care about the environment. In fact, when you went shopping for a carpet recently, you deliberately chose one made from recycled polyester soda bottles. Recycled? Perhaps it would be more accurate to say *downcycled*. Good intentions aside, your rug is made of things that were never designed with this further use in mind, and wrestling them into this form has required as much energy—and generated as much waste—as producing a new carpet. And all that effort has only succeeded in postponing the usual fate of products by a life cycle or two. The rug is still on its way to a landfill; it's just stopping off in your house en route. Moreover, the recycling process may have introduced even more harmful additives than a conventional product contains, and it might be off-gassing and abrading them into your home at an even higher rate.

The shoes you've kicked off on that carpet look innocuous enough. But chances are, they were manufactured in a developing country where occupational health standards—regulations that determine how much workers can be exposed to certain chemicals—are probably less stringent than in Western Europe or the United States, perhaps even nonexistent. The workers who made them wear masks that provide insufficient protection against the dangerous fumes. How did you end up bringing home social inequity and feelings of guilt when all you wanted was new footwear?

That plastic rattle the baby is playing with—should she be putting it in her mouth? If it's made of PVC plastic, there's a good chance it contains phthalates, known to cause liver cancer in animals (and suspected to cause endocrine disruption), along with toxic dyes, lubricants, antioxidants, and ultraviolet-light stabilizers. Why? What were the designers at the toy company thinking?

So much for trying to maintain a healthy environment, or even a healthy home. So much for peace, comfort, and safety. Something seems to be terribly wrong with this picture.

Now look at and feel the book in your hands.

This book is not a tree.

It is printed on a synthetic "paper" and bound into a book format developed by innovative book packager Charles Melcher of Melcher Media. Unlike the paper with which we are familiar, it does not use any wood pulp or cotton fiber but is made from plastic resins and inorganic fillers. This material is not only waterproof, extremely durable, and (in many localities) recyclable by convention means; it is also a prototype for the book as a "technical nutrient," that is, as a product that can be broken down and circulated infinitely in industrial cycles—made and remade as "paper" or other products.

The tree, among the finest of nature's creations, plays a crucial and multifaceted role in our interdependent ecosystem. As such, it has been an important model and metaphor for our thinking, as you will discover. But also as such, it is not a fitting resource to use in producing so humble and transient a substance as paper. The use of an alternative material expresses our intention to evolve away from the use of wood fibers for paper as we seek more effective solutions. It represents one step toward a radically different approach to designing and producing the objects we use and enjoy, an emerging movement we see as the next industrial revolution. This revolution is founded on nature's surprisingly effective design principles, on human creativity and prosperity, and on respect, fair play, and goodwill. It has the power to transform both industry and environmentalism as we know them.

Toward a New Industrial Revolution

We are accustomed to thinking of industry and the environment as being at odds with each other, because conventional methods of extraction, manufacture, and disposal are destructive to the natural world. Environmentalists often characterize business as bad and industry itself (and the growth it demands) as inevitably destructive.

On the other hand, industrialists often view environmentalism as an obstacle to production and growth. For the environment to be healthy, the conventional attitude goes, industries must be regulated and restrained. For industries to fatten, nature cannot take precedence. It appears that these two systems cannot thrive in the same world.

The environmental message that "consumers" take from all this can be strident and depressing: Stop being so bad, so materialistic, so greedy. Do whatever you can, no matter how inconvenient, to limit your "consumption." Buy less, spend less, drive less, have fewer children—or none. Aren't the major environmental problems today— global warming, deforestation, pollution, waste-products of your decadent Western way of life? If you are going to help save the planet, you will have to make some sacrifices, share some resources, perhaps even go without. And fairly soon you must face a world of limits. There is only so much the Earth can take.

Sound like fun?

We have worked with both nature and commerce, and we don't think so.

One of us (Bill) is an architect, the other (Michael) is a chemist. . . . [You] might say we came from opposite ends of the environmental spectrum. . . .

We met in 1991, when the EPEA [Environmental Protection Encouragement Agency] held a reception at a rooftop garden in New York City to celebrate the opening of its first American offices. (The invitations were printed on biodegradable diapers, to highlight the fact that conventional disposable diapers were one of the largest single sources of solid waste in landfills.) We began talking about toxicity and design. Michael explained his idea of creating a biodegradable soda bottle with a seed implanted in it, which could be grown on the ground after use to safely decompose and allow the seed to take root in the soil. There was music and dancing, and our discussion turned to another object of modern manufacture: the shoe. Michael joked that his guests were wearing "hazardous waste" on their feet, waste that was abrading as they spun on the rough surface of the roof, creating dust that people could inhale. He told how he had visited the largest chromium extraction factory in Europe—chromium is a heavy metal used in large-scale leather tanning processes—and noticed that only older men were working there, all of them in gas masks. The supervisor had explained that it took on average about twenty years for workers to develop cancer from chromium exposure, so the company had made the decision to allow only workers older than fifty to work with the dangerous substance.

There were other negative consequences associated with the conventional design of shoes, Michael pointed out. "Leather" shoes are actually a mixture of biological materials (the leather, which is biodegradable) and technical materials (the chromium and other substances, which have value for industries). According to current methods of manufacture and disposal, neither could be successfully retrieved after the shoe was discarded. From a material and ecological standpoint, the design of the average shoe could be much more intelligent. We discussed the idea of a sole coated with biodegradable materials, which could be detached after use. The rest of the shoe could be made of plastics and polymers that were not harmful, and which could be truly recycled into new shoes.

Incinerator smoke drifted from nearby rooftops as we discussed the fact that typical garbage, with its mixture of industrial and biological materials, was not designed for safe burning. Instead of banning burning, we wondered why not manufacture certain products and packaging that could be safely burned after a customer is finished with them? We imagined a world of industry that made children the standard for safety. What about designs that, as Bill put it, "loved all the children, of all species, for all time"?

Traffic was increasing on the streets below, a true New York traffic jam, with blaring horns, angry drivers, and increasing disruption. In the early evening light, we imagined a silent car that could run without burning fossil fuels or emitting noxious fumes, and a city like a forest, cool and quiet. Everywhere we turned, we could see products, packaging, buildings, transportation, even whole cities that were poorly designed. And we could see that the conventional environmental approaches—even the most well-intended and progressive ones—just didn't get it.

That initial meeting sparked an immediate interest in working together, and in 1991 we coauthored *The Hannover Principles,* design guidelines for the 2000 World's Fair that were issued at the World Urban Forum of the Earth Summit in 1992. Foremost among them was "Eliminate the concept of waste"—not reduce, minimize, avoid waste, as environmentalists were then propounding, but eliminate the very concept, by design. We met in Brazil to see an early version of this principle in practice: a waste-processing garden that was in essence a giant intestine for its community, turning waste into food.

Three years later, we founded McDonough Braungart Design Chemistry. Bill maintained his architectural practice and Michael continued to head the EPEA in Europe, and both of us started teaching at universities. But now we had a focused way to begin to put our ideas into practice, to turn our work in chemical research, architecture, urban design, and industrial product and process design to the project of transforming industry itself. Since then, our design firms have worked with a wide range of corporate and institutional clients, including the Ford Motor Company, Herman Miller, Nike, and SC Johnson, and with a number of municipalities and research and educational institutions to implement the design principles we have evolved.

We see a world of abundance, not limits. In the midst of a great deal of talk about reducing the human ecological footprint, we offer a different vision. What if humans designed products and systems that celebrate an abundance of human creativity, culture, and productivity? That are so intelligent and safe, our species leaves an ecological footprint to delight in, not lament?

Consider this: all the ants on the planet, taken together, have a biomass greater than that of humans. Ants have been incredibly industrious for millions of years. Yet their productiveness nourishes plants, animals, and soil. Human industry has been in full swing for little over a century, yet it has brought about a decline in almost every ecosystem on the planet. Nature doesn't have a design problem. People do.

35 ANDRÉS DUANY, B. 1949

Duany Plater-Zyberk & Company, Plan of Seaside, FL, 1978
Courtesy of Duany Plater-Zyberk & Company

American architect and urban planner Andrés Duany is intimately connected with the formation of New Urbanism, a design movement intended to address a variety of urban ills including congestion, sprawl, and the lack of affordable housing. Applicable on regional and local scales, its principles promote the creation of walkable and socially diverse neighborhoods that include homes, workplaces, and public amenities. Implementation of relevant zoning codes and ordinances to guide and regulate an area's growth is of paramount importance in the New Urbanist quest for what the architectural historian Vincent Scully has termed "The Architecture of Community."*

The town of Seaside, on Florida's Gulf coast, is the paradigmatic New Urbanist development. In the late 1970s, Duany and his partner/wife Elizabeth Plater-Zyberk designed the master plan of Seaside, modeled on a typical pre-1940s southern American town. A commercial and civic center forms the settlement's core, surrounded on three sides by residences and on the fourth by the ocean. Buildings display variety, however, Duany and Plater-Zyberk devised design codes to regulate formal and material vocabulary, street width and adornment, and building placement. Thus the visual diversity of Seaside is dependant on an overall aesthetic harmony.

Since Seaside's creation, the town has been a source of debate. Financially, it is successful and has almost reached built capacity, demonstrating that there is a public appreciation for the ordered community atmosphere Seaside provides. However, the town has been criticized as a traditional and nostalgic theme park for the privileged. Other charges have been leveled at New Urbanism as a planning and design strategy, yet the movement continues to grow. The comments below provide insight into the principles that generated New Urbanism, which, under the leadership of Duany, Plater-Zyberk and others, now flourishes both nationally and abroad.

---

* Vincent Scully, "The Architecture of Community," in Peter Katz, *The New Urbanism: Toward an Architecture of Community* (New York: McGraw-Hill, 1994).

"General Agreement on Architecture and Related Matters" (2003)

In response to an age rife with social stress, driven by economies so powerful that the entirety of the natural world is decisively affected by the pattern of human dwelling; for a design profession confused by the esoteric and the transient, we set forth these principles.

We are in agreement that:

The discipline of architecture should take substance from its own tradition and not be subjected to artistic or intellectual fashions. Architecture is not a consumer item.

The language of architecture should be in continual evolution but . . . not fall under the thrall of short fashion cycles.

Architecture should interact with the imperatives of economics and marketing but not be consumed by them. It is a role of the art of architecture to tame the savagery of commerce.

Architecture should engage the supporting disciplines of engineering and sociology but not be enslaved by them.

Certain critics—those who do not possess the craft and experience of building—should not be granted undue influence on the reputation of architecture and architects. Ar-

Andrés Duany, "General Agreement on Architecture and Related Matters," http://www.dpz.com/literature_andres_writings.htm. Courtesy of Duany Plater-Zyberk & Company. Reprinted with permission from the author.

chitects should develop an unmediated voice in the press, to explain their work themselves. (Architects should affect this demand by canceling their subscriptions to those publications that do not comply.)

Participation in a permanent avant-garde is an untenable position that consumes those who do. Architects at the peak of their abilities must not be marginalized merely because their time of fame has passed.

It is essential to eliminate the humiliation of architects performing for the opinion of an absurdly small number of critics. Such critics are empowered only because they are recognized as such by the architects themselves. This problem does not apply to architectural historians, who earn their standing through research and documentation rather than through personal preference. Historians support the knowledge base on which architecture stands and from which it evolves.

Buildings should be durable and mutable in balanced measure. This is crucial to the longevity required of urbanism.

The design schools should accept the responsibility of teaching a body of knowledge, and not attempt to incite individualism. Students should be exposed to the general vernacular and not just to the very few geniuses produced by each generation. Emulation of the exceptional does not provide an adequate model for professional training.

The architectural schools should be liberated from the thrall of sociologists, linguists and philosophers. Those who are primarily dedicated to other disciplines should depart to their own departments from which they can continue to educate architects in proper measure.

The wall between history and the design studio should be eliminated. History is to be a living continuum. The achievements of our predecessors [are] the basis of all human progress. Architecture cannot be the sole exception.

Students should be exposed to the apprenticeship system. There has been no more effective method of learning architecture. Most of the finest buildings of all time were the result of apprenticeship.

It is essential to our communities that architecture be practiced as a collective endeavor and not as a means of brand differentiation in pursuit of the attentions of the media.

Architects should retake responsibility for an urbanism that is currently abandoned to the statistical concerns of zoning, building codes, traffic and financing.

Architectural expression should assimilate the cultural and climatic context, no less than the will to form of the architect.

Architects honor the human scale in their designs, remembering that it is human beings whom we serve and whose environment we are creating. Buildings and spaces that alienate or intimidate the people who live or work in them, or the pedestrians who pass among them, are inhuman.

Buildings should acknowledge the character of a place. It is also necessary to acknowledge the opposite: that architectural influence can travel along cultural and climatic belts to positive effect.

Architecture should not become a pawn in the culture wars. It is a falsification of history to consider a style representative of this or that hegemony or liberation.

Architectural style should be independent of politics. The most cursory observation will reveal that buildings and cities are neither democratic nor fascist; that they easily transcend the ideology of their creators to become useful and beloved to other times. Buildings should incorporate authentic progress in material and production methods, but not for the sake of innovation alone.

Architects should harness those systems of production that make the best design available to the greatest number. Only those artifacts that are reproduced in quantity are consequential to present needs—we have the challenge of large numbers.

The techniques of mass production should affect the process of building, but it is not necessary that they determine the form of the building, or the urbanism.

It is essential to engage the mobile home industry, the prefabrication industry, and the house plan industry. These are efficient methods to provide housing. The current low quality of their production is the fault of non-participation by architects.

Architects should endeavor to publish their work in popular periodicals. How else will the people learn?

The techniques of graphic depiction should not determine the design of the buildings. Computer-aided design must remain an instrument for the liberation of labor and not become a determinant of form. Because a shape can be easily depicted does not necessarily mean that it should be constructed.

It is essential to recognize that each building should be coherently composed. A building cannot be the simulacra of an absent urbanism. Authentic variety can only result from a multiplicity of buildings. True urbanism is the result of many designers working in sequence.

Traditional and contemporary architectural styles should have equal standing, as they represent parallel, persistent realities. They may be used badly or well, but their evaluation should be on the basis of their appropriateness to context, and their quality, not to fashion.

It is essential to deny contemporary buildings dispensation for having been created in the so-called modernist era. They must be held to a standard as high as their predecessors'. After all, the means available to us are not less than theirs.

It is essential to acknowledge a preference for controls by known rules and properly constituted laws, rather than be subjected to the whims and opinions of review boards.

Architects should work concurrently with landscape architects in the process of design. Landscape architects must in turn abdicate their preference for autonomous layouts. The ground is not a canvas and nature is not material suitable for an installation piece.

Architects, like attorneys, should dedicate a portion of their time without compensation to those who do not otherwise have access to professional design.

Architects should participate in the political arena so as to affect the built environment at the largest scale. It is disastrous to create policy without the participation of those with an adequate design education.

Architects should debate those who through relativist argument undermine architecture's potential as a social and ecological instrument for the good. The academic imperative of weakening architecture and architects harms society.

We should not impose untested or experimental designs on the poor. The likelihood of failure in such cases has proven to be very great; and they are powerless to escape its consequences. Architects should experiment, if at all, with those wealthy enough to be patrons. They can afford to move out of their buildings if necessary.

It is essential to understand the difference between creativity, which we accept as necessary, and originality, which when pursued at all costs is destructive to architecture. The pursuit of originality condemns our cities to incoherence and the architect's life's work to unwarranted obsolescence.

Because so much of the craft of building has been lost, it is essential that architects allocate a portion of their time to its research and recovery; and to the sharing of the fruits of this endeavor by teaching and writing.

The architectural vernaculars of the world be the subjects of systematic study and that they be models for the design process. Good, plain, normative buildings must again be available everywhere and to all.

The analysis of everyday building should not result in the conclusion that the people will accept only mediocrity. It is pandering to give them only what they already know.

Buildings should incorporate passive environmentalism in siting, materials and the performance of their mechanical elements. Economic analysis alone will not reach this conclusion.

Architectural history should include not just the form-givers, but the masters of policy. Talented students who are not seduced by form making should be exposed to these role models. Municipal policy and administration is sorely in need of their abilities.

Architects should respond to context. If the context is not suitable, then the proper response is to inaugurate one that is so. Not until this is common practice will the proliferation of architectural review committees cease to bedevil both good and bad designers.

Architects must honor the human scale in their designs, remembering that it is human beings whom we serve and whose environment we are creating. Buildings and spaces that alienate or intimidate the people who live or work in them, or the pedestrians who pass among them, are inhumane.

36 FRANK GEHRY, B. 1929

Gehry Partners, The Stata Center for Computer, Information and Intelligence Sciences
Massachusetts Institute of Technology, Cambridge, MA, completed 2004
Photo by author

After studying architecture at the University of Southern California and urban planning at Harvard's Graduate School of Design, Frank Gehry worked in Los Angeles and Paris before opening his own practice in 1962. Since then, the Canadian-born architect has steadily earned a reputation for his unique and experimental designs. In the past decade, Gehry has gained international notoriety for his highly expressionistic, unconventional works, such as the titanium-clad surfaces of the Guggenheim Museum in Bilbao, Spain (completed in 1997) and the skewed, intersecting elements of the Stata Center at Massachusetts Institute of Technology (1998–2004). In addition to unexpected forms, Gehry has also used unusual materials; for the renovation of his own house in Santa Monica, California, Gehry juxtaposed common, inexpensive materials such as plywood, corrugated metal, and chain-link. Yet, in more recent years, he has incorporated advanced technologies into the design and fabrication of his works. Ultimately, Gehry's architecture is a product of personal decisions, of an "intuition" he likens to that of the artist. The resulting aesthetic, informed by the realities of materials and construction, is always one of transformation, of constant flux, of excitement and novelty. Some critics question the functionality of Gehry's buildings, feeling that his emphasis on form neglects both the user and the existing context. Others, however, are enthralled by his works; as Gehry's designs often read as both architecture and sculpture, he has found tremendous approval in both architectural and popular circles.

"Architecture and Intuition" (2003)

I was trained as a modernist. I came to school after the Beaux-Arts movement, and all my teachers said enough with that historic shit. Let's get on with it. I thought that historicism was a dead end. The painters and sculptors were doing stuff that was much more exciting; they were playing with ideas, forms, textures, and feelings that were infinitely more interesting to me. I wanted to discover how to make a building that had what I call juice—that is, feeling or a spirit. If you look at history, you find that over the centuries, numerous artists, sculptors, and architects have struggled to represent movement with inert materials. That was interesting to me. When I looked at sculpture, especially statues of the Indian goddess Shiva, I sensed the movement inside them. Then I thought to myself, cars have movement, planes have movement; there is movement all around us. How do you bring that into architecture? I started messing with those ideas.

Years ago, I did a trellis for Norton Smith. I wanted it to look like frozen motion, but I didn't know how to do it. I could draw and model it, but I didn't know how to build it, exactly, so I convinced Norton to let me construct it in sections. I built the first layer, and that was fine. I built the second layer and half of the third, and I was starting to get somewhere. Then he stopped me. He said he didn't want to spend any more money on my fancy ideas, and that it was going to be my unfinished symphony.

When some people started doing temples again—postmodern stuff—I reacted against it because of the way I was trained. If you're going to go back in history, you might as well go back millions of years—to fish—and I started drawing fish-like things. It was

---

Frank Gehry, "Architecture and Intuition," *The State of Architecture at the Beginning of the 21*st *Century*, ed. Bernard Tschumi and Irene Cheng (New York: Monacelli Press and the Trustees of Columbia University, 2003). © 2003 by the Monacelli Press Inc., and the Trustees of Columbia University in the City of New York. Reprinted with permission from the author and publishers.

intuitive. I started drawing, and I let it go to see where it would lead. I started making things. I made a thirty-five-foot-long fish sculpture for an exhibition, and I realized that when I stood next to it, I felt the movement. Other people sensed it, too. Even though it was an ugly piece of kitsch, it worked somehow. At thirty-five feet long, it was starting to approach an architectural scale. From there, I cut off the head and tail, and I made a fish room for the Walker Center in Minneapolis, at the request of Mildred Friedman, then curator of design. And it worked. We stripped it of some of the kitsch; we were making it more abstract and it started to work. After I learned how to build that, I took the next step and moved to a larger scale. It wasn't something I sat down and planned. If I knew what I was going to do, I wouldn't bother to do it—it would have been done already in my head.

When I was a kid, I studied the Talmud with my grandfather. The essence of the Talmud is the golden rule: "Do unto others as you would have others do unto you." That's the logic. It's not much more complicated than that. There was another saying when I was growing up: "If you step on a crack, you break your mother's back." So, when you're a kid, you don't step on a crack, because you don't want to break your mother's back. It's a childlike notion of power. I think we carry something of that sensibility into our adult lives; you think that if you stand on a certain place near a fulcrum you can move the universe. But if you go at things that way, your actions become so important and powerful that you can't do anything. You go into gridlock. For instance, I hired a kid who had studied with Peter Eisenman. He was talented, but his experience with Peter had caused him to view each line as so precious that he couldn't draw a line or make a wall. He strove for a perfection that he could never reach, and it paralyzed him. It's wonderful to search your psyche and to comb your life for meaning—for the meaning of the universe. But you're asking more than is humanly possibly of yourself. You are a product of nature. If you just follow your intuitions, you won't get out of line because gravity will hold you down. The culture around you, the building department, the economy, and the client will keep you in line, so in all likelihood, you will never destroy the world. You won't break your mother's back if you step on a crack. You can, however, do things that have an effect on the world. You just have to free yourself to let those things happen.

37

SARAH WHITING, B. 1964

WW Architects, IntraCenter, Lexington, KY, 1997.
Diagram of spatial "parentheses" that weave between form and program in a community center project.
Courtesy of WW Architects

As an assistant professor of history and theory at Princeton University's School of Architecture and cofounder, with Ron Witte, of the design firm WW in 1990, Sarah Whiting merges the academic and professional realms of architecture. In her essay "Going Public," Whiting draws on this personal experience to provide a firm yet encouraging directive for contemporary architects. She begins by taking architects to task for what she perceives to be their recent inability to advance the field of architecture. Specifically, Whiting addresses architecture's reliance on past conceptual strategies that, once radical, are today merely repetitious and ineffective. In the early twenty-first century, she asserts that an acknowledgement of public heterogeneity lacks the impact it had thirty years ago—then it was novel; today it is a given. Whiting argues that, due to the rich architectural and intellectual legacy bequeathed by our forerunners, architects are now in a position to do more than recycle the past; they "must engage, lead, catalyze—*act*" to "contour tomorrow's cultural landscape." Architects must work toward the future.

The primary focus of this article is contemporary, encouraging the establishment of a "projective" or "postcritical" practice in architecture (as opposed to the "critical" practice of the previous few decades). However, Whiting also invokes a historical point of reference, namely the Vitruvian standards by which we, in large part, continue to measure architecture; she asks, "are we really so far removed from commodity, firmness, and delight?" Regardless of the answer, such a question reminds us that, even while looking forward, we cannot escape our past.

"Going Public" (2003)

Public Inquiry

Architects have a fondness for things public. Discussions about the rebuilding of the World Trade Center have revolved primarily around the public nature of the site, students want their thesis projects to "explore public space," and the duality of public and private life has become the binary of choice for academic as well as journalistic inquiry. Increasingly, however, architecture faces a public problem. Our public interest has become schizophrenic of late: *theory's* investment in publicness tends toward pluralization, while *practice's* public is increasingly marked by an interest in singular consensus. Perhaps most problematic for those of us with egos (and just try to find an architect without one) is that neither pole encourages, or even allows for, architectural assertion. As an instrument of progress, our commitment to a collective *civitas* risks becoming a posture (instead of a stance). Our altruism may well have become the enemy of architecture's forward motion, even at the very moment when our understanding of the public has entered a vastly more sophisticated era.

Public Opinion

Unlike "hegemony," the public sphere is less on the side of rule, more open to opposing views. Unlike "culture," it is more obviously a site of intersections with other classes and cultures. . . . Public sphere invokes "identity," but does so with more emphasis on actions and their consequences than on the nature or characteristics of the actors.[1]

Sarah Whiting, "Going Public," *Hunch* 6/7 (Rotterdam: Berlage Institute, 2003). © Sarah Whiting and the Berlage Insitute. Reproduced with the permission of the author and *Hunch*.

[1] Bruce Robbins, "Introduction: The Public as Phantom," *The Phantom Public Sphere* (Minneapolis:University of Minnesota Press, 1993), xvii.

By 1993, when Bruce Robbins penned the words above as part of his introduction to *The Phantom Public Sphere*, critical theorists were already fully immersed in unpacking what *public* might mean. Decades of important writing have profoundly advanced our understanding of the multifaceted nature of this term. We are now acutely attentive to the dangers of oversimplification, homogenization, and marginalization. We know a great deal more today about the tricky terrain of politics, agency, and action. For better or worse, we even know enough to state unequivocally that we frankly don't know much at all. This writing has had an enormously positive influence upon schools of architecture, including a resurgence of interest in the work of Henri Lefebvre, Michel de Certeau and Michel Foucault, and a production of sophisticated analyses of buildings and cities across broad historic and geographic spans. An inadvertent parallel to this public labor, however, has been the emergent role of the architect as public crossing guard: a generator of and mediator among multiple publics. While mediation has been rendered a productive strategy by theorists like Fredric Jameson and K. Michael Hays or practitioners like Peter Eisenman and Rem Koolhaas, who already long ago understood mediation as an *active between* (that is, an engaged interaction that itself generates new possibilities rather than compromise), more often than not, mediation has been misunderstood within architecture to mean a *passive between*—a simple conciliation between two sides.[2]

---

[2] Mediation as an *active between* engages and shapes the two forces that it is negotiating rather than merely reacting to them. For examples of such strategies in writing as well as design please see (among other works by these authors) Fredric Jameson, *The Political Unconscious: Narrative as a Socially Symbolic Act* (Ithaca, NY: Cornell University Press, 1981); K. Michael Hays, "Between Culture and Form," *Perspecta* 21 (Cambridge, MA: MIT Press, 1984): 14–29; Peter Eisenman, "Architecture as a Second Language: The Texts of Between," *Threshold: Restructuring Architectural Theory,* Marco Diani and Catherine Ingraham (Evanston, IL: Northwestern University Press, 1989), 69–73; Rem Koolhaas, *Delirious New York* (New York: Oxford University Press, 1978).

Public Safety

We represent a broad-based citizenry, composed of public and private sector leaders, community activists, and multidisciplinary professionals. We are committed to reestablishing the relationship between the art of building and the making of community, through citizen-based participatory planning and design.[3]

The public design charrette, where residents, practitioners and local politicians work together to generate design solutions, epitomizes what has become a numbing drive for consensus or conciliation within an increasing majority of architectural and development projects. Lower Manhattan, for example, is now under the watch of millions of eyes. Will this hyper-supervision guarantee that the outcome of the WTC rebuilding project will be less banal than the harrowingly dull six schemes initially proposed? Probably not. The implication that the broadest of publics needs to approve the WTC proposition—or that it ever could reach consensus—is an assumption that should raise a red flag for architecture today. This assumption is precisely where architecture's public crisis lies and where architects, schools, and clients should take notice.

Ideologies of inclusiveness and accommodation have unknowingly become the progenitors of such forms of compromise. The neutralities that (don't) steer architectural actions in today's compromise urbanism find a strange resonance in the DNA of our intellectual upbringing. Could it be that *The Critical*, in its contemporary guise, has placed us into a Novocain-laced stupor where we can't recognize the simultaneous di-

---

[3] Charter of the New Urbanism, 1996, 1 [note: a pdf of the Charter is available on the CNU website: www. cnu.org. An expanded version of the Charter was recently issued in book form, the Charter of the New Urbanism, Michael Leccese (New York: McGraw Hill, 2000)].

lution and desiccation of what were once potent critical strategies?[4] Recognizing and exposing options, differences, and similarities should not become an end in itself. The richness of alternatives has become an opiate whose ingestion satisfies our desire for the extraordinary, while drawing us ever deeper into a public coma.

Public Image

In the Downtown Athletic Club each "plan" is an abstract composition of activities that describes, on each of the synthetic platforms, a different "performance that is only a fragment of the larger spectacle of the Metropolis. . . . Such an architecture is an aleatory form of "planning" life itself: in the fantastic juxtaposition of its activities, each of the Club's floors is a separate installment of an infinitely unpredictable intrigue that extols the complete surrender to the definitive instability of life in the Metropolis.[5]

When Rem Koolhaas defined the "Culture of Congestion" in *Delirious New York*, he looked back to look ahead: he exposed the often unconscious strategy of radical hybridity present in the psychological explorations of Surrealism but also in the normative modernism of American mid-century corporate architecture. In his own projects (La Villette, Euralille, Congrexpo, ZKM, Jussieu, etc.), Koolhaas developed, accelerated, and refined the hybrid ethos, breathing life into this strategy through an aggressive urban and architectural research program. The aura that Koolhaas's work legitimately produced has become something altogether different in its contemporary proliferation

---

[4] For more on *The Critical* as a specific movement in architectural theory, see Sarah Whiting, "Critical Reflections"; Peter Eisenman, "Autonomy and the Will to the Critical"; and R.E. Somol, "In the Wake of Assemblage," *Assemblage* 41 (Cambridge, MA: MIT Press, 2000), 88–93.

[5] Rem Koolhaas, "Definitive Instability: The Downtown Athletic Club," *Delirious New York* (1978; rpt. New York: Monacelli, 1994), 157.

as a generalized architectural strategy of our time, however. Radical programmatic juxtaposition has become a mere sign, an accepted stand-in for a radicalized public realm. In its propagation, hybridity has endlessly reproduced the *image* of a pluralized and invigorated public, but its effects have returned once again to the unconscious, re-peating *ad nauseum* the cross-programming strategies that were once radical but which are now only facile. Such strategies, which only twenty or thirty years ago created new worlds through the alchemy of juxtaposed conclusion, have become familiar in the hands of the less imaginative, and have only produced the repetitive inconclusiveness of hybridity as a *technique* rather than a *proposition*. The image of radicality in these de-rivative projects is not enough to veil their overwhelming nostalgia for a remembrance of radicality recently past.

Public Nature

I would rather look at a cultural landscape that is as desiccated as it is in actuality, rather than one that is falsely comforting.[6]

Of course, it is hard *not* to be nostalgic for the radicality of the late 1960s, 70s and 80s. And those working during that period were in turn nostalgic for the radicality of the 1910s, 20s and 30s. Juxtaposition, collage, rotation, dissection, assemblage, and other strategies were the "something borrowed, something new" for the second generation or neo-avant-garde—a new beginning that digested history as it decidedly stepped into the future. Rather than render repetition redundant,[7] which is what the superfi-

---

[6] Benjamin Buchloh, "Round Table: The Present Conditions of Art Criticism," *October* 100 (Cambridge, MA: MIT Press, 2002), 224.

[7] For more on the strategy of repetition, see R.E. Somol, "Dummy Text, or The Diagrammatic Basis of Contemporary Architecture," in Peter Eisenman, *Diagram Diaries* (New York: Universe, 1999), 6–25.

cial borrowing of these strategies does today, it is time to recognize them as a means embedded in a historical moment, not a timeless endpoint. Furthermore, while there is no doubt that we are fortunate to have inherited the ideologies of the neo-avant-garde, we don't need to treat them with kid gloves. As the *avant*³ (avant *x* avant *x* avant or neo-neo-avant-garde), we stand face to face with this historical pattern. In order to advance rather than recycle, we should revel in the conscious *manipulation* of borrowed techniques—in addition to forging new ones—in order to reflect our agendas. Our architectural ambitions can be honed through the exploitation of expanded architectural strategies. We are well equipped to identify today's architectural constituency (architecture's public) and to articulate architecture's commitments (are we really so far removed from commodity, firmness, and delight?). Architectural excellency is repeatedly defined according to criteria that are often out of date; the critical project is falsely comforting precisely because it was so important in advancing the discipline. The historical significance of the critical project is diluted, however, when we pretend that it can automatically impart architectural importance, as if criticality were simply a sprinkling of MSG. Today's cultural landscape *is* desiccated, but rather than burying our heads in the sand by trying to maintain a pretense of a landscape that has past, we need to exploit architecture today in order to contour tomorrow's cultural landscape.

Going Public

*"In this kind of world," Peterson said, "absurd, if you will, possibilities nevertheless proliferate and escalate all around us and there are opportunities for beginning again.*⁸

Wake up. Architects, students and theorists ought to sit up for a moment and take a look around. Thanks to decades of intellectual effort—the acumen of certain archi-

---

⁸ Donald Barthelme, "A Shower of Gold," *60 Stories* (New York: Penguin, 1982), 22.

tects, theorists, curators, schools, and publications such as *Oppositions* and *Assem-blage*—we are surrounded by a remarkably fertile field of *stuff*. Our disciplinary ambitions—formal, technological, material, and intellectual—are poised to flourish. We would do well to shed at least a good part of our Obedience Complex. Lesson learned (really); let's move on. We know now that the public realm is a heterogeneous field; let's exploit the possibilities of our own architectural expertise. Rather than lose ourselves among its heterogeneity, we should aspire to change this field's topography. In order to do so, architects must engage, lead, catalyze—*act*, rather than only *react*. Our expertise lies in defining forms, spaces, and materialities; we should not be afraid of the results and subjectivities (read: *biases*) that such definition implies. Unlike other disciplines in the liberal arts, architecture's relationship to critical theory is not entirely concentric. Rather than bemoan this fact or conclude that theory has no bearing on architecture—two options that guarantee architecture's intellectual suicide—architects interested in the progressive project have no choice but to take advantage of our ability to slip in and out of critical theory's rule. After all, hasn't critical theory itself defined the rule-zone as, at best, a fuzzy entity? New spatial orders for the public realm thrive in the oxygen of expectant uncertainty. Architecture's ability to skip across, float on top of, or choose to obey critical theory's frameworks gives us an exhilarating vantage point. Damn the torpedoes. Full steam ahead.

38

Shumon Basar's article, "The Poisonous Mixture," an entertaining and enlightening meditation on the architect's position in the early twenty-first century, serves as a fitting conclusion for this collection. Previously employed in the office of Zaha Hadid and an educator at the Architectural Association in London, Basar no doubt has seen many professionals grapple with the various forms of "impotence" that may afflict the contemporary architect. Cultural, political, economic, technological, and other changes prompt (often unforeseen) transformations in the architectural discipline, issuing a constant challenge to the architect's abilities and adaptive skills. Indeed, Basar writes from experience, noting the young architect's devastating acknowledgement of powerlessness and the subsequent freedom to be earned by relinquishing the idealistic and ultimately unrealistic desire to "achieve everything." This message, passed on through Basar's text and his related activities as an editor, author, lecturer, critic, and curator, may prove particularly relevant to architects who today struggle to find their place in our ever-changing world.

"The Poisonous Mixture" (2004)

The Deal

A dopey-looking architect is happily married to an improbably beautiful woman when a sudden recession strikes. In a fit of panic, they go to Las Vegas to try to save themselves. In a casino, the wife duly declines the advances of a suave, smoldering magnate. He persists, finally making an offer to the financially desperate couple: One million dollars to spend one night with the beautiful wife. After dismissing the outrageous proposal, the architect and his wife lie back in bed and, from the righteous silence hovering between them, the possibility of agreeing to the million dollars begins to seem not so obscene after all. What's "one night," they think, compared to the thousands of nights that their fortified, water tight marriage will indubitably contain. But once the deal is consumed, the very edifice of the marriage begins to fall apart, brick by brick, as the architect-husband becomes distraught with anxieties that his wife might actually have enjoyed the night she spent with "the client." Nothing, the architect realizes, will ever be the same.

The Detail

Woody Harrelson's character in the film *Indecent Proposal* suffers an ignoble fate because he didn't focus on the detail. He didn't understand how the torrid part—Robert Redford's plea for "just one night"—would relate to the fragile whole of his marriage. The good parable should teach us that one must not underestimate the latent dangers of imperfect detailing—that vigilance to detail should be second only to breathing for

Shumon Basar, "The Poisonous Mixture," in *Content*, ed. Rem Koolhaas et al. (Cologne: Taschen, 2004). © 2004 Taschen GmbH and Office for Metropolitan Architecture. Reprinted with permission from the author and publisher.

any self-respecting architect. "God is in the details," pronounced Germany's very own architectural St. Augustine, Mies van der Rohe, which probably came as a surprise to those who thought God had died and gone to heaven. Amen.

The Virtuous

Indecent Proposal was released the year I started my education in architecture. Very quickly, I felt the need to become au fait with the rules governing what is considered virtuous and what is sinful. Ever since Mies's unique brand of fastidious, materially terse architecture proliferated to become the DNA of the neutered world that surrounds us, architects have valorized, with religious ferment, the absolute gravitas of "detailing": that is, a strange fetishization of screws, joints, gaps, and junctions. In a further twist of obsessive perversity, the construction of the detail should be almost imperceptible and, above all, it should not show evidence of having been made by human hands. Along with wearing one's shirt with the top button closed (without a tie) and listening to freeform jazz while drafting, the (male) architect's pursuit of the controlled finish is a wayward, contagious infliction peculiarly at odds with the true unwieldy scale of architecture and the manifold, abstract dimensions in which it is situated.

The Battle

"Architecture is a poisonous mixture of power and impotence."[*] When I read this statement as a student, my idealism was violated in the way a child's world is slowly dismantled with the successive abduction of Santa Claus, Superman, and the Man in the Moon. "But surely," I protested, "if our concepts are bold enough, if our passion is hi-octane fueled, can't we achieve anything? Shouldn't we be able to achieve everything?" It's only when one begins to try to build something that one understands the

---

[1] Rem Koolhaas, lecture at Columbia University, 1989.

second half of architecture's dialectical recipe. Like Hercules, or Bruce Willis in *Die Hard*, the architect must fight a veritable battle against ever-embittered combatants who seem to want to see him fail. There are building regulations, bored bureaucrats, economic vicissitudes, nefarious political climates, unspoken histories, indifferent construction industries and the "public." And often, above all of these harbingers of impotence, the architect faces The Client in a relationship that can be as infernal or beautiful as any marriage. This litany is sometimes referred to as "external forces," implying that the nature of practice is the reciprocity between this "outer realm" and the "inner realm"—the seat of the architect's creativity and will. Understanding the character of architecture's "impotence" might, I thought a few years later, be the key to liberation: how to unlock idealist delusion and give way to practicable strategy.

The Schism

There are two piles of images on my desk. The first includes a series of diagrams and flowcharts showing how a firm, OMA, has recently been extending its operations and presence by affiliating itself with diverse companies and experts. The other pile is a series of close-up photographs of three buildings in Holland, revealing how various joints, gaps, surfaces, and apertures have held out over time.[2] Cracks, oxidation, deterioration, patination, a panel falling off here, dead flies: a mesmerizing smear of decay in color. Leafing through the two sets of images is like looking at two possible future outcomes of a single decisive present.

The Inevitable

The pictures of aging buildings are a Dorian Gray-like reminder of the inevitable perishability of everything. It might sound portentous to claim that it is the fear of

---

[2] Netherlands Dance Theater, The Hague; Kunsthal, Rotterdam; Educatorium, Utrecht.

death that both plagues and motivates architects. This would assume that buildings are physical personifications of their authors, estranged metonyms, or abandoned look-alikes. Any building is however marked by the mortality of its material assemblage. It can go wrong at any time, and might do so in public. The author is unable to hide from the unforeseen problems—the imperfections—of the creation. This may be why James Stirling never revisited his finished buildings: he claimed it was too much like visiting ex-loves. Perhaps going back is so terrifying because, if the building is the architect, any tectonic failures are tantamount to corporeal failures. It's like staring at your own expiry, and realizing that there is nothing you can do to stop it.

The Tactical

"The important thing is to be aware one exists."[3]

I organize the diagrams into a matrix of my table and behold a spray of acronyms—OMA, AMO, VPRO, 2x4, IDEO; proper names—Prada, Harvard, Ove Arup; and a miscellany of individuals, some of whose names I recognize and others I don't. In relation to the photos of decay, these diagrams seem to outline an exploratory search for external, abstract organization—abstract not in the sense of "not-there," but in the way that freedom is abstract. The various permutations of letters and names look like a desire to discover tactics—tactics of ensuring one's freedom. Having been taught that the only way architects can generate the conditions of their freedom is by building more and better, getting bigger commissions and ending up with a fat cigar and a helipad, the spidery networks of interlaced diversification that orbit OMA look insane, and therefore the right thing to be doing. I can't help but think that the inward-looking species of architect—frozen by its love for frozen things—seems doomed to D-list subjugation.

---

[3] Jean-Luc Godard, *Pierrot Le Fou* (London: Lorimar, 1969).

These bubble diagrams on the other hand, linking Chinese TV broadcasting with notions of rethinking Europe, attest to an unbridled locomotive where Surrealistic juxtapositions begin to operate at the level of culture, economics, and language.

The Cure

It isn't just a question of accepting that there are waves, and agreeing to surf them. Imagine, like Leonardo da Vinci, that you can create weather, and with weather, the mother of all waves. It could strike anywhere (New York, China, Las Vegas, the Ruhr Valley, Portugal . . .) so one has to appear as though one can and will be everywhere at once. Make friends with culture (that's where the money is), hang out with fashion (it works for Christina Aguilera), celebrate superficiality (it's today's depth), be brutal and soft (we want it both ways), see the treasure in Junk (there is no such thing as obsolescence), spawn tribute clones (it's the true measure of fame), ditch piety and ennoble promiscuity (when have the youth ever been wrong?) and most of all, realize that power isn't something worth believing in, you have to live it. From architecture's funeral pyre, a new Andrew Lloyd Webber musical could be born. The project of architecture, if it is to survive intact and potent, must transcend its former self: it has to wake up and realize that the true and only important task is the vigilant corruption of the chain of causality that begins with "client" and ends in "building." Appear self-aggrandizing? Accept Machiavellian tendencies? Dance like John Travolta? Sure. Just don't look inwards, look out. The most powerful effect of impotence is the desire to find the cure.

SUGGESTIONS FOR FURTHER READING

The following is a selected list of additional readings pertaining to the authors featured in this collection. I have included works that provide a general overview of their respective subjects and that are, on the whole, intelligible to a non-architectural audience.

Dictionaries

Ching, Francis D.K. *A Visual Dictionary of Architecture*. New York: John Wiley & Sons, 1996.

Curl, James Steve. *A Dictionary of Architecture and Landscape Architecture*. 2nd ed. New York: Oxford University Press, 2006.

Fleming, John, Hugh Honour, and Nikolaus Pevsner. *The Penguin Dictionary of Architecture and Landscape Architecture*. 5th ed. New York: Penguin, 2000.

Surveys of the History and Theory of Architecture from Prehistory to the Present

Ching, Francis D.K., Mark M. Jarzombek, and Vikramaditya Prakash. *A Global History of Architecture*. New York: John Wiley & Sons, 2006.

Kostof, Spiro. *A History of Architecture: Settings and Rituals*. 2nd ed. New York: Oxford University Press, 1995.

Kruft, Hanno Walter. *A History of Architectural Theory from Vitruvius to the Present*. New York: Princeton Architectural Press, 1996.

Moffett, Marian, Michael Fazio, and Lawrence Wodehouse. *Buildings Across Time*. 2nd ed. New York: Mc-Graw-Hill, 2004. Includes CD-Rom.

Trachtenburg, Marvin and Isabelle Hyman. *Architecture: From Pre-History to Postmodernism*. 2nd ed. New York: Prentice Hall, 2003.

Surveys of the History and Theory of Modern Architecture

Colquhoun, Alan. *Modern Architecture*. New York: Oxford University Press, 2002. Focuses on the history and theory of twentieth-century European architecture.

Curtis, William J. *Modern Architecture Since 1900*. 3rd ed. New York: Prentice Hall, 1996.

Frampton, Kenneth. *Modern Architecture: A Critical History*. 3rd ed. New York: Thames and Hudson, 1992. Suitable for those already possessing basic knowledge of twentieth-century architecture.

Mallgrave, Harry. *Modern Architectural Theory: A Historical Survey, 1673–1968*. New York: Cambridge University Press, 2005.

Architectural Anthologies and Readers

Benson, Tim and Charlotte, eds. *Architecture and Design 1890–1939*. New York: Whitney Library of Design/Watson Guptil Publications, 1975. Organized thematically, texts address the history, theory, and development of architecture.

Conrads, Ulrich, ed. *Programs and Manifestoes of 20ᵗʰ Century Architecture*. Cambridge, MA: MIT Press, 1975. Primary documents from 1903 through 1960 by prominent figures of modern architecture.

Gilmore, Elizabeth, ed. *From the Classicists to the Impressionists: Art and Architecture in the Nineteenth Century*. Vol. 3 of *A Documentary History of Art*. Garden City, NY: Anchor Books, 1966. Essays arranged thematically and preceded by brief biographical/contextual essays about the authors.

Harrison-Moore, Abigail, and Dorothy Rowe, eds. *Architecture and Design in Europe and America, 1750–2000*. Malden, MA and Oxford: Blackwell Publishing, 2006. Historical and contemporary essays that address the history and theory of architecture and design.

Hayes, K. Michael, ed. *Architecture Theory Since 1968*. Cambridge, MA: MIT Press, 1998. Advanced theoretical essays by key practitioners and thinkers; includes editor's commentary in form of general introduction and brief essays preceding entries.

Lefaivre, Liane, and Alexander Tzonis, eds. *The Emergence of Modern Architecture: A Documentary History from 1000 to 1810*. New York and London: Routledge, 2004. Excerpts by architects and architectural commentators; synthesizing introduction by Tzonis and helpful keyword cross-references.

Mallgrave, Harry Francis, ed. *An Anthology from Vitruvius to 1870*. Vol. 1. of *Architectural Theory*. Malden, MA and Oxford: Blackwell Publishing, 2006. Over 200 excerpts by architects and architectural thinkers from Vitruvius through Semper, along with general introduction and contextualizing introductory essays. Volume II (addressing 1870 through 2000) expected in winter 2007.

Nesbitt, Kate, ed. *Theorizing a New Agenda for Architecture, 1965–1995*. New York: Princeton Architectural Press, 1996. Essays by architectural figures, arranged thematically.

Ockman, Joan, ed. *Architecture Culture 1943–1968*. New York: Rizzoli Press, 1993. Excerpts by architects and architectural commentators; contains introductory essay and helpful briefs preceding each excerpt.

Roth, Leland M., ed. *America Builds: Source Documents in American Architecture and Planning*. New York:

HarperCollins/Icon Editions, 1983. Texts on the development of American architecture and urbanism from 1624 though 1980; contains contextual introductions for each excerpt.

Vitruvius and Roman Architecture

MacDonald, William. *An Introductory Study. The Architecture of the Roman Empire*. Vol. 1. Revised ed. New Haven: Yale University Press, 1982. A detailed examination of the form, construction, and symbolic meaning of major Roman monuments as they relate to culture and society.

Smith, Thomas Gordon. *Vitruvius on Architecture*. New York: Monacelli, 2004. A recent translation of five of the ten Vitruvian books; includes hypothetical recreations of Vitruvius's lost sketches.

Ward-Perkins, John B. *History of World Architecture: Roman Architecture*. New York: Phaidon Press, 2004.

Abbot Suger and Medieval Architecture

Coldstream, Nicola. *Medieval Architecture*. Oxford and New York: Oxford University Press, 2002. Addresses European architecture from 1150 to 1550.

Saalman, Howard. *Medieval Architecture*. New York: George Braziller, 1962. A concise survey.

Leon Battista Alberti and Italian Renaissance Architecture

Grafton, Anthony. *Leon Battista Alberti: Master Builder of the Italian Renaissance*. Cambridge, MA: Harvard University Press, 2002.

Murray, Peter. *The Architecture of the Italian Renaissance*. London: Batsford, 1963. Reprinted by Schocken Press, 1997. A popular and well-received survey of Renaissance architecture.

Wittkower, Rudolf. *Architectural Principles in the Age of Humanism*. London: Warburg Institute and University of London, 1949. 5th ed. New York: Academy Press, 1998. Addresses architects of the Renaissance, emphasizing relationship between architecture and culture. Considered a classic text on Renaissance architecture.

Andrea Palladio

Burns, Howard. *Andrea Palladio: The Complete Illustrated Works*. New York: Universe, 2001.

Palladio, Andrea, Vaughn Hart, and Peter Hicks. *Palladio's Rome*. New Haven: Yale University Press, 2006. First compilation and English translation of Palladio's illustrated guidebooks to Rome, originally published in 1554.

Summerson, John. *Inigo Jones*. London: Oxford University Press, 1964. New Haven: Paul Mellon Centre for Studies in British Art and Yale University, 2000. Discusses life and work of British architect Inigo Jones (1573–1652), often recognized as the foremost practitioner of Palladian architecture in England.

Claude Perrault

Herrmann, Wolfgang. *The Theory of Claude Perrault*. London: A. Zwemmer, 1973.

Pérez-Gómez, Alberto. *Architecture and the Crisis of Modern Science*. Cambridge, MA: MIT Press, 1983. Reprint 1985. Addresses shifts in architectural thought and design resulting from the scientific revolution.

Etienne-Louis Boullée and Eighteenth-Century Architecture

Bergdoll, Barry. *European Architecture 1750–1890*. New York: Oxford University Press, 2000. Considers social and contextual ideas in relationship to the historical and theoretical development of the period.

Laugier, Marc-Antoine. *An Essay on Architecture*. Translated by Wolfgang and Anni Herrmann. Los Angeles: Hennessy & Ingalls, Inc., 1977. Includes brief biographical essay on Laugier.

Middleton, Robin, and David Watkins, eds. *Architecture of the Nineteenth Century*. Milan: Electra, 2003. Detailed survey of architecture from the Enlightenment through the 1800s; Part I covers the eighteenth century.

Rosenau, Helen. *Boullée & Visionary Architecture*. London: Academy Editions; New York: Harmony Books, 1976. Addresses Boullée's life and work; contains an English translation of his *Architecture, Essay on Art*.

Eugène-Emmanuel Viollet-le-Duc and Nineteenth-Century Architecture

Bergdoll, Barry. "The *Dictionnaire raisonné*: Viollet-le-Duc's Encyclopedic Structure for Architecture." In *The Foundations of Architecture: Selections from the Dictionnaire raisonné,* by Eugène-Emmanuel Viollet-le-Duc. Translated by Kenneth D. Whitehead. New York: George Braziller, Inc., 1990. Discusses biographical information of Viollet-le-Duc, his concept of structural rationalism, and places him within a cultural and theoretical context. Also see Bergdoll's *European Architecture 1750–1890* listed above.

Middleton, Robin, and David Watkins, eds. *Architecture of the Nineteenth Century*. Milan: Electra, 2003. Detailed survey of architecture from the Enlightenment through the 1800s; Part II addresses the nineteenth century.

Viollet-le-Duc, Eugène-Emmanuel, and M.F. Hearn (ed). *The Architectural Theory of Viollet-le-Duc: Readings and Commentaries*. Cambridge, MA: MIT Press, 1990. Selections from Viollet-le-Duc's works, with contextual essays and commentary by the editor.

Viollet-le-Duc, Eugène-Emmanuel. *Lectures on Architecture*. 2 volumes. Translated by Benjamin Bucknall. New York: Dover Publications, 1987. Transcriptions of lectures on topics of architecture from history through construction and ornament.

Louis Sullivan

Frazier, Nancy. *Louis Sullivan and the Chicago School.* New York: Knickerbocker Press, 1999. Examines work of Sullivan and his contemporary Chicago architects.

Morrison, Hugh. *Louis Sullivan: Prophet of Modern Architecture*, revised ed. New York: W.W. Norton & Company, 2001. An introduction to the life and work of Sullivan; includes bibliography of Sullivan's writings and a list of his buildings.

Sullivan, Louis. *Kindergarten Chats and Other Writings.* New York: Dover Publications, 1980. Collected texts by Sullivan; reprint of 1918 edition.

Frank Lloyd Wright

Levine, Neil. *The Architecture of Frank Lloyd Wright.* New York: Princeton Architectural Press, 1996. A thorough survey and evaluation of Wright's work; takes into account his writings, philosophies, and personal life.

Wright, Frank Lloyd. *Frank Lloyd Wright: An Autobiography.* Petaluma, CA: Pomegranate Communications, 2005. First published in 1932.

Adolf Loos

Gravagnuolo, Benedetto, Aldo Rossi, and Roberto Schezen. *Adolf Loos: Theory and Works.* Translated by Marguerite McGoldrick. 4th ed. London: Art Data, 1995. Biographical overview, contextualization, and commentary precede extensive documentation of Loos's architectural works.

Tournikiotis, Panayotis. *Adolf Loos.* Translated by Marguerite McGoldrick. New York: Princeton Architectural Press, 2002. Monograph on Loos addressing his life, architectural designs, and writings.

Antonio Sant'Elia

Caramel, Luciano, and Alberto Longatti. *Antonio Sant'Elia, The Complete Works.* New York: Rizzoli, 1988. Commentary on Sant'Elia's sketches and designs.

Da Costa Meyer, Esther. *The Work of Antonio Sant'Elia: Retreat into the Future.* New Haven: Yale University Press, 1995. Comprehensive examination and analysis of Sant'Elia's life and work.

Geoffrey Scott

Dunn, Richard M. *Geoffrey Scott and the Berenson Circle: Literary and Aesthetic Life in the Early 20th Century.* Lewiston, NY: Edwin Mellen Press, 1998. Biography and contextualization of Scott.

Reed, Henry Hope. Foreword to *The Architecture of Humanism: A Study in Taste*, by Geoffrey Scott. New York: W.W. Norton & Company, Inc., 1974. Contextualizes and discusses importance of Scott's text.

Ruskin, John. *The Seven Lamps of Architecture*. New York: Dover Publications, 1989. British social and architectural critic associated with the ethical and naturalism "fallacies" discussed by Scott; originally published in 1849.

Le Corbusier

Boesiger, Willy. *Le Corbusier: Oeuvre complete* (or *Complete Works in Eight Volumes*), 11th ed. Boston: Birkhäuser Press, 1995.

Jenger, Jean. *Discoveries: Le Corbusier*. New York: Harry N. Abrams, 1996. Concise overview of Le Corbusier's life and work.

Le Corbusier. *Le Modulor*. Translated by Peter de Francia and Anna Bostock. Boston: Birkhäuser, 2000. Details Le Corbusier's universal measuring system based on the proportions of the human body; contains English translations of volumes 1 and 2, originally published in French in 1950 and 1955 respectively.

Walter Gropius and the Bauhaus

Fitch, James Marston. *Walter Gropius*. New York: George Braziller, Inc., 1960. A concise monograph.

Giedion, Sigfried. *Walter Gropius*. New York: Dover Publishing, 1992. Extensive discussion and analysis of Gropius's oeuvre; first published in 1954.

Gropius, Walter. *The New Architecture and the Bauhaus*. Cambridge, MA: MIT Press, 1965. Details Gropius's notion of the Bauhaus as a meeting ground for art and industrial production; originally published in 1935.

Whitford, Frank. *Bauhaus*. New York: Thames & Hudson, 1984. Historical overview of the Bauhaus's development as an institution and an artistic culture.

Henry-Russell Hitchcock and Modern Architecture—International Exhibition, 1932

Hitchcock, Henry-Russell. *Modern Architecture: Romanticism and Reintegration*. New York: Da Capo Press, Inc., 1993. First attempt to analyze and contextualize modern architecture within the trajectory of architectural history; first published in 1929, three years before the Museum of Modern Art exhibition.

———. "The International Style Twenty Years After." *Architectural Record* (Aug. 1951): 89–97. Reprinted in *Architecture Culture*, edited by Joan Ockman (see Anthologies section above). An evaluation, reconsideration, and partial repudiation of the formulaic principles concerning modern architecture presented in the exhibition and accompanying publication twenty years earlier.

Riley, Terence. *The International Style: Exhibition 15 and the Museum of Modern Art*. New York: Rizzoli and the Trustees of Columbia University, 1992. Catalogueue published for exhibition honoring the sixtieth anniversary of the MOMA International Style exhibition; examines formation, format and content of the original show.

R. Buckminster Fuller

Fuller, R. Buckminster. *Critical Path*. New York: St. Martin's Press, 1982. Appraisal of humanity's problematic situation during the late twentieth century and suggestions for continued survival; posed by many as the culmination of Fuller's thoughts.

———. *Operating Manual for Spaceship Earth*. New York: Princeton Architectural Press, 2000. Discussion and suggested corrections for the dangers facing our planet; originally published in 1969.

Sieden, Lloyd Steven. *Buckminster Fuller's Universe: His Life and Work*. New York: Perseus Books Group, 2000. Explanation of Fuller's life, philosophies, and projects.

Philip Johnson

Johnson, Philip. *The Architecture of Philip Johnson*. New York: Bulfinch Press, 2002.

———. *Philip Johnson: Writings*. New York: Oxford University Press, 1979. Collected essays by Johnson through the 1970s.

Schulze, Franz. *Philip Johnson: Life and Work*. Chicago: University of Chicago Press, 1996. Comprehensive biography of Philip Johnson.

Louis Kahn

Brownlee, David B., and David G. DeLong. *Louis I. Kahn: In the Realm of Architecture*. New York: Universe Publishing, 1991. Addresses Kahn's life, philosophies, and work.

Leslie, Thomas. *Louis I. Kahn: Building Art, Building Science*. New York: George Braziller, Inc., 2005. Uses cases studies to examine Kahn's innovative engineering and technological achievements.

Kahn, Nathaniel, dir. *My Architect*. DVD. New York: New Yorker Video, 2005. Film documenting Louis Kahn's son's search to learn about his father.

Scully, Vincent. *Louis I. Kahn*. New York: George Braziller, Inc., 1962. First monograph on Kahn.

Twombly, Robert, ed. *Louis Kahn: Essential Texts*. New York: W.W. Norton & Company, Inc., 2003. Kahn's most influential essays from 1944 through 1973; includes introductory essay by the editor and suggestions for further readings.

Aldo van Eyck

Ligtelijn, Vincent, ed. *Aldo van Eyck, Works*. Translated by Gregory Ball. Boston: Birkhäuser, 1999. Documentation and analysis of Van Eyck's work; prepared in commemoration of his eightieth birthday.

Strauven, Francis. *Aldo van Eyck: The Shape of Relativity*. Revised and updated English edition. Amsterdam: Architectura & Natura, 1998. Monograph, originally published in Dutch.

Archigram

Archigram, eds. *Archigram: Magazine for New Ideas in Architecture*. Vols. 1–9 (1961–1970). Issues of *Archigram*, containing work, thoughts, and commentary of contributors.

Sadler, Simon. *Archigram: Architecture without Architecture*. Cambridge, MA: MIT Press, 2005. Contextualizes and discusses Archigram's formation, development, and reception.

Robert Venturi and Denise Scott Brown

Brownlee, David B., David G. Delong, and Kathryn B. Hiesinger, eds. *Out of the Ordinary: Robert Venturi, Denise Scott Brown and Associates: Architecture, Urbanism, Design*. Philadelphia: Philadelphia Museum of Art, 2001. Accompanying text for an exhibition on Venturi, Scott Brown and Associates; includes analytical and contextualizing essays on the architects and their work.

Venturi, Robert, and Denise Scott Brown. *A View from the Campidoglio: Selected Essays 1953–1984*. Edited by Peter Arnell, Ted Bickford, and Catherine Bergart. New York: Icon Editions/Harper & Row Publishers, 1985. Collection of essays on Venturi and Scott Brown's architectural ideas and influences.

Von Moos, Stanislaus. *Venturi, Rauch, & Scott Brown: Buildings and Projects*. New York: Rizzoli, 1987. Extensive analysis and commentary by author, documentation of projects from the mid-1960s to mid-1980s.

————. *Venturi, Scott Brown, and Associates: Buildings and Projects, 1986–1997*. New York: Rizzoli, 1999. Analysis and commentary by author, documentation of projects from the mid-1980s to the 1990s, and an interview with Venturi and Scott Brown.

Aldo Rossi

Ferlenga, Alberto, ed. *Aldo Rossi: The Life and Works of an Architect*. Germany: Konemann Press, 2002. Builds upon 1999 exhibition on Rossi's oeuvre curated by Ferlenga; discusses biographical information in conjunction with architectural production.

Moneo, José Rafael. *Theoretical Anxiety and Design Strategies in the Work of Eight Contemporary Architects*. Cambridge, MA: MIT Press, in association with Harvard University, Graduate School of Design, 2004.

Considers Rossi alongside seven other contemporary architects, including Venturi, Scott Brown, Eisenman, Gehry, and Koolhaas.

Rossi, Aldo. *A Scientific Autobiography*. Translated by Lawrence Venuti. Cambridge, MA: MIT Press, 1981. Based on Rossi's notebooks from the ten years between 1971 and 1981, the original date of publication.

Hassan Fathy

Fathy, Hassan. *Natural Energy and Vernacular Architecture: Principles and Examples with Reference to Hot Arid Climates*. Chicago: United Nations University and University of Chicago Press, 1986.

Richards, James M. *Hassan Fathy*. Singapore: Concept Media; London: Architectural Press, 1985. Criticism and interpretation of Fathy's work and architectural approach in Egypt.

Steele, James. *An Architecture for the People: The Complete Works of Hassan Fathy*. London: Thames and Hudson, 1997.

Peter Eisenman

Eisenman, Peter, et al. *Five Architects*. New York: Wittenborn & Company, 1972. Reprint, New York: Oxford University Press, 1975. Projects by and commentary on the work of five New York architects later characterized as the "Whites"—Eisenman, Graves, Gwathmey, Meier, and Hejduk—as opposed to the "Grays"—Stern, Moore, and others. Originally published in 1972.

Frank, Suzanne Shulof, and Peter Eisenman. *Peter Eisenman's House VI: The Client's Response*. New York: Watson-Guptill Publications, 1994. Owners of Eisenman's House VI discuss the joys and difficulties of construction, occupation, and renovation.

Galofaro, Luca. *Digital Eisenman: An Office of the Electronic Era*. Architecture and Informatics Series. Translated by Lucinda Byatt. Boston: Birkhauser Press, 1999. Explores the ways in which Eisenman now uses digital technologies to assist design.

Oppositions Reader: Selected Readings from a Journal for Ideas and Criticism in Architecture, 1973–1984. Edited by K. Michael Hays. New York: Princeton Architectural Press, 1998. Essays by Eisenman and others, taken from *Oppositions*, a journal coedited by Eisenman and produced by the Institute of Architecture and Urban Studies; introductory essay by Hays contextualizes Eisenman's philosophy.

Charles Jencks and Postmodern Architecture

Jencks, Charles. *Late Modern Architecture*. New York: Rizzoli, 1980. Discussion of 1960s and 1970s architecture, building upon and departing from modern architecture.

————. *The New Paradigm in Architecture: The Language of Postmodernism*. New Haven: Yale University Press, 2002. A retrospective of postmodern architecture beginning with the 1960s.

Klotz, Heinrich. *The History of Postmodern Architecture*. Translated by Radka Donnell. Cambridge, MA: MIT Press, 1990.

Portoghesi, Paolo. *Postmodern*. Translated by Ellen Shapiro. New York: Rizzoli, 1983. Discusses postmodernism and provides dozens of architectural examples.

Demetri Porphyrios

Porphyrios, Demetri. *Classical Architecture*. London: Academy Editions 1991. 2nd ed. London: Papadakis Publishing, 2006.

————, ed. *Classicism Is Not a Style*. London: Architectural Design and Academy Editions, 1982. Essays on contemporary classical architecture by architects such as Aldo Rossi, Giorgio Grassi, Leon Krier, and Porphyrios; accompanying designs by these and other practitioners.

Juhani Pallasmaa

Holl, Steven, Juhani Pallasmaa, and Alberto Pérez-Gómez. *Questions of Perception: Phenomenology of Architecture*. Tokyo: A+U, 1994. 2nd ed., San Francisco: William K. Stout Publishers, 2006.

Pallasmaa, Juhani. *The Eyes of the Skin—Architecture and the Senses*. London: Academy Editions, 1996. 2nd ed., London: John Wiley & Sons, 2005.

Bernard Tschumi and Deconstructivist Architecture

Broadbent, Geoffrey. *Deconstruction: A Student Guide*. London: Academy Editions, 1991.

Kipnes, Jeffrey. *Perfect Acts of Architecture*. New York: MOMA; London: Thames & Hudson, 2001. Commentary on and documentation of Tschumi's *Manhattan Transcripts*, as well as Koolhaas's Exodus or Voluntary Prisoners of Architecture, Eisenman's House VI, and Libeskind's *Chamber Works: Architectural Meditations on Themes from Heraclitus*.

Tschumi, Bernard. *Architecture and Disjunction*. Cambridge, MA: MIT Press, 1997. Essays written by Tschumi between 1975 and 1991.

Rem Koolhaas

Koolhaas, Rem, and Bruce Mau. *S, M, L, XL*. New York: Monacelli Press, 1995. Collection of essays, thoughts, and projects by Koolhaas and others at OMA; often focuses on issues of complexity found in the contemporary metropolis.

Patteeuw, Véronique, ed. *Considering Rem Koolhaas and the Office for Metropolitan Architecture: What is OMA?* Rotterdam: NAi Publishers, 2003. Accompanying publication for traveling exhibition on the work of Koolhaas and OMA.

Daniel Libeskind

Kipnes, Jeffrey. *Perfect Acts of Architecture* (see Tschumi section above).

Libeskind, Daniel. *Breaking Ground: Adventures in Life and Architecture.* New York: Riverhead Books, 2004. Libeskind's autobiography.

Schneider, Bernhard. *Daniel Libeskind: Jewish Museum Berlin—Between the Lines.* Translated by John William Gabriel. Munich and New York: Prestel Publishing, 1999. Discusses the history and design of Libeskind's Jewish Museum.

Greg Lynn

Di Cristina, Giuseppa, ed. *Architecture and Science.* Chichester, West Sussex, UK: Wiley-Academy, 2001. Essays and work by architects such as Lynn, Eisenman, Gehry, and Libeskind who employ a topological approach to architecture aided by computer-based technology.

Lynn, Greg, ed. *Folding in Architecture.* Architecture Design Profile. London: Academy Editions, 1993. Revised edition, Chichester, West Sussex, UK; Hoboken, NJ: Wiley-Academy, 2004. Essays about the possibilities afforded by computer-aided design and its implications for architecture.

———. *Folds, Bodies, and Blobs: Collected Essays.* Brussels: La Lettre Volée, 1998. Writings on issues such as form, proportion, and geometry and how they are impacted by computer-aided design.

Norman Foster

Foster, Norman. *Reflections.* Munich and London: Prestel Publishing, 2006. A compilation of Foster's essays on architecture, arranged thematically.

Pawley, Martin. *Norman Foster: A Global Architecture.* New York: Universe Press, 1999. A survey of Foster's work from the beginning of his career to the late twentieth century.

Samuel Mockbee

The Home Maker: Samuel "Sambo" Mockbee. Video recording. Princeton: Films for the Humanities & Sciences, 2002. Shows footage of constructed works by Mockbee and students of the Rural Studio; commentary by Mockbee, clients, and others. Originally broadcast 7 January 2002 as a segment of *Nightline*, with host Ted Koppel.

Mockbee, Samuel. *Samuel Mockbee and the Rural Studio: Community Architecture*. Edited by David Moos and Gail Trechsel. Birmingham, Alabama: Birmingham Museum of Art; New York: Distributed Art Publishers, 2003. Exhibition catalogue.

William McDonough and Sustainable Architecture

McDonough, William. "Design, Ecology, Ethics, and the Making of Things," in *Theorizing a New Agenda for Architecture,* edited by Kate Nesbitt (see Anthologies section above). Speech given in 1993 at Cathdral of St. John the Divine in New York City.

William McDonough Architects. *The Hannover Principles: Design for Sustainability*. New York: William McDonough Architects, 1992. Recommendations for environmentally friendly and sustainable design; commissioned by city of Hannover, Germany, for the 1992 Earth Summit.

McLennan, Jason F. *The Philosophy of Sustainable Design*. Kansas City, MO: Ecotone Publishing Company, 2004. Discussion of the history and potential future of sustainable design; addresses technologies, materials, and leading practitioners and includes a list of additional readings on green design.

Todd, Nancy Jack. *A Safe and Sustainable World: The Promise of Ecological Design*. Washington, D.C.: Island Press, 2005. Written for nonspecialists, this book discusses possibilities for an environmentally friendly existence.

Andrés Duany

Bressi, Todd. *The Seaside Debate: A Critique Of The New Urbanism*. New York: Rizzoli, 2002. Discussions and critiques of New Urbanism by architects, planners, and academics.

Duany, Andrés, Elizabeth Plater-Zyberk, and Jeff Speck. *Suburban Nation: The Rise of Sprawl and the Decline of the American Dream*. New York: North Point Press, 2001. Critique of suburban problems and a reevaluation of suburban planning based on New Urbanist concepts.

Katz, Peter. *The New Urbanism: Toward an Architecture of Community*. New York: McGraw-Hill, 1993. A series of case studies, including Seaside, Florida, that demonstrate principles and techniques of New Urbanism.

Frank Gehry

Dal Co, Franceso, and Kurt W. Forster. *Frank O. Gehry: The Complete Works*. New York: Phaidon Press, 2003.

Gehry, Frank O., and J. Fiona Ragheb. *Frank Gehry, Architect*. New York: Solomon R. Guggenheim Foundation, 2003. Exhibition catalogueue.

Lindsey, Bruce. *Digital Gehry: Material Resistance, Digital Construction*. Boston: Birkhauser Press, 2002. Discussion of Gehry's use of digital technologies.

Sarah Whiting

Somol, R.E., and Sarah Whiting. "Notes around the Doppler Effect and Other Moods of Modernism." *Perspecta, The Yale Architectural Journal* 33. Cambridge, MA: MIT Press, 2002. Calls for a more projective, propositional direction for architectural practice and discourse.

Whiting, Sarah. "Bas-Relief Urbanism: Chicago's Near South Side," in *Mies in America*, edited by Phyllis Lambert. New York: Harry N. Abrams, 2001. Examines Mies's design for the campus of Illinois Institute of Technology as an urban model.

"Projective Landscape: A Conference on Projective Practice." Held at the Delft University of Technology (16–17 March 2006). http://www.projectivelandscape.nl/. Conference organized to discuss projective as opposed to critical architectural practice; website contains videos of conference lectures and discussions.

Shumon Basar

Basar, Shumon, and Markus Miessen, eds. *Did Someone Say Participate? An Atlas of Spatial Practice*. Cambridge, MA: MIT Press, 2006. Texts that address issues of space, contemporary architectural and interdisciplinary practices.

Zizek, Slavoj. *Looking Awry: An Introduction to Jacques Lacan through Popular Culture*. Cambridge, MA: MIT Press, 1991. Main psychoanalytic theories of Lacan explained and examined through investigations of popular film and literature.